SEEKING THE WELFARE
OF THE CITY

SEEKING THE WELFARE OF THE CITY

Toward an Evangelical Appropriation
of the Pneumatology of Colin Gunton
for Public Theology

by
NAOMI NOGUCHI REESE

☙PICKWICK *Publications* • Eugene, Oregon

SEEKING THE WELFARE OF THE CITY
Toward an Evangelical Appropriation of the Pneumatology of Colin Gunton for Public Theology

Copyright © 2025 Naomi Noguchi Reese. All rights reserved. Except for brief quotations in critical publications or reviews, no part of this book may be reproduced in any manner without prior written permission from the publisher. Write: Permissions, Wipf and Stock Publishers, 199 W. 8th Ave., Suite 3, Eugene, OR 97401.

Pickwick Publications
An Imprint of Wipf and Stock Publishers
199 W. 8th Ave., Suite 3
Eugene, OR 97401

www.wipfandstock.com

PAPERBACK ISBN: 978-1-6667-8216-5
HARDCOVER ISBN: 978-1-6667-8217-2
EBOOK ISBN: 978-1-6667-8218-9

Cataloguing-in-Publication data:

Names: Reese, Naomi Noguchi, author.

Title: Seeking the welfare of the city : toward an evangelical appropriation of the pneumatology of Colin Gunton for public theology / Naomi Noguchi Reese.

Description: Eugene, OR : Pickwick Publications, 2025 | Includes bibliographical references.

Identifiers: ISBN 978-1-6667-8216-5 (paperback) | ISBN 978-1-6667-8217-2 (hardcover) | ISBN 978-1-6667-8218-9 (ebook)

Subjects: LCSH: Gunton, Colin E. | Holy Spirit.

Classification: BT121.3 .R44 2025 (paperback) | BT121.3 .R44 (ebook)

VERSION NUMBER 012325

Contents

CHAPTER 1
Introduction | 1
   Thesis Statement | 3
   Review of the Literature | 3
   Gunton's Contribution | 9
   The Shape of this Study | 12
   Significance of the Project | 13
   Why Gunton as a Theologian of the Holy Spirit? | 14

CHAPTER 2
The Promise of Gunton's Pneumatology: The Eschatological Spirit | 17
   The Promise of Gunton's Pneumatology: Transformation of the Whole Creation | 18
   The Legacy of Augustine and the Eschatological Spirit: Transcendent and Personal Spirit | 25
   Biblical Evidence for the Eschatological Spirit | 36
   Gunton Critiqued | 44
   Conclusion | 45

CHAPTER 3
Gunton's Doctrine of the Triune God and Pneumatology | 47
   Being and Becoming: The Relation between the Immanent and Economic Trinity | 48
   The Triune Creator and the Creation: Maker of the Earth | 50
   The Triune Creator's Relation to the Creation: Not Constrained, Yet Involved | 55
   Doctrine of Providence: The Triune God Who Works Toward the One Goal | 62
   The Triune God and the Missio Dei | 67
   Bradley Green's Critique Revisited | 72
   Conclusion | 74

CHAPTER 4
The Trinitarian God: The Two Hands of the Father, the Son and the Spirit | 77
    Divine Love: Universality and Particularity | 78
    The Actuality of Atonement: The Universality and Particularity of Christ | 81
    Christ: The Mediator of Creation | 87
    Christ: The Mediator of Redemption | 90
    The Holy Spirit: Relation to Jesus of Nazareth | 97
    Critique | 105
    Conclusion | 110

CHAPTER 5
Gunton's Doctrines of Anthropology, Ecclesiology, and Pneumatology | 112
    The Church: Trinitarian Community | 113
    Anthropology: The Triune God | 120
    The Eschatological Spirit, the Church and Culture | 127
    Critique | 133
    Conclusion | 137

CHAPTER 6
Seeking the Welfare of the City: Public Theology for the USA in the Twenty-First Century | 140
    A Brief History of Public Theology | 141
    Seeking the Welfare of the City: The Aim of Public Theology | 143
    How Should We Engage in Public Theology? Public Theologians, Thinkers and Colin E. Gunton | 146
    Criteria for Discerning the Spirit's Work in Relation to Public Theology | 180
    Conclusion | 183

CHAPTER 7
Conclusion | 187

Bibliography | 195

Chapter 1

INTRODUCTION

WHAT IS PUBLIC THEOLOGY?[1] There are many definitions of this discipline and none is universally accepted. A general definition many would agree with, however, is that public theology is theology which is done in order to influence public arenas by "witnessing to a truth that is relevant to what is going on in the world and to the pressing issues which are facing people and societies today"[2] by restoring the place of Scripture in public discourse. Although there is no universally accepted definition of public theology, the following definition supported by Stephen Holmes captures the most prominent features of a public theology which reflects evangelical commitments.

> Public theology is a category of theology that seeks to engage contemporary realities with theological truth, and to understand how to identify the relevance of biblical texts and values for particular societal and cultural contexts. Christian theology claims to be able to address all aspects of reality because there is nothing that exists beyond God's knowledge or control. Moreover, for theological

---

1. E. Harold Breitenberg rightly points out the diversity of definitions of public theology. He compares this to the television game show *To Tell the Truth*. "As I recall, every now and then all three contestants in a round would stand up, because all three were in fact the person they claimed to be. This, I think, is true for public theology" (70). Nonetheless, he describes five approaches to defining public theology: "the interpretive, historical, and descriptive, and the methodological and the constructive" (70). See Breitenberg, "To Tell the Truth," 55–96.

2. Forrester, *Truthful Action*, 127–28.

engagement with cultural realities to work effectively, theology must be able to take its place in the marketplace of ideas. Indeed, theology offers a powerful and compelling account of the nature of that marketplace and all other cultural realities. Further, public theology must be done with a view toward the transformation of the world. In other words, public theology cannot stop at analysis, but must move on to engagement and to active transformation which calls for things to be different. Missiological intention is therefore an important aspect of public theology.[3]

Since the Enlightenment, Christian theology has been significantly marginalized by the scientific revolution. Even to the present day, the place of theology in the university is disputed. Further, with the rise of postmodernism in the twentieth century, many people seek to understand truth in strictly cultural terms. There is, therefore, a significant need for theology to engage with culture.

In the history of public theology, the Holy Spirit's role in creation has been underexplored. Likewise, theology in general has neglected this eschatological aspect of the Spirit's work. Colin E. Gunton sees one of the causes of such neglect in theology to be a long-held belief in dualism: Viewing reality as a dichotomy between this world and the world to come rather than "seeking a realization of the next in the materiality of the present."[4] Further, Clark Pinnock contends, "So much more attention has been given to the Spirit's work in redemption than the Spirit's work in creation. . . . We have read the Bible for its spiritual truth and neglected the material dimensions of its message."[5] In both cases, the Spirit's work is diminished and a holistic picture of public theology within the scope of the *Missio Dei* is lost. Such theology fails to portray a trinitarian God and, consequently, fails to adequately represent the divine purpose for the world.

---

3. Stephen Holmes, email message to author, on February 1, 2010. For the purpose of this study, his formula will provide a working definition for public theology.

4. Gunton, *Promise*, 50. Gunton holds Augustine's theologoumenon—the Spirit is the love that unites the Father and the Son—to be the main cause of this neglect. He contends, "Augustine's single minded desire to fit the Spirit into his scheme has meant that the essential features of the economy scarcely feature" (Gunton, *Promise*, 50).

5. Pinnock, "Role of the Spirit in Creation," 49.

INTRODUCTION

THESIS STATEMENT

Hence, a theology is needed that recaptures the eschatological aspect of the Spirit's work over creation, and Colin E. Gunton's pneumatology contains the resources to meet this need. The thesis of this work is that Gunton's pneumatology which is trinitarianly formulated and eschatologically conceived can move us toward a full-bodied, holistic and trinitarian public theology that takes into account the triune God and consequently helps resolve long-standing theological problems. Ultimately, it enables us to see the world through the eyes of the eschatological Spirit and to look beyond traditional modes of Christian cultural engagement that have been counterproductive. A pneumatology which is firmly grounded in a trinitarian theology is necessary for the further development of public theology. It is only within this framework that we can understand the divine intention of redemption toward the creation and have a holistic understanding of the mission of the triune God for the created world. In so doing, we will be able to discern how we should engage with culture as a participant in the divine redemption.

The objective of this study, therefore, is to show how the promise of Gunton's pneumatology can contribute to a more robust, holistic, and trinitarian public theology. It is to *identify* the distinctive function of the Spirit in the transformation of creation in order to *restore* an emphasis on the trinitarian God who acts toward the goal of the perfection of his creation. Ultimately, it is to discern the relation between the trinitarian God and our understanding of the world to discover our mission for the world. It will be argued that the Spirit's "eschatological action of perfecting the created order: of enabling it to become that which it was created to be"[6] needs to be the center of focus to achieve this end.

REVIEW OF THE LITERATURE

In the theological literature, the matter of cultural engagement has been a passion for many theologians both past and present. Scholars such as Augustine, John Calvin, Abraham Kuyper, H. Richard Niebuhr and James Davison Hunter are among the prominent theologians whose work greatly contributed to showing *how* and *why* Christians should engage with the public square.

---

6. Gunton, *Father, Son and Holy Spirit*, 30.

St. Augustine, in *The City of God*, critiqued pagan culture in response to pagan denunciation of Christianity for the fall of Rome in AD 410. Augustine not only offered a fair and reasonable critique of pagan culture, but also showed the fundamental differences in the nature of the two cities. Augustine held that "One city [the city of man] is that of men who live according to the flesh," while "The other [the City of God] is of men who live according to the spirit."[7] One is formed by the "love of God," while the other is formed by the "love of self."

Augustine argues that despite the differences in the nature of these two cities, they intermingle from the time of Cain and Abel to the end of time. Yet, the life of the citizen of the heavenly City is like that of a sojourner who is "captive and an alien."[8] Although the two cities are equally afflicted by the fallenness of this world, they are different in faith, hope and love.

Both cities seek peace, yet the kind of peace they seek is different. For the city of man, they seek peace by overpowering and imposing on their fellow men because the city is a "city of contention."[9] On the other hand, "the peace of the heavenly City lies in a perfectly ordered and harmonious communion of those who find their joy in God and in one another in God."[10] Still, the heavenly City seeks peace in this world because although "faith can assure our exodus from Babylon, . . . our pilgrim status, for the time being, makes us neighbors."[11] Although ultimate peace cannot be enjoyed in this fallen world, as long as the two cities intermingle, the city of God seeks peace in order to make good use of the "peace" of Babylon.

John Calvin's contribution to cultural engagement is significant. Although Calvin follows in the steps of Augustine, what separates him from Augustine is his much more holistic view of culture and God's creation. Calvin argues that God as the Creator formed the world and sustains us by his provision (e.g., justice, wisdom, genuine truth) so that human life will flourish in order to pursue the end that God has intended for us. Calvin

---

7. Augustine, *City*, XIV 1, 295.

8. Augustine, *City*, XIX 17.

9. Augustine, *City*, XV 4.

10. Augustine, *City*, XIX 13. Augustine argues that the city of God has a "peace of its own, namely, peace with God in this world by faith and in the world to come by vision." Augustine, *City*, XIX 26.

11. Augustine, *City*, XIX 26.

writes, "We must learn to expect and ask all things from him, and thankfully ascribe to him whatever we receive."[12]

Further, Calvin reveals the Spirit's work in the creation of culture. This is a very significant point in Calvin's perspective on cultural engagement. In Gen 1:2, Calvin sees the power of the Spirit who sustains and preserves the creation. But, he extends this power to the life of the believer and unbeliever.[13] The pursuit of cultural attainment, economic development, or the enjoyment of food were not evil in themselves in the eyes of Calvin. Rather, what made them evil is the heart of humankind. God's curse will be upon humankind if they follow after their own selfish ambitions.

Abraham Kuyper was one of the pivotal figures in public theology.[14] Kuyper argued that there are various social and cultural spheres of human life. Although there is a plurality of these spheres, the sovereignty of God extends to all of them and they are intended to function according to the divine will.

Kuyper states that common grace is a gift from God because the world would have been destroyed by sin without it.[15] And if there were no world, there would be no culture. Hence, common grace is the foundation of culture and God achieves his great plan for the world through common grace. The original creation will survive in the end and culture without sin will continue in the new earth.[16]

Kuyper contends that in contrast to particular grace, common grace is not spiritual, but temporal and material. Yet, he acknowledges a connection between the two types of grace[17] despite the polar dualism (spiritual and natural) between them. Nonetheless, Kuyper finds the source of these two kinds of grace unified in Christ who is the mediator of creation and redemption.[18]

---

12. Calvin, *Institutes*, 1.2.1.

13. Calvin, *Institutes*, 2.2.15.

14. His famous statement in the inaugural speech at the Free University of Amsterdam in 1880, "there is not a square inch in the whole domain of our human existence over which Christ, who is Sovereign over all, does not cry: 'Mine!'" has inspired many Christians. Kuyper, "Sphere Sovereignty," 488.

15. Kuyper, "Common Grace," 167–68. Henry Van Til criticizes this as lacking Scriptural evidence. See Van Til, *Calvinistic Concept of Culture*, 134–35.

16. Kuyper, "Common Grace," 175.

17. Kuyper, "Common Grace," 169. Kuyper argues, "Special grace presupposes common grace. Without the latter the former cannot function" (169).

18. Kuyper, "Common Grace," 186–87.

In *The Spirit in Public Theology: Appropriating the Legacy of Abraham Kuyper*, Vincent E. Bacote explores Kuyper's view of the Spirit's cosmic work in an attempt to show the distinctiveness and uniqueness of the work of the Spirit. The language that Kuyper used to describe the Spirit's activity in creation (e.g., perfecting work, animating principle of all life, and restraint of sin), Bacote argues, overlaps with his description of the operation of common grace. Therefore, the Spirit's work in creation is a missing link and can be understood as an unacknowledged force underlying Kuyper's public theology. Although Kuyper did not make a direct connection between the Spirit and common grace in his discussion of common grace, Bacote argues that there is a strong connection between the Spirit's cosmic work and common grace.

In the middle of the twentieth century, H. R. Niebuhr attempted to clarify the relationship between Christ and culture in his book *Christ and Culture*. He introduced a fivefold typology drawn from the history of Christian thought: Christ against culture, Christ of culture, Christ above culture, Christ and culture in paradox, and Christ as the transformer of culture. Niebuhr's five typologies are highly influential and are often treated as the standard options for thinking about the relationship between Christian faith and cultural context.

Niebuhr states that the Christ against culture and the Christ of culture types are the two extreme boundaries since the adherents of the former type completely reject culture whereas those of the latter type wholly embrace it. In between these two extremities Niebuhr identifies the remaining three types: Christ above culture, Christ and culture in paradox and Christ as the transformer of culture. For these types, the question is not whether to reject or accept culture, but how to live a responsible life in the world while remaining faithful to Christ.

Niebuhr contends that although creation is tainted by sin, its original nature is not diminished to such an extent that it must be destroyed. "The problem of culture is therefore the problem of its conversion, not of its replacement by a new creation; though the conversion is so radical that it amounts to a kind of rebirth."[19] Niebuhr thus rejects the idea that culture is evil, but argues that culture is "corrupted order rather than order for corruption."[20] Humans continue to cultivate what God created in the beginning.

19. Niebuhr, *Christ*, 194.
20. Niebuhr, *Christ*, 194.

Richard Mouw, following Kuyper's theological conception of culture, argues for the significance of Christian cultural engagement in *When the Kings Come Marching In: Isaiah and the New Jerusalem*. Mouw contends that some culture, despite its wickedness (e.g., the ships of Tarshish), will enter the New Jerusalem (Rev 21:26). This is because it is God's original intention to fill the earth with "process, pattern, and products of culture formation" by human participation.[21] Hence, although it is perverted and distorted by human sinfulness, God will redeem and transform culture at the end.[22] As the Psalmist says, "The earth is the Lord's, and everything in it" (Ps 24:1): he will reclaim what belongs to him in the end.

Yet, Mouw argues that this does not indicate that Christians have power to transform culture. Although we are asked to participate in filling the earth by forming the artifacts and institutions of culture, it is Christ who transforms culture at the end of time. Mouw states, "Human culture will *someday* be transformed. Does this mean, then, that we must begin that process of transformation here and now? Are we as Christians called to transform culture in the present age? Not, I think, in any grandiose or triumphalistic manner. We are called to *await* the coming transformation."[23] Christians must wait for Christ's coming to consummate all things. But, as we wait, we should not wait passively, but rather actively seek the Holy City, which involves sharing the suffering of Christ.

More recently, *To Change the World: The Irony, Tragedy, and Possibility of Christianity in the Late Modern World* by James Davison Hunter has received considerable attention. While Hunter argues that Christians should engage with culture, he differs with the traditional views on the critical point of whether Christians can change the world.

Hunter contends that whether it is through politics or popular culture, it would be naïve to believe that Christians have the power or ability to change the world—or to even know how to change the world.[24] Therefore,

21. Mouw, *When the Kings Come*, 11.
22. Mouw, *When the Kings Come*, 11.
23. Mouw, *When the Kings Come*, 129; italics in original.
24. Hunter bases much of his reasoning on sociological evidence, such as a theory he finds compelling concerning how a society changes. On this view, changes in society typically take place when people of power work together, rather than a great number of ordinary people working together to change what is traditionally believed. Another sociological concept is the correlation between social conditions and one's beliefs: "Strong and coherent beliefs require strong institutions enveloping those who aspire to believe." Suffice it to say that in our modern, pluralistic situation such coherent beliefs are weakening. Hunter, *To Change the World*, 202. See my chapter 6 for further details.

Hunter proposes a "theology of faithful presence" as a new approach. He writes, "A theology of faithful presence begins with an acknowledgement of God's faithful presence to us and that his call upon us is that we be faithfully present to him in return."[25] Hence, this approach condemns tyranny and coercion. On the contrary, faithful presence calls for sacrificial love in honoring God.

Accordingly, through our faithful presence, Christians should seek "new patterns of social organization that challenge, undermine, and otherwise diminish oppression, injustice, enmity, and corruption and, in turn, encourage harmony, fruitfulness and abundance, wholeness, beauty, joy, security, and well-being."[26] We cannot seek the welfare of the city by force or coercion. But, by following the example of Christ which exemplified the peace of God on earth, Christians should seek peace in this pluralistic age and exemplify the love of God to our neighbor.

Having briefly surveyed the history of literature in public theology, one is struck by the strange absence of the Spirit as the eschatological Spirit: The Spirit's work is somehow neglected in the paradigms of Christ and culture and the usefulness of culture. This is an odd trend since transformation of the world is seemingly a desideratum for most of these theologians.[27]

Further, these theologians do not approach the issues from a trinitarian perspective due to the absence of the eschatological Spirit. Indeed, the relation between the trinitarian God and the created world is hardly explained. Also, the relation between the Spirit and Christ is largely unexamined.[28]

Furthermore, a strong dualism between this world and the world to come (the temporal and the spiritual) arises because the eschatological Spirit is neglected. This world is not destined to be discarded and forgotten. Rather, it is "destined for perfection, completedness"[29] along with humankind.

---

25. Hunter, *To Change the World*, 243.

26. Hunter, *To Change the World*, 247–48.

27. Though Calvin and Kuyper have given considerable thought to the Spirit's work in cultural engagement, it is nonetheless true that their understanding of the Spirit's work remains within the boundaries of preservation and revelation (common grace), while overlooking the transformative (cosmic pneumatology) aspects of the Spirit's activity.

28. This is especially highlighted by Bacote who attempts to illuminate the uniqueness of the Spirit's role within a trinitarian paradigm. His investigation of cosmic pneumatology is commendable, yet he separates the Spirit from Christ, pneumatology from Christology. See Bacote, *Sprit in Public Theology*.

29. Gunton, *Christ*, 45.

In light of these considerations, public theology must draw upon the resources of trinitarian theology—especially the role of the eschatological Spirit—and public theology must be examined within the scope of the *Missio Dei* so that the relation between the trinitarian God and our understanding of the world will be clarified. In so doing, we rightly locate the eschatological action of the Spirit at the center of public theology.

GUNTON'S CONTRIBUTION

This research project examines Colin E. Gunton and his pneumatological contribution to public theology because Gunton's pneumatology provides what has been lacking in public theology, namely the eschatological action of the Spirit. Gunton's pneumatology offers a renewed understanding of the Holy Spirit who transforms and perfects the created world through the Spirit's eschatological action. The Spirit is the agent of perfection and transformation of the world whose function is distinctive, yet in unity with Christ. The Spirit enables the world to become transformed so that "all things may through being perfected praise the one who made them."[30]

Hence, the emphasis is on the Spirit's function as "the giver of community"[31] in contrast to traditional theological conceptions of the Spirit such as a gift or the bond of love. Put differently, the focus is on the transcendent (economic) rather than the immanent Spirit.[32] Gunton contends, "In the economy it is the action of the Spirit not simply to relate the individual to God, but to realize in time the conditions of the age to

---

30. Gunton, *Christ*, 96.

31. Gunton, *Christ*, 49.

32. Gunton asserts, "The Spirit is better identified in terms of transcendence than of immanence." Gunton, "God the Holy Spirit," 108. To identify the Spirit's work in the world is to "show that there is a way of God's action towards us and his world which is not separable from his action in Christ, but not reducible to it either." Gunton, "God the Holy Spirit," 112.

come."[33] As noted earlier, this eschatological dimension of the Spirit's work has been largely neglected over the history of Christian theology.[34]

In this light, Gunton makes a significant contribution to public theology in the following areas. First, Gunton's robust pneumatology that emphasizes the eschatological function of the Spirit provides vital resources that have been lacking in public theology. In the history of public theology, the Spirit's work has been mainly understood in terms of common grace, preserving and maintaining. However, with the fresh approach of Gunton's pneumatology, we are able to develop *how* and *why* the Spirit works within the public square to bring the created world to the intended end. In other words, Gunton's pneumatology enables us to set public theology within the scope of the *Missio Dei*.

Second, Gunton's pneumatology rightly places public theology in relation to a trinitarian God. As stated above, theological concepts of cultural engagement in the past have hardly reflected trinitarian commitments due to the absence of the Spirit. This has resulted in a grave failure to understand the mission of the trinitarian God who acts toward one goal—the transformation of the world.[35] However, Gunton's trinitarian treatment of

---

33. Gunton, *Promise*, 50. Gunton's argument for the eschatological Spirit's action in the economy is firmly grounded in the intimate relationship between the Son and the Spirit since Gunton discerns the Spirit's action through the unity that the Spirit shares with the Son in the divine purpose for the world. In other words, Gunton discerns the Spirit's work in the economy based on his understanding of the trinitarian God who seeks to move toward the one goal of the transformation of the world. Therefore, if pneumatology is separated from Christology, the wholeness of the Spirit's work cannot be discerned because we are talking about the trinitarian God who works together to move toward the one goal.

34. Gunton gives credit to Irenaeus and St. Basil for the theological concept of the eschatological Spirit. Irenaeus's two hands of God is especially foundational to Gunton's pneumatology: Whatever is achieved in perfecting and redeeming the created order is the work of the Father, mediated by the Son and Spirit. If the Spirit perfects the created world, he must do so through the Son, the mediator of creation, for there is no other way. Gunton also appeals to the Cappadocians' concept of the trinitarian God whose being is the persons in relation to each other and argues that each person is made known by action to each other.

The biblical references to which Gunton appeals to establish the eschatological dimension of the Spirit's work are the following: Gen 1:2, 2:7; Exod 31; Ps 33:6; 104:20b–30; Ezek 37:9, 12; Rom 8:21; Rev 21–22. Gunton reads Rom 8:20 against the backdrop of Gen 3:17 and concludes that "Apart . . . from the Spirit's act of eschatological renewal, the destiny of the whole creation, man and nature alike, is futility and death." See Gunton, "Spirit Moved Over the Face of the Waters," 193.

35. For example, although Kuyper and Mouw argue that some cultural artifacts will

this issue (drawing on the Cappadocians and Irenaeus's two hands of God) shifts direction to an approach in which the triune God makes himself known to his creature.

Consequently, such an approach helps resolve long-standing theological problems, including the unbiblical divorce of redemption and creation. The presence of the eschatological Spirit enables us to recognize the trinitarian God who interacts with the world through the two hands of the Father, the Son and the Spirit. Thus, there is no separation between redemption and creation, or soteriology and creation. The Spirit who transforms and resurrects humanity also enables creation to achieve its intended purposes.

Third, and similarly, Gunton's pneumatology restores the relationship between Christ and the Spirit. Viewing God's relation to the created world through the lens of Irenaeus's two hands of God, Gunton is able to distinguish, yet unite, the work of Christ and the Spirit in creation and redemption. Christ is absolutely necessary in the transformation of the world since he is the mediator of creation. However, equally important is the Spirit's presence in the restoration of the world. Therefore, Christ who is the mediator of creation and the Spirit who is the agent of perfecting the creation cannot be separated because they are the two hands of the Father who is the creator of the world. Separating the work of the Son from the Spirit, or pneumatology from Christology, fails to capture the reality and unity of the Spirit's work.

Finally, Gunton's robust pneumatology which is conceived trinitarianly brings a fresh approach to public theology. By placing public theology in the sphere of the Trinity, Gunton enables us to see the world through the eyes of the eschatological Spirit. This, in my opinion, significantly widens the approaches that Christians can take to cultural engagement. While Gunton himself did little work in this area (e.g., he did not provide criteria for discerning the Spirit's activity), he certainly paved the way to further develop a trinitarian public theology from a pneumatological perspective.

---

enter the New Jerusalem in the end, the reasons for this (other than the cultural mandate or the Lordship of Christ) have not been provided. I believe what is needed to supply this deficiency is a robust understanding of the trinitarian God and eschatology in order to understand the purpose and end of public theology within the scope of the *Missio Dei*.

THE SHAPE OF THIS STUDY

In order to identify the contributions derived from the promise of Gunton's pneumatology, we will sketch the relation and interaction of the Spirit's eschatological action with the trinitarian God, creation, Christology, anthropology and ecclesiology. The objective is to identify the various facets of the Spirit's eschatological action and ultimately to comprehend the relation between the trinitarian God and our understanding of the kind of world in which we live in hopes of drawing out practical applications for cultural engagement for the twenty-first century.

Chapter 2 will sketch Gunton's fresh approach to pneumatology, which is trinitarianly and eschatologically conceived. The method employed is twofold. In the first part, Gunton's eschatological Spirit as the agent of the transformation of the world will be examined. I will endeavor to provide a general idea of Gunton's pneumatology, especially what it accomplishes and how it is relevant to public theology. The latter part will examine Gunton's theological conception of the Spirit as personal and transcendent.[36] This part also examines the biblical evidence which undergirds Gunton's argument for the eschatological Spirit.[37]

Chapters 3 and 4 will engage the core of Gunton's pneumatology—his recasting of Irenaeus's two hands of the Father, which underlies Gunton's promise. These two chapters thus aim to exegete Gunton's recasting of Irenaeus's two hands of the Father. Again, the approach is twofold. Chapter 3 will focus on the trinitarian God who acts toward one goal: the transformation of creation. The aim is to delineate the reality of God who mediates with the world through his two hands. Gunton's doctrine of providence and his conception of God's acts and being will be examined in order to further understand the triune God who acts toward one goal.

Chapter 4 will examine the latter part of Gunton's recasting of Irenaeus: The Son and the Spirit as the two hands of the Father. The aim of this chapter is to focus on the relation between the Spirit and Christ regarding the transformation of creation. Hence, special attention is given to elucidating the unique relation between them: The Spirit who is the agent of transformation is distinct from Christ who is the mediator of creation, yet

---

36. This study will closely examine Gunton's interpretation of the Cappadocians, especially St. Basil, in contrast to that of St. Augustine in order to illuminate Gunton's argument from the Eastern Fathers.

37. Scriptures that will be examined include Gen 1:2, 2:7, 3:17; Pss 33:6, 104:20b–30; Ezek 37:9, 12; Rom 8:20–21; Rev 21–22.

the Spirit cannot work apart from Christ because they are the two hands of the Father. The ultimate aim of these chapters is to show that there is no dual purpose in God's divine plan for creation, but one.

Chapter 5 will shift attention from the relations among the triune God to the relation between the eschatological Spirit and the Church as well as the relation between the the eschatological Spirit and humanity. The goal is to sketch how humanity is located in the mission of God and how the Spirit works in relation to humanity to achieve this end within the context of the Church.[38] Hence, the relation between the Church and the Spirit will be explored. Further, the concept of human personhood, especially focusing on the image of God and our relation with the Spirit, will be examined.

Chapter 6 will attempt to draw upon the resources uncovered in previous chapters to outline applications for Christian engagement of the public square for the twenty-first century. In this chapter, a brief overview of the history of public theology and principles of engagement focusing on the theme "seeking the welfare of the city" will be presented. Then, I will examine six prominent U.S. public theologians and thinkers in order to determine whether pneumatology plays any significant role in their public theology. Next, I discuss Gunton's contribution to public theology. The chapter concludes with criteria for discerning the Spirit's work in society.

SIGNIFICANCE OF THE PROJECT

The significance of this study can be found in two areas. First, in terms of public theology, to my knowledge, no public theologian has approached public theology from the standpoint of the Spirit's work in creation. Hence, this represents a fresh approach to public theology. Gunton's robust pneumatology provides a strong theological foundation for the Spirit's eschatological action in creation. In so doing, Gunton broadens the horizons of public theology: God is the triune God who acts toward one goal which is the transformation of his entire creation, both humanity and the created world.

In terms of Gunton's pneumatology, to my knowledge, no one has ever attempted to examine how Gunton's pneumatology can contribute to public theology. Hence, this is a unique attempt to apply Gunton's pneumatology to the discipline of public theology.

---

38. For the purpose of this study, the focus is on the Western Church.

WHY GUNTON AS A THEOLOGIAN OF THE HOLY SPIRIT?

Colin E. Gunton is considered one of the most prominent theologians of our time. His contribution to the renewal of systematic theology in Britain in the last thirty years of the twentieth century is significant.[39] At his sudden death in 2003, he was Professor of Christian Doctrine at King's College, London. Gunton was a prolific writer and treated numerous topics in theology including creation, the Trinity, Christology, atonement, pneumatology, ecclesiology, anthropology, revelation, and others. On the topic of pneumatology, Gunton wrote numerous articles and book chapters and presented a variety of lectures. Although he did not produce a stand-alone book on pneumatology, Gunton's keen interest in the topic is evident and his contribution widely acknowledged.[40]

Gunton received his theological education at Oxford. In his dissertation, which was revised and published in 1978 as *Becoming and Being*, Gunton examined Karl Barth and process philosopher Charles Hartshorne on God's being as becoming. Gunton found "Barth's actualism an alternative to both transcendentalist theologies of substance and immanentist metaphysics of the world process."[41] Yet, Gunton criticized Barth's view of pretemporal divine election since it minimized the significance of God's action in the world.[42] Gunton thus took up the task of finding a more satisfactory way to describe God's relation to the world. He sought to create a theological formula to best explain the mediation of God while respecting

---

39. Webster, "Systematic Theology after Barth," 258. Cf. Schwöbel, "Tribute to Colin Gunton," 16–17.

40. The lack of a stand-alone volume on pneumatology is explained by the fact that for Gunton the Spirit is best explored in relation to the Trinity as a whole. Gunton's theological method, which treated a wide spectrum of doctrinal loci in the light of the Trinity, did not allow pneumatology to stand alone. Gunton's books such as *Father, Son and Holy Spirit*; *The Promise of Trinitarian Theology*; and *The One, the Three and the Many* are good examples of this.

41. Webster, "Systematic Theology," 258. Webster explains that Gunton argued that "Barth's doctrine of God, with its inseparability of God's aseity and God's action in the economy, offers an alternative . . . to both classical theism and Hartshorne's neoclassical replacement." Webster, "Gunton and Barth," 20.

42. Webster explains Gunton's worries: "Barth's notion of pretemporal divine election subtracts from the genuinely historical character of the world and of God's action in the world: divine history appears to be finished in advance, and so the eschatological movement of creation to its perfection is compromised as the past is allowed to become the center of gravity in God's dealings with the world. In effect, divine pretemporality threatens genuine creaturely temporality." Webster, "Systematic Theology," 259.

God's freedom and to answer the question of how God interacts with the world despite the ontological differences between God and the creation.

Perhaps Gunton's focus on the Holy Spirit had its beginning in his desire to understand the mediation of the triune God with creation. His eagerness to understand the relation of the triune God with creation ultimately led him to emphasize the personhood of the Holy Spirit as well as the eschatological aspect of his work in creation. Gunton came to realize that the divine mediation had not been approached trinitarianly, but rather binitarianly. He came to believe that the presence of the Holy Spirit had to be reconsidered in order to appropriately understand the mediation of the triune God for the created world.

The restoration of the Spirit's personhood and his eschatological work results in a sea change in how we understand God and creation. First, Gunton's robust pneumatology enables us to see the eschatological aspect of the Spirit which signifies the restoration/transformation of the created world along with humanity. Second, Gunton's robust pneumatology gives the Spirit distinctiveness. Gunton argues, "The Spirit, contrary to what is often assumed, *is God's transcendence*" while the Son "realizes God's immanence in history—he becomes flesh."[43] Hence, Gunton's robust pneumatology introduced a clear and necessary demarcation between the Son and the Spirit in transforming and redeeming creation.

Paul Cumin argues, "To begin with Jesus for Gunton is to begin from the Spirit, and only as such to truly begin with Jesus."[44] This is because, Gunton contends, "Christology which is abstracted from a discussion of the relation to it of pneumatology is not Christology rooted in the actual human career of the incarnate Lord."[45] Hence, Gunton proposes, "We shall accordingly approach the doctrine of the Trinity according to the way of knowing, beginning with the economy of the Spirit and moving from there to the economy of the Son, the economy of the Father, and thence to the doctrine of the triunity of God."[46] The Spirit is thus the foundation of knowing the triune God.

---

43. Gunton, *Christian Dogmatic Theology*, 2.7.34.15. Unpublished quotation found in Cumin, "Taste of Cake," 67; italics in original.

44. Cumin, "Taste of Cake," 66.

45. Gunton, *Promise*, xxx.

46. Gunton, *Christian Dogmatic Theology*, 2.7.33.1, quoted in Cumin, "Taste of Cake," 66.

Gunton's pneumatology unearthed the work and person of the Spirit in the transformation of creation. Consequently, it enables us to see the relation between God and creation from a fresh perspective: Creation is to be redeemed along with humanity because of the eschatological Spirit. Furthermore, Gunton's pneumatology calls for a fresh way of knowing the triune God: The economy of the Spirit is the starting point of the doctrine of God's triunity.[47] Hence, Gunton's contribution to pneumatology is significant, and Gunton is truly a theologian of the Spirit.

---

47. As much as this is a strength of Gunton's pneumatology, it can also be a weakness depending on how this methodology is applied to the doctrine of God. Gunton is right to argue that pneumatology plays a significant role in understanding Christology (e.g., the sinlessness of the Son). And as we will see in the following chapters (e.g., chapters 3 and 4), Gunton's robust pneumatology produces much fruit in the development of Christology and consequently the doctrine of God. Yet, a theological dilemma arises when he applies this methodology to gain a glimpse of the inner life of the triune God from the economy. Gunton, pointing to Jesus, contends, "What it is to be a human person in this case [in the sense of Scotus's view] is identical with what it is to be a divine person." Gunton, *Act and Being*, 147. Thus, Gunton hints at univocity between God and humanity in personhood. And this is due to the fact that Gunton develops the personhood of Christ based on his understanding of the Spirit's work in the economy: Personhood, whether it is divine or human, is shaped by the eschatological Spirit. See my chapter 5 for further discussion.

CHAPTER 2

THE PROMISE OF GUNTON'S PNEUMATOLOGY

THE ESCHATOLOGICAL SPIRIT

GUNTON'S ROBUST PNEUMATOLOGY PROVIDES vital resources that have been lacking in public theology. Unlike the traditional concept of the Spirit, Gunton's pneumatology has significant emphasis on the eschatological function of the Spirit. To some degree, Gunton's pneumatology is about eschatology:[1] How the Spirit works to fulfill the divine eschatological plan in accordance with Christ. In this way Gunton has indeed developed a fresh concept of pneumatology.

---

1. For example, in *Christian Faith*, Gunton divides the book into three parts: The triune creator God, Christ, and the eschatological Spirit. See Gunton, *Christian Faith*. In this layout, it is the eschatological Spirit, not the sanctifying Spirit, that Gunton identifies as the third person of the Trinity. To be sure, Gunton does not neglect the Spirit's role in sanctification. Instead, Gunton defines sanctification in the light of the eschatological work of the Spirit. "Sanctification means being made holy, and it is the purpose for which justification is conferred. The holiness of the community is not primarily the holiness of the individuals within it—though that is a part of it—but that of a people bound together because they share in the life of worship, proclamation, teaching, sharing and good works." Gunton, *Christian Faith*, 148. Gunton's pneumatology thus maintains the vital aspect of sanctification. Yet, one must be informed that Gunton's construal of sanctification is rather different. The primary emphasis is not "the holiness of individuals" but rather "that of a people bound together." Also, it is not to be set apart, but rather "the way upon which they are set." Gunton, *Christian Faith*, 148.

Until this point, the exact promise of Gunton's pneumatology has not been identified. Hence, this chapter aims to identify first *what* Gunton's pneumatology promises. This chapter is an attempt to provide a general idea of Gunton's pneumatology, namely what it accomplishes and how it is relevant to public theology. This will in turn answer *how* and *why* Gunton's pneumatology fills gaps in public theology. As Gunton promises, "In the light of Trinitarian theology, everything looks different."[2] We must therefore seek to understand what he promises in his pneumatology. How everything looks different in light of Gunton's pneumatology is the question to be answered.

Having identified Gunton's pneumatology, his understanding of the Holy Spirit as the eschatological Spirit is examined next. The purpose of this section is to examine the underpinnings of Gunton's pneumatology that is trinitarianly formed. The method which will be employed is twofold. In the first part, Gunton's theological conception of the Spirit as person will be examined, while the second part will examine the Spirit as transcendental Spirit.

Third, the biblical evidence for the eschatological Spirit will be examined. This section focuses on the biblical soundness of Gunton's pneumatology. Again, the method will be twofold. First, the biblical evidence for the perfection of the whole creation will be examined. Next, the biblical evidence for the eschatological Spirit will be considered. These latter two sections, the theological and biblical basis for the eschatological Spirit, are intended to demonstrate the theological and biblical soundness of Gunton's pneumatology that is eschatologically oriented and trinitarianly formed. Finally, the promise of Gunton's pneumatology will be defined in the last section.

THE PROMISE OF GUNTON'S PNEUMATOLOGY: TRANSFORMATION OF THE WHOLE CREATION

Basil of Caesarea is perhaps the most significant theologian in relation to Gunton's pneumatology. Gunton states, "It is Basil who makes, I think, the most important point."[3] Basil's stance on the work of the Spirit is clearly eschatological: "The original cause of all things that are made, the Father . . .

---

2. Gunton, *Promise*, 7.
3. Gunton, *Father, Son and Holy Spirit*, 81.

the creative cause, the Son . . . the perfecting cause, the Spirit."[4] Moreover, Basil's attribution of the work (*ad extra*) to the three persons is trinitarianly formulated.[5]

Gunton's appreciation of Basil, therefore, is the basis for his eschatological Spirit who perfects the creation at the end. However, behind the eschatological Spirit, there is a trinitarian God whose being consists of three persons in communion. And that is the center of both Basil's and Gunton's theology. Gunton contends, "To say that the Spirit is the perfecting cause of creation is to make the Spirit the eschatological person of the Trinity: the one who directs the creatures to where the creator wishes them to go, to their destiny as creatures."[6] More succinctly, "the Spirit is God being eschatological."[7]

Hence, for Gunton, the eschatological Spirit is a *person*, not *substance*, whose mission is to perfect the created world in accordance with Christ. And it is not a *modalistic* God, but rather the *trinitarian* God whose being consists of three persons who "receive and give each other what they are."[8] Indeed, the work of the Spirit is inseparable from that of the Father and the Son. Nonetheless, as significant as Gunton's eschatological Spirit and its

---

4. Basil of Caesarea, *On the Holy Spirit* XV 36 and 38.

5. Gunton's indebtedness to Basil is clear. Gunton follows Basil and argues, "It should be said that creation, reconciliation and redemption are all to be attributed to the Father, all realized through the work of his two hands, the Son and the Spirit, who are, of course, themselves substantially God." Gunton, "End of Causality?," 77. Gunton, referring to the Apostles' Creed, contends that the Creed's attribution of creation to the Father, salvation to the Son, and life in the church to the Spirit encourages modalism. Hence, as seen in Basil also, the original cause of all things should be attributed to the Father, and the Son and Spirit should be construed as his two hands who work to achieve what the Father wills for the world. Such statements also indicate Gunton's dislike of Augustine and his criticisms of Western theology. Gunton is well known for his critique of Augustine for failing to understand the achievement of the Cappadocians in the divine ontology. As a consequence, Gunton argues that Augustine "allowed the insidious return of a Hellenism in which being is not communion, but something underlying it." Gunton, *Promise*, 10. This, Gunton asserts, resulted in a modalistic, Platonistic view of God which encouraged individualism rather than unity and relation, and God as mind (intellect, knowledge) rather than personal agents (action). This issue has been addressed in recent volumes. See, for example, Green, *Colin Gunton and the Failure of Augustine*; Johnson, *Rethinking the Trinity and Religious Pluralism*; McNall, *Free Corrector*; McNall, "Gunton and Augustine," 269–84.

6. Gunton, *Father, Son and Holy Spirit*, 81.

7. Gunton, *Father, Son and Holy Spirit*, 76.

8. Gunton, "Spirit as the Lord," 83.

contribution to pneumatology is, how exactly Gunton's pneumatology can make a difference in public theology is the question that we seek to address.

The Spirit Who Transforms: Unveiling of the Eschatological Spirit

Gunton defines the work of the Spirit as "perfecting" as discussed above. Drawing from this definition, we can identify two main points. The first point is the dynamic nature of creation: the transformation/perfection of the world. If the Spirit is the eschatological Spirit who perfects, the creation must be the object of such perfection. Indeed, the Spirit is the agent of the age to come.

Nonetheless, the Spirit's work has been construed as immanent rather than transcendent.[9] In fact, it is common to stress the immanent aspects of the Spirit such as strengthening believers and guiding them to follow Christ.[10] In other words, the Spirit is often seen as a "substantial force" that we possess within us rather than a person who acts as an agent of the age to come.[11] Gunton contends, "The Spirit is better identified in terms of transcendence than of immanence. The Spirit may be active within work, but he does not become identical with any part of the world."[12] It is therefore the Spirit that transforms/perfects the entire creation. And this transformation does not indicate a return to the protological state of the creation, but rather "redirection" or movement towards the completion of the creation. Gunton refers to this as a "'return'. . . but of a process by which that which was in the beginning is not so much restored to a former integrity as returned perfected to the Father through the Son and by the Spirit—an eschatological rather than protological return."[13]

The second point, which arises from the first, is that if the Spirit is the eschatological Spirit who brings the transformation of the world, our reconciliation with God through the Spirit is the means of effecting such

---

9. Gunton provides an extensive discussion on how the Spirit's work has been understood as immanent contrary to its true nature in history in *Theology through the Theologians*. Gunton, *Theology through the Theologians*, 105–8. As a result, the aspect of his work which is transcendent has been overlooked. Gunton traces the root of the problem to the fountainhead of Western theology, Augustine.

10. Luke 12:12; John 14:26; 16:8–11; Rom 8:24; etc.

11. Gen 1:2, 2:7; Exod 37; Ezek 37:9, 12; Luke 1–2; Rom 8:21; etc.

12. Gunton, *Theology through the Theologians*, 108.

13. Gunton, *Theology through the Theologians*, 127.

transformation. Gunton contends that reconciliation is "the Father's determination to bring all things into *relation* to himself through Christ."[14]

To be sure, *relation* is an important concept because it determines rightness with God. If one's relation with God is skewed, he/she cannot remain right with God. Gunton thus defines sin as a "false relation to God."[15] It is "the disruption or distortion of the relation of personal beings with the personal creator God."[16]

The Spirit opens the hearts of men and invites us to restore our relation with God.[17] Restoring our relation with God, which is reconciliation, enables us to become what we are created to be. Accordingly, our relation with each other along with the created world will be restored—this is the means of the "transformation of God's whole creation." Gunton summarizes, "Spirit relates to one another beings and realms that are opposed or separated. That which is or has spirit is able to be open to that which is other than itself, to move into relation with the other. . . . By his Spirit God enables creation to be open to him."[18]

The Spirit is the agent of perfecting. The Spirit should not be seen as something that works within our inner-self only, but rather acts to effect the transformation of the whole creation, humanity (soul and body) and the world. And to achieve this goal, the Spirit enables us to open ourselves to God so that the relation which was disrupted by sin will be restored. As a result, we will place ourselves in right relation with God along with each other and the created world (unity). In so doing, we will be conformed to become what we are created to be (particularity). "To enable the whole creation to realize its own proper way of being before God"[19] is indeed the mission of the eschatological Spirit.

---

14. Gunton, *Theology through the Theologians*, 120.

15. Gunton, *Christian Faith*, 139.

16. Gunton, *Christian Faith*, 59.

17. In regard to the action of the Spirit "opening" or "relating," Gunton contends, "there is biblical evidence to suggest that there are two main aspects to a theology of spirit in general. The first is that spirit is to do with the crossing of boundaries." Gunton, *One, the Three, and the Many*, 181. This is the first aspect of the Spirit's work, while the Spirit's work of particularity is another aspect.

18. Gunton, *One, the Three and the Many*, 181.

19. Gunton, "Pneumatology," 647.

Unity and Particularity of the Spirit: The One and the Many

Having examined Gunton's pneumatology, the eschatological Spirit, we now aim to sketch how this eschatological Spirit actually works in our world to bring perfection. That is, we wish to examine *if* and *how* Gunton's pneumatology can impact our contemporary reality. This is a critical point because public theology is the theology that "seeks to engage contemporary realities with theological truth."[20] A pneumatology that has no bearing on reality cannot provide resources to further the development of the discipline.

Gunton argued that the root problem of Modernity was the displacement of God from our society. From the beginning of Western thought, the concept of God (or gods) has served to create unity for society. However, in Modernity, humanity, who sought their own autonomy and freedom, displaced God with human reason and will. Ironically, humanity did not find freedom. Instead, they found themselves in other forms of slavery. Gunton states, "When the one is displaced by the many, the displacement happens in two ways: either the many become an aggregate of ones, each attempting to dominate the world, . . . or the many become homogenized, contrary to their true being, into the mass."[21]

Further, Gunton argues that in pursuit of freedom, humanity sought disengagement from others. Freedom was thought to mean being completely free from any "eternal grounding of life." However, what they did not realize was that true freedom exists only in the relation that allows space between God and humanity.[22] Gunton states, "My contention is that the distinctive failures of our era derive from its failure of due relatedness to God, the one, the focus of the unity of all things."[23] For the answer to this dilemma, Gunton looks to God whose being consists of three persons in communion: a perfect balance of the one and the many.[24]

---

20. Holmes, email message, February 1, 2010.

21. Gunton, *One, the Three, and the Many*, 33.

22. Gunton defines person to mean being in relation with God as well as with each other and the rest of the creation. "This means, first, that we are in the image of God when, like God but in dependence on his giving, we find our reality in what we give to and receive from others in human community." Gunton, *Promise of Trinitarian Theology*, 113–14. In seeking freedom, humanity sought to be disengaged from God and others, which undermined his very purpose for existing.

23. Gunton, *One, the Three and the Many*, 38.

24. Gunton contends that otherness and relation are necessary in any relation since "only that which is other than something else can be related to." Gunton, *Promise of Trinitarian Theology*, 171. As we see in the Trinity, otherness and relation exist. Gunton

To overcome the disengagement of society, Gunton argues that the Spirit opens humanity to enter into relation with God. God is "the source of all being, meaning and truth. It would seem reasonable to suppose that all being, meaning and truth, even as created and as distinct from God, is in some way marked by its relatedness to its creator."[25] And as we relate to God, we become related to each other. Hence, there will be no more disengagement, but unity between God and humanity through the Spirit.

On the other hand, although there is unity, if there is no otherness, it would be mere homogenizing. Otherness must exist in this unity just as in the Trinity. While the Spirit enables humanity to enter into relation with God, he also particularizes humanity.[26] In other words, the Spirit particularizes them by uniting them with God—unity (one) and particularity (many) are two sides of the same coin. Gunton, in agreement with Richard of St Victor, illustrates the validity of the Spirit's work of particularity.

> The third person of the Trinity is essential if there is to be true otherness in the Godhead. . . . In that sense, we may say that the Spirit's function in the Godhead is to particularize the *hypostases*

---

thus states, "Neither a collectivist nor an individualist conception of human being in the world is adequate to the way we are. In this respect, the trinitarian conceptuality at the very least gives food for thought about what it is to be human in society. . . . Indeed, in our fragmented and perplexed society, it may be that theology has here insights with redemptive possibilities." Gunton, *Promise of Trinitarian Theology*, 204.

25. Gunton, *One, The Three and The Many*, 167.

26. Gunton's concept of "particularity" is rather abstract. David Höhne defines particularity as follows: "Particularity is best understood as the product of mutually constitutive relations." Höhne, *Spirit and Sonship*, 1. He further states, "The Spirit perfects, that is, gives ontological direction to the *hypostases* of everything in creation towards the Father, through the Son. This allows us 'to develop an ontology of the material particular as that which is destined to achieve a distinctively finite completeness or perfection in space and through time.'" Höhne, *Spirit and Sonship*, 25. To be concise, it is a relation in otherness. Höhne's book is very helpful in understanding Gunton's notion of particularity. A concrete example of what particularity may look like in biblical accounts which Gunton draws from is the relation between Jesus and the Spirit (Luke 1–2, 4). Höhne engages in extensive exegetical studies on Luke chapter 4 to identify the Spirit's work of particularity as well as to examine whether Gunton's argument for particularity is biblically based. In regard to Basil's influence on Gunton's pneumatology, Höhne rightly points out that particularity is perhaps Gunton's own theological invention: "It cannot be denied that *De Spirit Sancto* is replete with the language of perfection but to suggest that this includes concrete substantiality is a matter of inference rather than observation." Höhne, *Spirit and Sonship*, 13. This is an interesting point since it reveals how Gunton came to formulate his own pneumatology distinct from Basil. Particularity will be further examined in chapter 4.

> ... or persons of Father and Son: to liberate them to be themselves, to be particular persons in community and as communion.[27]

Hence, otherness in unity exists through the particularizing work of the Spirit. As a result, a perfect balance between unity and otherness is restored. In other words, humanity's true freedom is restored through being related to God who is the source of all things.

Moreover, this particularity influences what sort of society will be formed. Gunton writes, "All particulars are formed by their relationship to God the creator and redeemer and to each other. . . . Their reality consists, therefore . . . not in the universals they instantiate, but in the shape of their relatedness with God and with other created hypostases."[28] There is no society that is "context-less: it takes shape in a world which is not irrelevant to its being, as the garden was in some way integral to the being of Adam and Eve."[29]

As we are united to God and each other and being particularized through the Spirit, the world will be redirected to what it was first intended to be. And a community that is central to this eschatological perfecting is none other than the church. Gunton states, "The eschatological destiny of creation is a kind of community: the bringing of all the creation to the Father in Christ. The Church is called to be the community that plays a central part in the perfecting through the Spirit."[30]

In light of the above, we can conclude that Gunton's pneumatology is relevant to public theology because the eschatological Spirit who particularizes and unites humanity overcomes the problems that are presented by Modernity. One could argue that the overcoming of Modernity is indeed part of the process of perfecting creation by the eschatological Spirit. Unity transcends disengagement from each other, while particularity transforms mere homogeneity. Since there is no society that is context-less, the type of being that lives in the world determines the form of society. If so, Gunton's pneumatology has a strong bearing on contemporary reality. Stated briefly, Gunton's pneumatology aims to present a more holistic view of perfection: The perfection of the whole created world.

---

27. Gunton, *One, the Three and the Many*, 190; italics in original.
28. Gunton, *One, the Three and the Many*, 207.
29. Gunton, *One, the Three and the Many*, 219.
30. Gunton, *Theology through Theologians*, 203.

THE LEGACY OF AUGUSTINE AND THE ESCHATOLOGICAL SPIRIT: TRANSCENDENT AND PERSONAL SPIRIT

We have examined above Gunton's pneumatology that is eschatologically (transcendent) oriented and trinitarianly (persons) formulated. Further, we have applied his pneumatology to the modern problem of the one and the many that arise from a false conception of unity and diversity in order to illustrate that Gunton's pneumatology can engage contemporary realities with theological truth.[31]

In this section, we will examine Gunton's pneumatology in the light of his critique of the Augustinian legacy. In this examination, special attention will be given to Gunton's conception of the Spirit as personal and transcendent since these are the hallmarks of Gunton's pneumatology. And by the same token they are the main charges that Gunton brings against Augustine.

Before proceeding, a word of caution is in order. As mentioned above,[32] Gunton's critique of Augustine has generated much debate among scholars. Many scholars have argued that Gunton's criticism of Augustine is unfair and unfounded. In the years following Gunton's passing, something of a consensus has emerged that Gunton's criticism of Augustine was misguided. However, Joshua McNall argues that while he agrees that Gunton went too far, he also sees merit in some of Gunton's arguments, since "not all his charges may be easily dismissed."[33] One such charge, McNall argues, is Gunton's concern about Augustine's later influence. McNall explains that Gunton's main concern was not "providing a full-orbed reading of the bishop in his context," but was how Augustine's theology may have negatively influenced the tradition—the Augustinian legacy. McNall adds that Augustine's so-called "inward turn"[34] is one example of this, and Gunton

---

31. Gunton contends, "Modernism and postmodernism alike work for the destruction of particularity and for homogeneity, the former in subordinating the particular to rigid and universal patterns of thought and behavior, the latter failing to make any links between things at all, and so treating everything as of equal value." Gunton, *One, the Three and the Many*, 74.

32. See n5.

33. McNall, "Gunton and Augustine," 270.

34. Augustine's "inward turn" refers to Augustine's attempt to "find a kind of 'trinity' within his rational mind, which consists of the triad of memory, understanding and will" (McNall, "Gunton and Augustine," 276).

"was quite right to lament the unintended consequences that drip down from Hippo Regius."[35]

In this chapter, I follow McNall's lead on Gunton and Augustine. Gunton's criticism of Augustine must be examined carefully and cautiously. Yet, I echo McNall that some of Gunton's criticisms should not be quickly dismissed. Gunton may have overplayed his hand criticizing Augustine, making his arguments less persuasive. Nonetheless, I contend that Gunton is still worth listening to, especially considering his work on the eschatological Spirit. And Gunton's critique of Augustine's bond of love and dualism arising from the inward turn are points that are worthy of further examination in order to unfold the eschatological aspect of the Spirit.

Platonic God Verses Trinitarian God: Augustine, the Fountainhead of Western Theology

There is a trinitarian God behind the eschatological Spirit in Gunton's pneumatology. Clearly, Gunton's pneumatology cannot be fully appreciated apart from the doctrine of the Trinity. As Hans Schaeffer states, "The doctrine of the Trinity is the centre of Gunton's theology."[36] Christoph Schwöbel explains that Gunton's pneumatology was developed "alongside the exposition of the doctrine of the Trinity as persons in communion."[37]

Gunton's theological commitment to the doctrine of Trinity arises from his conviction that "In some way, God must be Father, Son and Spirit always, to the heart of his being. The doctrine of the Trinity is the doctrine that attempts to do just that: to identify the God who comes among us in the way that he does; to enable us to see as much as we need of the nature

---

35. McNall, "Gunton and Augustine," 270.

36. Schaeffer, *Createdness and Ethics*, 36. Schaeffer continues, "It is this doctrine that renders possible a correct treatment of both God as God and world as world. It not only leaves room for stressing the ontological difference of both God and world, but is also the way in which both divine and human essence are somehow warranted; the Trinity is 'the space to be human'. The doctrine of the Trinity is the way to avoid common misconceptions of the relation between God and human being that cross the spectrum from pantheism to personalism" (36).

37. Schwöbel, "Shape of Colin Gunton's Theology," 192. Schwöbel adds, "It [the theology of the Holy Spirit] forms a constitutive part of it [the doctrine of the Trinity], perhaps that part which distinguishes Gunton's Trinitarian Theology most clearly from that of his most frequent conversation partners, like Robert Jensen and John Zizioulas." Schwöbel, "Shape of Colin Gunton's Theology," 192.

of our God."³⁸ For Gunton, then, God is necessarily the Trinity who has thus revealed himself to humanity. To misunderstand this point is to fail to perceive God as he truly is.

However, Gunton laments that Western theology has gone astray in perceiving the trinitarian God, and places the greatest blame upon Augustine's theology.³⁹ The basis of Gunton's accusation against Augustine is that Augustine, being influenced by Platonism, fused it with Christianity. As a result, the God construed by Augustine was not the triune God who is Father, Son, and Holy Spirit. Rather, it was a platonic God whose being is unknown substance (*substantia*). Indeed, Augustine's analogy of the human mind is an excellent proof of platonic influence over Augustine's theology.⁴⁰

In addition, Augustine's platonic influence caused Western theology to divorce the immanent Trinity from the economic Trinity. Gunton

---

38. Gunton, *Father, Son and Holy Spirit*, 12.

39. Robert W. Jenson who was Gunton's supervisor at Oxford recalls how Gunton came to dislike Augustine. "In his Oxford dissertation, Gunton—fairly or not—fathers the classical theism of Western Christian theology on Thomas Aquinas, as Aquinas is a great thinker and a chief shaper of the tradition. This view of Aquinas will remain. . . . But gradually, Augustine would replace Aquinas as the one chiefly blamed for those aspects of the theological tradition that Gunton, at time of the dissertation, labeled classical theism, and against which he never ceased to argue." Jensen, "A Decision Tree of Colin Gunton's Thinking," in *Theology of Colin Gunton*, 9–10. For those familiar with Gunton's work, it is amusing to discover that it was not Augustine whom Gunton first found fault with, but actually Aquinas.

40. It is an interesting question how much Augustine was actually influenced by Platonism. Diogenes Allen and Eric O. Springsted state, "Augustine . . . was one of the great Christian Platonists. Both he and Gregory of Nyssa . . . used the idea of Plotinus about the three divine hypostases to gain a deeper understanding of God." Allen and Springsted, *Philosophy for Understanding Theology*, 56. Robert Letham states, "Until recently, it was considered almost axiomatic that Augustine was influenced by Neoplatonism. From this, it is claimed, comes his overwhelming stress on the one divine essence and his great difficulties recognizing real distinctions for the three. In turn, this has left a legacy for the Western church: a modalistic tendency that blurs the distinctness of the persons." Letham, "Triune God," 100. Though Letham implies ("Until recently") that this traditional view of Augustine's Platonism isn't as monolithic as it once was, he does not elaborate on opinions to the contrary. On the other hand, Bradley G. Green defends Augustine. Bradley contends that despite the fact that Augustine preferred substance over relation, "Augustine is also clear that essence and substance *language* is a secondary concern to the *concepts* and *realities* themselves. Augustine does not argue that these terms must be used, but admits that a main impetus for trying to speak truthfully about God are the twin errors of tritheism and modalism." Green, *Colin Gunton and the Failure of Augustine*, 167. Although scholarly opinion is divided on this issue, it is fair to say that Augustine had some degree of platonic influence as Augustine himself admits in his *Confessions*. McNall echoes the same sympathy. McNall, "Guton and Augustine," 278–79.

contends, "To conceive God primarily in terms of intellect, with priority given to contemplation rather than action, renders the conception antithetical to a concept of God whose being is known primarily through his historical and particular action."[41] Augustine, whose idea of God mainly derives from *conceptual analysis* (e.g., the inner structure of human mind) rather than from the *actions* of God, failed to give due attention to the economic Trinity. The importance of the economic Trinity is minimized, while the immanent Trinity is appropriated apart from the economic Trinity where God's being and actions are revealed through Jesus Christ.[42]

Consequently, Gunton was determined to undo the damage that was caused by Augustine and Platonism. The trinitarian God had to be restored, and the platonistic God exposed. Furthermore, the significance of the economic Trinity had to be recovered in order to formulate a trinitarian ontology, "questions about the being of the God whose work is done both by Christ and by the Spirit who was understood to be in such close relation to him."[43]

Personal Spirit: Ontology

As noted above, the major factor that caused Augustine to lead Western theology astray, Gunton argues, was his misconception of the ontology of God. God is necessarily trinitarian. To perceive God as he truly is requires trinitarian thinking—God is three persons in communion.

In search of a solution, Gunton looked to the Cappadocians for a different perspective. Gunton states, "The achievement of the Cappadocians, an achievement which Augustine has failed adequately to understand, was to create a new conception of the being of God, in which God's being was

---

41. Gunton, *Act and Being: Towards a Theology of the Divine Attributes*, 40.

42. McNall argues that among all of Gunton's charges against Augustine, Augustine's inward turn to look for the *vestigial trinitatis* "remains viable" because it "proved influential in shaping certain modern tendencies [e.g., individualism and dualism]." McNall, *Free Corrector*, 231–32. This is a significant point in the formulation of the doctrine of God. As Gunton observed, "Because God is triune, we must respond to him in a particular way, or rather set of ways, corresponding to the richness of his being." Gunton, *Promise of Trinitarian Theology*, 4. If so, whether to turn inwardly (to the mind) or outwardly (to revelation) determines our approach to God and God's relation to humanity and the rest of creation. This, in my view, is the core of Gunton's argument against Augustine, and deserves further investigation.

43. Gunton, *Promise of Trinitarian Theology*, 8.

seen to consist in personal communion."[44] And this new concept of ontology ought to be the necessary foundation for Western theology.

As described above, Augustine's depreciation of person due to his Platonic debts is problematic because it promotes a view of God in which the divine being is "an unknown substance underlying the three persons rather than being constituted by their relatedness."[45] Gunton argues, "From at least the time of Augustine onwards the modalist temptation to posit a God lying behind his acts has been one of the perennial pitfalls of our tradition, Catholic and Evangelical alike."[46]

At the root of this problem, Gunton argues, is Augustine's failure to understand the meaning of *hypostasis*: particularity and unity. Gunton states,

> In all this, Augustine is taking a clear step back from the teaching of the Cappadocian Fathers. For them, the three persons are what they are in their relations and therefore relations qualify them ontologically, in terms of what they are.[47] Because Augustine continues to use relation as a logical rather than an ontological predicate, he is precluded from being able to make claims about the being of the *particular* persons, who, because they lack distinguishable identity tend to disappear into the all-embracing oneness of God.[48]

---

44. Gunton, *Promise of Trinitarian Theology*, 53.

45. Gunton, *Promise of Trinitarian Theology*, 43. Gunton also explains, "By contrast, the Cappadocian development, which Augustine so signally failed to appropriate, is that there is no being anterior to that of the persons. The being of God is the persons in relation to each other." Gunton, *Promise of Trinitarian Theology*, 74.

46. Gunton, *Father, Son and Holy Spirit*, 33. In fact, Gunton attributes modalism to Augustine: "The latter [Augustine] is modalist in direction, if not actually modalist, in the sense that the three persons of the Trinity tend to be conceived as posterior to an underlying *deitas* or being of which they are, so to speak, outcrops." Gunton, *Promise of Trinitarian Theology*, 74.

47. In other words, "Relation is an ontological category: relation constitutes who and what we are." Gunton, *Triune Creator*, 206.

48. Gunton, *Promise of Trinitarian Theology*, 41–42. In contrast to the Cappadocians, Gunton argues that Augustine could not "escape an individualistic concept of the person." Gunton, *Promise of Trinitarian Theology*, 95. In Augustine's mind, a person is identified with respect to himself, not in relation to others (e.g., the Father is a person not because of his relation to the Son and Holy Spirit, but with respect to himself). Therefore, Augustine's person is static and closed in. "Consequently . . . his concept of God escapes transformation, and he denies what for Basil was the heart of the matter: the 'three somethings subsist from one matter (material) which, whatever it is, is unfolded in these three.'"Gunton, *Promise of Trinitarian Theology*, 95.

In contrast to the Cappadocians, Augustine was unable to grasp the dynamic nature of the being of God.

Augustine's failure to appreciate the Cappadocian ontology also resulted in his misconstrual of pneumatology so that the Spirit's personhood was greatly undermined. For example, on the Augustinian view the Spirit is the bond (*vinculum*) of love that unites Father and Son. Yet, this bond of love is hardly perceived as a "person" when it should be on account of the ontology of the triune God. Instead, the Spirit is construed as a mere link that unites the Father and the Son within the Trinity because the concept of *hypostasis* is missing from Augustine's pneumatology. As a result, the Spirit's outward action is diminished: His activity of going beyond the Trinity to complete the love of the Father is disregarded.

To be sure, a link is unable to relate or act, while a person can. Thus, in Western theology there is a tendency to see the work of the Spirit as a "process, as the means of God's causal action upon us, rather than . . . his free personal relation with us."[49] We are unable to see the Spirit as a person who relates us to the Father because we are unable to "identify the God who comes among us in the way that he does."[50]

Since the identity of the Spirit was misconceived, the action of the Spirit also suffered. That is, because we were unable to identify the Spirit as a person who acts outwardly, we were unable to see his eschatological action which arises from his identity/distinctiveness as a person of the Trinity. Gunton contends, "The Spirit is indeed to be understood as the one who completes the relations of Father and Son. The difference is that the introduction of the eschatological note changes radically the way in which the relationship is understood: not a closed circle, but a self-sufficient community of love freely opened outwards to embrace the other."[51]

---

49. Gunton, *Theology through the Theologians*, 109.

50. Gunton, *Father, Son and Holy Spirit*, 12. McNall judges that Gunton's charge against Augustine on the bond of love as the third person of the Trinity is "the weakest point in Gunton's argument against Augustine." He contends that in *City of God*, Augustine identifies "the Sprit as the goodness (*bonitas*) and holiness (*sanctitas*) of God" and thereby captures the outward movement of the Spirit toward creation (Mcnall, "Gunton and Augustine," 274). While McNall is insightful, Gunton's criticism about the bond of love seems to include Augustine's shortcoming to capture the Spirit as a person—since a bond or link falls short of personhood. As a result, the personhood of the Spirit is undermined. The Spirit must be conceived as a person rather than a link, while the Spirit's movement must turn outward instead of inward. This is the eschatological character of the Spirit.

51. Gunton, *Theology through the Theologians*, 128.

No longer is the Spirit seen as an immanent power that works as God's causal action upon us. Rather, the Spirit is a person who seeks free personal relations with others. Gunton argues, "The Holy Spirit is then indeed the dynamic of the divine love, but one that seeks to involve the other in the movement of giving and receiving that is the Trinity; that is, to perfect the love of Father and Son by moving it beyond itself."[52] Therefore Gunton concludes, "The perfection of the divine love is revealed by the fact that it is neither self-love nor the merely reciprocal love of two for each other, but a love intrinsically oriented to community."[53]

Conceptualizing the being of God apart from the economic Trinity fails to perceive God as he truly is, chiefly by overshadowing the eschatological nature of the Spirit. To unfold the Spirit's work, one must look to the economy where God's action is revealed through Son and Spirit. Gunton states, "In the economy it is the action of the Spirit not simply to relate the individual God, but to realize in time the conditions of the age to come."[54] Therefore, "We must return to the economy of divine action in the Spirit's action in time and space to enquire whether there can be found a more comprehensive articulation of the Spirit's action than has been customary in the tradition."[55] The divorce between the immanent and the economy must be reconciled; the dynamic nature of the ontology of the divine being must be recovered. In so doing, we will unfold the eschatological Spirit.

Transcendent Spirit: Creation and Redemption

If the Spirit is the eschatological Spirit, what can we assume about creation? As Green rightly points out, "There *are* no eschatological activities apart from creation and redemption."[56] In other words, if the Spirit is "*to perfect*

---

52. Gunton, *Theology through the Theologians*, 127.
53. Gunton, *Theology through the Theologians*, 127.
54. Gunton, *Theology through the Theologians*, 127.
55. Gunton, *Theology through the Theologians*, 112.
56. Green, *Colin Gunton and the Failure of Augustine*, 57n126; italics in original. This is perhaps the most critical point of Gunton's eschatological Spirit since it appears to threaten the freedom of God in choosing to create. Green contends, "Gunton seems to waffle on whether this "outward" move towards the world in creation and redemption is somehow necessary or required. The thrust of Gunton's logic is that at the heart of what it means for the Spirit to be the Spirit is the whole realm of the Spirit's eschatological activities, but there are no eschatological activities apart from creation and redemption." Green, *Colin Gunton and the Failure of Augustine*, 57n126. Green rightly points out the

the love of Father and Son by moving it beyond itself,"[57] a creation is the place where the mission of the Spirit must be accomplished.

Gunton contends that creation is a project. It is a place where God's creation (humankind and the material world) is to be perfected by the Spirit and conformed to God's own particularity. Like a human project, it takes time and requires space. Hence, creation is not timeless or without space. On the contrary, it will require time and space for its perfection. Creation is good, but it is yet to be completed. Gunton explains,

> That which is made in the beginning is very good, yet remains to be perfected: perfect and to be perfected. It is not yet subdued, all things not yet brought together under one head, even Christ (Eph. 1:10). Eschatologically speaking, even "in the beginning," before the fall, things are not yet as they are created to be, because there is a task laid upon those created in the image of God and it involves both the moral and the cultural, insofar as they can be separated.[58]

Traditionally, the Genesis story has been understood as God creating a perfect world: perfection that has no room for progression. The corruption that we see today is due to the sin of Adam. Sin entered into the world and corrupted God's creation. Therefore, creation needs to be restored by Christ. Certainly, redemption is constitutive of the perfection/salvation of the world. Yet, this is not the whole picture of what God intends for his creation.

Gunton asserts, "What is realized in the incarnate involvement of the Son in time and space is the redirection of the creation to its original destiny, a destiny that was from the beginning in Christ, for all creation is

---

seeming implication: God needs to create since his nature requires the existence of a creation. To my knowledge, Gunton never discusses this tension in any of his writings. When Gunton talks about the freedom of God in his creative activity, he often appeals to the concept of mediation to secure the freedom and independence of God from the creation. To some extent, using the concept of mediation is the preferred recourse for Gunton to resolve any issues that may arise in the relation between God and creation. In chapter 4, I will discuss whether Gunton's eschatological Spirit can assure the freedom of God. The main point to be examined is how or whether the concept of mediation might provide theological warrant for the freedom of God in the light of Gunton's eschatological Spirit. It is certainly true that despite some apparent obstacles, Gunton's argument for the eschatological Spirit is supported by scripture (Gen 1:2, 2:7; Ezekiel 37; etc.) The issue here is how we should resolve theologically what Scripture already attests to us.

57. Gunton, *Theology through the Theologians*, 127; italics in original.

58. Gunton, "Reformation Accounts of the Church's Response to Human Culture" 79–80.

through and to the Son."⁵⁹ Hence, the perfection of creation "is not perfect in the sense of complete."⁶⁰ In other words, creation is designed to go somewhere. God did not intend only to rescue the world (redemption), but also to perfect it (creation). Creation was made through Christ, yet this creation is not only to be rescued by him who is the mediator of creation and redeemer of the world, but also is to be consummated in him for God's glory.

Gunton blames Western theology, especially Augustine, for failing to recognize the intricate relation between creation and redemption which is so significant for understanding the divine plan for the created world. If one fails to see this connection in the light of Christ, his mediating work of creation and redemption, Gunton contends that the divine purpose for God's creation cannot be fully uncovered. Consequently, the eschatological thrust of creation was completely undermined.

Gunton argues that Christ is replaced by platonic forms in Augustine's theology due to dualism.⁶¹ Christological mediation—creation and incarnation—was excluded because Christ was not the one whom the created order was created by, but "by *intellectual forms* or patterns."⁶² Accordingly, the incarnation of Christ was reduced to divine intervention to rescue the soul of humankind from the sins of the world, while it should be construed as God's continuous work for the perfection of the world.⁶³ Such severing of creation and redemption caused the omission of Christological mediation in God's divine plan for the world, as well as the neglect of the eschatological work of the Spirit.

---

59. Gunton, *Christ and Creation*, 94.

60. Gunton, *Triune Creator*, 202.

61. McNall agrees with Gunton to some extent on Augustine's tendency toward dualism. While McNall illustrates how Gunton misconstrued Augustine on material goodness, he says, "Gunton was not wrong, however, to note that a certain material dualism remained a problem for Augustine—even if it was a malady from which he was being progressively 'healed.'" McNall, "Gunton and Augustine," 278.

62. Gunton, *Triune Creator*, 202; italics in original.

63. Gunton is clear that the incarnation is not simply God's intervention to save the world from sin. That is, Christ would have become incarnated even if sin had not entered the world. "The ways of God for his creation involve Christ, the one through whom he created and continues to uphold the universe *in any case*, and therefore he would have come—even had sin not dictated the *form* of his coming. Sin and evil are, then, in Edward Irving's words, the *formal* cause of the incarnation, determining the shape it takes, in the suffering and death of Jesus." Gunton, *Christian Faith*, 67–68.

Moreover, the dualism that resulted from Platonism devalued the goodness of the material. As a result the creation is to be left behind for destruction at the end, despite its goodness and beauty. Gunton argues that such dualism is echoed loudly in Augustine's *City of God*. Gunton, thereby, calls for a "re-examination of the place of eschatology in our understanding of the relation of the two cities."[64]

Gunton, having understood the eschatological significance of creation, contends that contrary to the traditional construal, creation should not be understood as something to be left to decay, but a place that will be perfected. Creation provides the milieu of the divine drama of eschatology. Therefore, creation has significant meaning. And this significance comes from none other than Christ who is the mediator of creation and redemption. Gunton explains,

> The *material* world's fundamental meaningfulness is demonstrated by the fact that the one through whom it took shape became material. . . . The incarnate dies as the result of his engagement with a fallen world, and by his death calls it back to its true destiny. Thus by the incarnation the material world is affirmed as the place where there can be meaning, while through the cross of the crucified it is redeemed from meaninglessness.[65]

The significance of the creation in the scheme of the divine eschatology cannot be underestimated, and stands in contrast to an ontology of creation that views it as inferior and expendable. Gunton concludes, "The teaching that the one through whom the world was made became part of that world, even in its fallenness, affirms the readiness of that world for human knowledge, action and shaping."[66]

Augustine's weak Christology and pneumatology resulted in a lack of eschatology in his theology, Gunton argues. Failing to recognize the unity between creation and redemption, creation became irrelevant to the divine salvation. Further, it confused the whole picture of salvation.[67] The sig-

---

64. Gunton, *Promise of Trinitarian Theology*, 172.
65. Gunton, *Christ and Creation*, 122–23; italics in original.
66. Gunton, *Christ and Creation*, 123.
67. Gunton delineates the concept of salvation: "The eschatological completion of the project, inaugurated at the creation and re-established by Jesus, is thus anticipated in all forms of human action and worldly event that are enabled by the Holy Spirit as he relates the world to the Father through Jesus Christ, crucified, risen and ascended." Gunton, *Promise of Trinitarian Theology*, 192. Schaeffer's interpretation of Gunton's definition of salvation is concise and helpful: "Salvation history is the history of creation as a whole, a

nificance of creation was undermined when it needed to be acknowledged. Creation is an essential part of the divine plan of salvation because it provides a place for the divine drama of eschatology, not to mention that the One through whom the creation was created became part of the material world by choosing to come in the form of a man.

Understood in these terms, creation is also the object of salvation because the eschatological Spirit is also the perfecting cause of the creation. Gunton states, "Rom 8 is not just nice rhetoric for when we want to feel ecologically pious, but intrinsic to a sustained pneumatology, in which Paul moves from Christ, through the community of redemption, to the way in which the human creation is not to be perfected apart from the liberation of the world in which it is set."[68] In fact, Christ's resurrection body is the central example of perfection of the material world: "A body or, perhaps better, whole person perfected by the Spirit, the first fruits of the perfecting of all the creation, the form of which all human beings have been created."[69]

And the Spirit works according to the Son, "the first fruits of the perfecting of all the creation," in order to particularize humanity and the world by relating them to God and each other. As the Spirit enables humanity to realize their ultimate destiny, the created world will be liberated from its bondage. If we are being in communion, we cannot truly *be* apart from our environment. What surrounds us influences us as we also influence what surrounds us. This is the "conception of the Spirit as realizing the condition of the age to come particularly through the creation of community."[70]

In this section, we have examined the theological basis of Gunton's pneumatology. Gunton asserted that Augustine's failure to understand the Cappadocians' ontology and his platonic influence distorted not only Augustine's doctrine of God, but also his pneumatology. As a result, the personhood of the Spirit is undermined and the eschatological/transcendent aspect of the Spirit is silenced. Gunton's call for a new ontology and an attendant pneumatology that is primarily eschatological is persuasive. The trinitarian God must be recovered; the platonic God must be dismissed. To reveal a "more comprehensive articulation of the Spirit's action,"[71] the

---

timeful project of God, which deprives history of its assumed timelessness and anthropocentrism." Schaeffer, *Createdness and Ethics*, 69.

68. Gunton, "Reformation Accounts of the Church's," 81.
69. Gunton, "Reformation Accounts of the Church's," 81.
70. Gunton, *Promise of Trinitarian Theology*, 51.
71. Gunton, *Theology through Theologians*, 112.

trinitarian God whose being consists of three persons in communion who work together to achieve the perfection of the world must be recovered.

BIBLICAL EVIDENCE FOR THE ESCHATOLOGICAL SPIRIT

Having examined Gunton's critique of the Augustinian legacy and the eschatological Spirit, we must now turn to Gunton's biblical basis for the eschatological Spirit. In this section, first, the nature and orientation of the creation will be examined in hopes of identifying the necessity of eschatological work over the creation. To accomplish this, Gunton's exegetical work on Genesis is closely examined along with other important scriptures that present strong arguments for the Sprit's eschatological work. Secondly, we will examine passages that speak directly of the eschatological work of the Spirit in hopes of showing that the concept is firmly supported by scripture.

Biblical Evidence for the Perfection of the Whole Creation

The text of Genesis is clearly of great importance in relation to the doctrine of creation. Much controversy about the theological and exegetical interpretation of Genesis has shown the potential difficulties of the text. Nonetheless, Gunton traces much misunderstanding of Genesis back to Augustine.

Gunton accuses Augustine of following Origen, who was also swayed by Platonism in interpreting Genesis. As a result, Augustine misconstrued the "biblical orientation on creation" and led Western theology astray.[72] According to Gunton, three points that Augustine misconstrued are, first, a dualistic view of creation. Contrary to Augustine who divided the created world between the intellectual and the material, creation is to be perceived as one. Second, contrary to Augustine's contention, the image of God should be defined relationally rather in terms of possession of reason. Third, in regard to the relation between human and non-human creation, continuity within discontinuity should be acknowledged because of the createdness of both.

At the heart of all of these problems is Augustine's failure to give due weight to the economy. Gunton states,

---

72. Gunton, *One, the Three, and the Many*, 2–3.

> It is when he [Augustine] attempts a theological reading that the problems begin to appear, chief among them the fact that he is unable to interpret the text in the light of the economy, the biblical account of God's actions taking place in time, with the result that his understanding of divine action becomes abstract and essentially at variance with the spacious movement of the author of Genesis."[73]

Further, Augustine misconstrues the omnipotence of God in his creating activities by claiming that if God takes time to create, he is limited to time or bounded by this means of creation, which obscures the self-limitation of God in creation. The dynamic nature and orientation of the creation cannot be overlooked, Gunton asserts, because "This is a key to a theology of the Spirit—that God creates a world which requires time both to be and to become what it is created to be."[74]

Gunton refers to Genesis 1 to argue that chaos existed at the beginning of the world. In 1:2, the scripture states that "the Spirit of God was hovering over the waters." Although Gunton acknowledges that in general the preferred translation of אֱלֹהִים רוּחַ is "wind" rather than Spirit, he points out that "the reference is to the 'powerful presence of God moving mysteriously over the face of the waters ... hovering and ready for action.'"[75] Gunton thus concludes that even in Genesis the eschatological work of the Spirit, that is working against what is not God's, must be acknowledged.

Gunton argues that the instruction of 1:28 "to subdue the earth" describes the chaotic condition of the created world. God had not completed his creating activities. Furthermore, Genesis 2 indicates that there was no hospitable environment outside of the garden for Adam and Eve. Gunton concludes, "In that regard, chapters 1 and 2 are saying much the same. The world is of such a kind that it requires obedient human activity to enable the achievement of that for which it was created. Creation is perfect—'very good'—but remains to be perfected, in part by faithful human action."[76]

Interestingly, in relation to God's action in the creation, Gunton once again finds a Christological link between the creation and redemption. However, this time, the nature of the link is different. Gunton refers to

---

73. Gunton, "Between Allegory and Myth," 56.
74. Gunton, *Father, Son and Holy Spirit*, 108.
75. Gunton, *Father, Son and Holy Spirit*, 108.
76. Gunton, *Father, Son and Holy Spirit*, 110.

Christ as the wisdom of God (1 Cor 1:24, 30),[77] who reveals the manner of God's action towards the creation. The one through whom the creation was created is the crucified Lord who suffered on the cross. That is to say that Christ as the wisdom of God has shown the nature of God's wisdom in his creating and redeeming activity. Gunton explains, "This is not to suggest that God takes time to achieve wisdom—after all, is not his wisdom mediator of the creation from the beginning?—but that it is part of his wisdom in action that it allows, or, better enables, things to take their course."[78]

Moreover, Gunton contends that the wisdom of God not only enables the creation to take its own course to perfection over spans of time, but also takes into account the human condition in its createdness along with its fallenness.[79] Gunton states,

> It is, by its very nature, directed to a completion that *takes time*. And so divine action centred in the death of Jesus is action which is fully appropriate both to human fallenness and to its need of time in order to be itself. For the cross is where God engages with the human condition as it actually is, representing both its temporal structures and the nature of those who are in need of being redirected to their proper course.[80]

As the text of Genesis 1 and 2 shows, the nature of the creation requires time to be perfected. In the same way, the cross of Christ, which is the pivotal moment of God's plan of redemption, also demonstrates the necessity of re-direction as well as the progressive nature of the redemptive plan. Canonically, the cross is not only the point of divine intervention to deal with the falleness of the world, but also a mark that signifies the unfolding of the dynamic divine plan of the perfection of the whole

---

77. Gunton explains the nature of the wisdom of Christ. "The wisdom is primarily neither a way of fitting human life into the order of creation . . . nor a focus of a general continuity between the mind and the world. It is, rather, a *form of divine action* in which the relation between creator and creation is realized in a highly particular way." Gunton, *Father, Son and Holy Spirit*, 110; italics mine.

78. Gunton, *Father, Son and Holy Spirit*, 135–136.

79. Gunton speaks of the relation of God to time. "A more adequate account of the relation of God to time is to be found in maintaining the delicate balance between, on the one hand, creation, and redemption, and on the other, divine action and human response. The breaking in of the future kingdom does require obedient and active human response. But, given human fallibility and falleness, that can take shape only on the basis of the past divine creation and reconciliation by means of which is laid the foundation of present and future redemption." Gunton, *One, the Three and the Many*, 93.

80. Gunton, *Father, Son and Holy Spirit*, 136; italics in original.

creation: The One through whom the creation was made (Genesis 1; John 1:3) continues to bring the creation to perfection so that all will be put under him (Eph 1:22) in order that all the creation will glorify God in the end (Revelations 21–22).

Further, Jesus who is the wisdom of God is not only the action of God towards the creation, but also a "form of that right human being which realizes the truth of being."[81] Christ exemplifies with his body what it is to be perfected as God's creature. Gunton writes, "The doctrine of the resurrection is not first of all about immortality, but about God's purposes for his creation, and especially his human creation. . . . Whatever happens 'after death' it is continuous both with what happened before—life in the body—and with the life of the whole material creation."[82] Hence, no dualism exists between the material and immaterial, or body and soul. In short, the resurrection of Christ manifests the irrefutable fact that the whole human being, not only the soul (immaterial) but also the body (material), will be perfected. And Gunton extends this material perfection to the created world.

Gunton states that Rom 8 makes clear that the created world will be saved along with humanity. In light of the background of Gen 3:17, the created world is also in need of redemption, and its redemption relies on humanity: "The creation waits in eager expectation for the sons of God to be revealed" (Rom 8:19). Thus, the created world shares a common destiny with humanity. Whether they fall or rise, the destiny of the creation is tied to them.

Consequently, human responsibility for the created world is immense. As Gen 1:28 makes clear, this responsibility was given to humanity by God. God told Adam to take care of the earth, which was a calling to act as God's representative in ruling the earth. Therefore, failing to exercise our calling to take care of the world will result in the decay of the created realm.

Another important aspect of this relation is that as much as the creation needs humanity for its salvation, humanity also needs the creation. Gunton explains, "The crucial lesson to be learned from Romans 8 and its background in Genesis 1–3 is that it is a mistake to treat what we can call the material creation or the natural world in abstraction from its being in some way ordered to the human race."[83] Again, as the resurrection of

---

81. Gunton, *Father, Son and Holy Spirit*, 142.

82. Gunton, *Christian Faith*, 152.

83. Gunton, *Father, Son and Holy Spirit*, 111.

Christ shows, the whole person was resurrected. This signifies the fact that in the divine eschatological plan, there is a place for the material creation because of "its being in some way ordered to the human race." And Christ's resurrection is the promise of that. Gunton concludes,

> The resurrection of flesh, of the whole person, is the completion of the promise inherent in Genesis 1.26–7, because those created in the image of God are to be perfected in the context in which they are created. Likewise, the promise of Revelation 21.1–4 is that there will be a new heaven and a new earth, so that God will truly be praised in the completion and perfection of all his works.[84]

The study of creation clearly shows its dynamic nature. Yet, its perfection cannot be achieved apart from humanity. As Christ's resurrection testifies, the whole *creation* (human and non-human) must be perfected. Therefore, the eschatological work of the Spirit is necessary to accomplish this end. And this is indeed the divine plan of salvation for the whole world so that in the end all glory will be given to God by his entire creation.

The work of the Spirit is mysterious. As scripture says, "the wind blows wherever it pleases. You hear its sound, but you cannot tell where it comes from or where it is going" (John 3:8). Nonetheless, despite the mysterious nature of the Spirit's activity, there is sufficient scriptural evidence for the eschatological work of the Holy Spirit. Gunton contends, "A distinctive feature of the New Testament characterisation of the Spirit's action is their thoroughgoing eschatological emphasis. In Paul, the Spirit is the presence now, by anticipation, of that which belongs to the age to come."[85] Scriptures that demonstrate the eschatological character of the Spirit include: Down payment, 2 Cor 1:22; First-fruits, Rom 8:23; the Pentecost event, Acts 2:17–21; judgment, John 16:8; Luke 3:16. Gunton asserts that "for Scripture the Spirit is God being eschatological."[86]

Gunton finds further evidence in other parts of the Scripture. Gunton argues that Gen 1:2 suggests the Spirit's eschatological work. Palms 33:6 shows the Spirit's creating work in contrast to the Word. Other scriptures also signify the Spirit's work as the free, life-giving power of God (Gen 2:7; Ezek 37:1–14; Ps 104: 29b–30; Luke 1–2; etc.). In such verses the specific function of the Spirit, the life-giving power of God, is revealed. The Spirit freely moves in and towards the creation as a life-giving Spirit and

---

84. Gunton, *Christian Faith*, 154.
85. Gunton, *Theology through the Theologians*, 119.
86. Gunton, *Father, Son, and Holy Spirit*, 76.

maintains and renews the life of the creation. Gunton writes, "The Lord's Spirit gives the breath that is a life, a theme to which we must give central attention in any theology of the Spirit and the creation."[87]

Among these texts Ezek 37:1–14 is especially significant because of its intricate relation to the resurrection of Christ. Gunton argues that the resurrection of Christ is the fulfillment of Ezek 37:1–14, the promise which is inherent in these verses. Accordingly, the nature and person of the Spirit can be revealed by the manner of the Spirit's work over the dry bones. In fact, the eschatological work of the Spirit will become more distinct in the first two chapters of Luke because there is, Gunton argues, continuity between Luke's pneumatology in the first two chapters and the life-giving power of God. Gunton states,

> The Spirit's freedom in relation to the creation is expressed paradigmatically in the forming of the Son's body in the womb of Mary. It is in the incarnation and particularly in relation to the humanity of Christ in general that we discern a unique particularizing of the activity of the Spirit as the life-giving power of God in and towards his creation.[88]

Besides, as we see in the story of the temptation of Jesus in Luke 4, it is the Spirit who empowers the Son to resist temptation. Gunton writes, "The Spirit, therefore, is not conceived, as tends to be the case with Augustine, as the immanent possession of Jesus, but as God's free and life-giving activity in and toward the world as he maintains and empowers the human activity of the incarnate Son."[89] Such a being cannot be a mere substance or force. Gunton explains,

> The Spirit is on such an account not so much an endowment as the one sent from the Father who in personal divine action enables the incarnate Son to be himself. *That is why the Holy Spirit is rightly called a person, a hypostasis. By this is meant at least a centre of action rather than merely a 'substance'—in the usual sense—or 'force'.*[90]

Hence, the Holy Spirit is a personal Spirit who moves outwardly towards the creation to enable it to enter into union with God.

---

87. Gunton, *Father, Son and Holy Spirit*, 110.
88. Gunton, "Spirit in the Trinity," 126.
89. Gunton, "Spirit in the Trinity," 127.
90. Gunton, *Theology through Theologians*, 116; italics in original.

Another significant aspect of the life-giving power of God in Ezek 37:1–14 is the shift of our focus from spiritual perfection—that is, the Spirit only perfecting the soul—to the perfection of the material such as body and society. As examined above, spiritual perfection has been the sole focus of transformation/redemption. Yet, the dry bones that the Spirit raised to life foreshadow the resurrection of Christ and therefore signify the promise of the resurrection of a whole person, not just a soul.[91] Gunton contends, "An adequate account of the Spirit's perfecting action will embrace the human, the non-human, and the two in relation."[92]

Gunton illustrates how the Spirit works in our context of two realms—a human (soul and body) and non-human (the wider creation). Gunton's concern is "with the way in which the Spirit enables human action to interact with the creation in such a way as to enable it to be perfected."[93]

Gunton looks to Exod 31:1–11 to show that the Spirit of God was upon Bezalel, son of Uri, to equip him with the skills and ability to build a tabernacle as the Lord commanded.[94] In light of this, he then draws an

---

91. Gunton proposes a new concept of perfection that embraces the material along with the immaterial. He states, "Whatever we are to make of Leviticus' teaching on holiness, there seems little doubt that it is concerned with material—bodily and social—and not 'spiritual' perfection in a narrow sense." Gunton, "Reformation Accounts of the Church's," 80. Gunton defends this by claiming that a proper account of the Spirit's perfecting action indicates that it does not remain in the realm of the non-material, but moves on to perfect the material. Further, Gunton contends, "To say God is spirit is to say, I believe, not that he is non-material—though, of course, that does not have to be denied—but, positively, that he is able to transcend the ontological divide between the Creator and created, in order to transform and perfect the *material* world." Gunton, "Reformation Accounts of the Church's," 80–81. This new conception of "perfecting" or "spiritualizing" is significant in understanding the Spirit's eschatological work as well as the divine plan of salvation for his creation.

92. Gunton, "Reformation Accounts of the Church's," 80.

93. Gunton, "Reformation Accounts of the Church's," 80.

94. Victor P. Hamilton comments on the Spirit of God that came upon Bezalel and his colleagues to equip them with skills and knowledge for building the tabernacle. He suggests that although the Spirit gives new gifts and abilities to humanity, "more often than not, I suspect, the Spirit takes gifts already present and refocuses and redirects them in ways of his choosing." Hamilton, *Exodus*, 522. He draws an inference from David playing a lyre before Saul (1 Sam 16:18, 23) and concludes that the same thing can apply to the case of Bezalel. Perhaps the significance of Hamilton's interpretation is that the Spirit can use the skills or knowledge that God's people have developed over the years to build a tabernacle that is not only a place of worship, but also a recreation of God's Kingdom. This implies that as with Bezalel, we also are expected to participate in God's recreation of his cosmos. The eschatological Spirit, thereby, promotes humanity's participation in God's perfection of the world.

analogy between God the Creator and Moses. As God saw that his creation was good (Gen 1:31), Moses looked at the tabernacle (Exod 39:43). As God rested on the seventh day of his creation (Gen 2:2), Moses was commanded by God to remind his people to observe the Sabbath (Exod 31:3).[95]

Such analogies enable us to see the parallel that exists between God and humankind in the activity of creating and remind us of the cultural mandate of Gen 1:28. Gunton contends, "It seems to me to be right to understand the mandate of Genesis 1.28 as not a permission but a command to so engage with the created order to enable it to join the human species in praise of its creator."[96] Gunton calls such creating activities "culture."[97]

This becomes much clearer in light of Rom 8:18–21. Humanity is not alone in participating in God's creating activities. As the Spirit was upon Bezalel to equip him to build a tabernacle, the Spirit will be upon the people of God to fulfill our calling. Thus, partnership between the Spirit and humanity is absolutely necessary to achieve the perfection of the creation. As one can see in Romans 8, Paul exhorts the Romans to live in the Spirit. Then, he makes clear that the creation cannot be liberated apart from humanity. What this implies is that "Specific forms of symbolic actions [worship,

---

95. The theme of building a tabernacle has significant implications for the work of the eschatological Spirit as we can see that the phrase רוּחַ אֱלֹהִים appears in this verse (Exod 31:3) for the third time (e.g., Gen 1:2, 41:38). With this in mind, Peter Enns comments that to build a tabernacle is not simply to build a place of worship, but to create a heaven on earth which implies the creative force of the eschatological Spirit. Enns adds, "The references to the Sabbath are intended to connect the building of the tabernacle to creation." Enns, *Exodus*, 507; italics in original. Therefore, the creation story of Genesis foreshadows Exodus. This implies that a tabernacle is a place where God recreates the cosmos. Israel is a new people of God—that is, God's new creation, while the tabernacle is a microcosm of the created order. In other words, "God is truly recreating heaven in *space* and *time*." Enns, *Exodus*, 546. If so, this is indeed an ideal illustration or analogy of what Gunton appeals to—the eschatological Spirit who works in two realms, the human and the created world, to bring perfection to the entire creation.

96. Gunton, *Father, Son and Holy Spirit*, 123.

97. Gunton observes, "In this context, culture, we might say, is that set of activities in which those made in the image of God share in the divine perfecting of that which was made in the beginning." Gunton, "Reformation Accounts of the Church's," 80. Gunton emphasizes that the criteria to determine what true culture is in this fallen world must be explicitly Christological. Nonetheless, he contends, "Christ is to be found not only where the gospel is consciously lived." Gunton, "Reformation Accounts of the Church's," 90. He thus implies the possibility that the Spirit's eschatological work can be manifested in areas or persons without God. Gunton appeals to the mysteriousness of the Spirit, but also to the "mysterious and indefinable reality we call life—that realm which . . . is peculiarly that of the Lord." Gunton, *Father, Son and Holy Spirit*, 124.

communion, etc.] place human life in relation to God, human social order and the material world. The action of the Spirit is required if those actions and their social context are to achieve what they are designed to do."[98] There is no society that is context-less. Human action affects the form of society. Yet, human action must be empowered and guided by the eschatological Spirit to enable the creation to achieve its end.

GUNTON CRITIQUED

There are, of course, scholars who challenge the viability of a "Trinitarian theology" such as Bernhard Nausner and Richard M. Fermer[99] who hold that Gunton is unable to deliver on his promise due to significant theological flaws in his system.

Some of the criticisms offered by Nausner and Fermer include the following. First, in regard to Cappadocian theology (which they argue doesn't actually exist), Gunton along with John Zizioulas misinterprets the Cappadocians. This results in reducing *ousia* to *koinonia*. Second, Gunton's concept of personhood is difficult to apply to human beings—for example, the assertion that personhood consists of relation and otherness. When applied to humans, since Gunton does not hold to an *ousia*, but a relational ontology, it raises the question of "who or what does the relating."[100] Third, Gunton oversimplifies the problems of modernity (homogeneity and subjectivism). As a result, he fails to capture a more comprehensive view of modern problems (e.g., human experience and socialization). In their view, since Gunton did not grasp the real problems of the modern world, his trinitarian theology that promises that everything looks different is unable to offer a solution for the modern world.[101]

Nausner and Fermer's charges against Gunton's trinitarian theology are worthy of examination. These are significant points that if ultimately

---

98. Gunton, *Father, Son and Holy Spirit*, 122.

99. Nausner, "Failure of a Laudable Project," 403–20; Fermer, "Limits of Trinitarian Theology as a Methodological Paradigm," 158–86.

100. Nausner, "Failure of a Laudable Project," 416.

101. Cf., Green, "Gunton and the Theological Origin of Modernity." Similarly, Green also points out the problem of Gunton's oversimplification of the problems of modernity: "I will suggest that because Gunton's analysis of the nature and origin of modernity is somewhat flawed, likewise Gunton's suggestion for what provides healing in the light of modernity indeed may be flawed." Green, "Gunton and the Theological Origin of Modernity," 171.

true have the potential to damage the foundation of Gunton's trinitarian theology. Nonetheless, I argue that Gunton's trinitarian theology still has much to offer the modern world. As Fermer himself admits, "Many of the aims of the Trinitarian theology that have been examined are laudable."[102] Indeed, Gunton's pneumatology, which is a constitutive part of his trinitarian theology, is a case in point.

CONCLUSION

In light of the preceding discussion, we can conclude that Gunton's pneumatology, which is trinitarianly formed and eschatologically conceived, can shed new light on our world and life in this world. Gunton claims, "In the light of the theology of the Trinity, everything looks different."[103] This is because, Gunton argues, the theology of the Trinity, particularity and unity, reveals to us the nature of our world and life in this world. Therefore, everything looks different in the light of Gunton's Trinitarian theology and especially when his pneumatology is considered as part of it.

Gunton's pneumatology promises many things. The eschatological Spirit is a personal Spirit who moves outwardly to invite humankind to enter into relation with God. Similarly, the eschatological Spirit is a transcendent Spirit who brings perfection to the world for God's glory. Hence, the restoration of our relation with God as well as the transformation of God's creation is promised. And this promise does not remain solely with humankind, but extends to our created world. But, among all of these, most importantly, Gunton's pneumatology promises that God is a God who comes among us. He is not a static God, unmoved and aloof. On the contrary, his nature, the divine love that is not content to remain within himself, moves him to reach out beyond himself.

Furthermore, Gunton's pneumatology promises our place in this drama of transformation. God calls humanity to participate in the divine plan of the perfection of the world. Hence, we have responsibilities to fulfill. We are neither onlookers nor sole receivers of the divine plan of perfection. The created world depends in part on us for its liberation from bondage. It is our calling and duty to take care of the world by representing the Creator in our stewardship of the world. And from this perspective, Gunton's pneumatology promises to be a theology that bears upon life. It is no longer a

102. Fermer, "Limits of Trinitarian Theology as a Methodological Paradigm," 185.
103. Gunton, *Promise of Trinitarian Theology*, 7.

theory, but a reality that shapes our existence in order to influence what is around us.

Gunton's pneumatology offers contributions to the area of public theology because it is a theology that calls for radical consequences for human life as well as the created world. In other words, it is a pneumatology that confronts us with the divine plan of perfection: It takes us out of the darkness to place us under the sun to see that God is already working among us in carrying out his mission to the whole world and calling us to participate.

Gunton's pneumatology that is trinitarianly formed and eschatologically conceived is a welcome resource for public theology because it complements what is lacking in public theology. On the one hand, the Spirit is a person—not a thing or a link—who moves beyond the Trinity to seek relation. On the other hand, the Spirit is eschatological—He perfects the world by particularity and unity. In these ways, Gunton's pneumatology is helpful to further develop public theology.

Yet one area that requires further examination is whether Gunton is able to justify the eschatological Spirit in relation to the divine freedom. That is, whether he can continue to defend his claim that it is not by necessity that God creates, but by his essence (the divine love) that God creates as an expression of his love. As we examine the various facets of the Spirit's eschatological action in relation to the trinitarian God, Christology, and anthropology, this issue must be revisited to assess the validity of Gunton's claim.

CHAPTER 3

GUNTON'S DOCTRINE OF THE TRIUNE GOD AND PNEUMATOLOGY

THE DOCTRINE OF GOD is significant because it influences all other areas of theology (Christology, Pneumatology, Incarnation, Atonement, etc.). Depending on one's theological methodology, God can be construed very differently (relational versus non-relational, etc.).

Gunton argues for the trinitarian God who is the Father, the Son and the Spirit. God is relational because he is constituted by the three persons in communion. In particular, Gunton argues for the eschatological Spirit. In the previous chapter, we saw that Gunton lamented how Western theology had overlooked the eschatological character of the Spirit due to the fact that God is conceived as substance rather than a person, and passive rather than active.

In this way, Gunton seems to say that there is consistency between God's being and action. That is, God's action must originate in his being. If so, it is important to examine Gunton's doctrine of God to determine whether it provides a sufficient basis for the eschatological Spirit. To accomplish this end, we will first examine the relation between the immanent Trinity and economic Trinity. This is an attempt to understand the basis of Gunton's theological methodology for the doctrine of God. Second, we will examine the triune Creator and the creation. The purpose of this section is to identify who God is and what the creation is in relation to God in hopes of establishing that God relates to the creation regardless of the ontological differences between the two.

Third, the nature of this relation will be examined. The primary focus of this section is God's aseity: whether and how God's aseity can be preserved in his relation to the world. Accordingly, the source of the relation will be examined, and the function of the source will be discussed to show that God relates to the world without undermining his sovereignty. Fourth, the last two sections will examine the actions of God in providence and salvation. The purpose of these sections is to examine how God's relation to the world can be transformative and redemptive. This will in turn answer why such a relation is necessary to achieve God's ultimate purpose for the world.

BEING AND BECOMING: THE RELATION BETWEEN THE IMMANENT AND ECONOMIC TRINITY

As discussed in chapter 2, Gunton places significant emphasis on person (*hypostasis*) rather than substance (*ousia*). God is three persons in communion. Thus, God is dynamic rather than static. Because God is necessarily trinitarian, to perceive God as he truly requires trinitarian thinking. Hence, conceptualizing the being of God apart from the economic Trinity fails to properly grasp the ontology of God. Nonetheless, Western theology has failed to adequately understand the concept of *hypostasis*. Accordingly, God's being was conceptualized apart from the economic Trinity. The consequence was the divorce of the immanent Trinity from the economic Trinity. Gunton laments, "There seems to be little clarity about how the two are related: how the identity of God as Father, Son and Holy Spirit relates to the kind of things that have been, and are said of the kind of being that God is."[1]

Gunton attempts to formulate the doctrine in a way that addresses this division. He looks to Karl Barth for the answer, as he looked to the Cappadocians for their relational ontology.[2] Gunton employs Barth's *being*

1. Gunton, *Act and Being*, 1. John G. Flett, interacting with Karl Barth's theology, also expresses his concern in regard to the schism between the two trinities: "The transition between who God is *in se* and his act of reconciliation is '*first a divine* problem—the problem of God's *own* being,' for it is a problem of how 'in anticipation his existence includes within itself our existence with him. How can the one *be* true and the other *become* true?'" Flett, *Witness of God*, 200; italics in original.

2. See Gunton, *Becoming and Being*. This is Gunton's dissertation at the University of Oxford under the guidance of Robert Jenson. In this volume, Gunton makes a

in becoming to find a solution for the schism between the two trinities.³ Gunton argues,

> Barth uses the concept of divine becoming to show that there is no breach between God's action and his being. In the incarnation God demonstrates his freedom "to become unlike Himself and yet to remain the same", and it is this revelation of himself which ought to be the source of any conclusions we draw about what he is in eternity.⁴

Gunton contends that in the person of Jesus Christ, God's action is revealed to the world. "The doctrine of the Trinity is what must be true if the biblical witness to revelation is indeed witness to the event that is God. . . . the doctrine of the Trinity is *our* interpretation of God's *self interpretation* of himself to us."⁵ God's action originates in his essence. In other words, what God reveals of himself in the incarnated Son is true to his being.⁶ "God's essence and work are not twofold but one."⁷ No schism therefore exists between the immanent and economic Trinity.

---

comparison between Charles Hartshorne and Karl Barth on the doctrine of God, "being and becoming." Both theologians contested the classical concept of God in which God's being is static. Gunton, agreeing with Barth, argues for a new way to conceive of God as "being and becoming." Gunton further elaborates on this concept in his *Act and Being*.

3. The concept of "becoming" is significant. Depending on how the term is defined, one can end up with very different pictures of God. In regards to Barth's concept of "becoming," T. F. Torrance describes it as follows: "The fact that in the incarnation God became man without ceasing to be God, tells us that his nature is characterized by both repose and movement, and that his eternal Being is also a divine *Becoming*. This does not mean that God ever becomes other than he eternally is or that he passes over from becoming into being something else, but rather that he continues unceasingly to be what he always is and ever will be in the living movement of his eternal Being. His becoming is not becoming on the way toward being or toward a fullness of being, but is the eternal fullness and the overflowing of his eternal unlimited Being. Becoming expressed the dynamic nature of his Being. His Becoming, as it were, the other side of his Being, and his Being is the other side of his Becoming. His Becoming is his Being in movement and his Being in movement is his Becoming." Torrance, *Christian Doctrine of God*, 242.

4. Gunton, *Act and Being*, 97.

5. Gunton, *Becoming and Being*, 130; italics in original.

6. Gunton raises an important related question: "Why then must there be any distinction at all between outward activity and essence, or between 'economic' and 'immanent' trinity?" Gunton, *Becoming and Being*, 147. He answers that this is to maintain the freedom of God, calling the distinction "an asymmetry of understanding, by which God's freedom is preserved." Gunton, *Becoming and Being*, 147.

7. Barth, *Church Dogmatics*, 371 (page citations are to reprint edition).

In the same way, Gunton argues, we can determine that God, who is triune, is essentially a relational being.

> The being of God is thus *self-related* being. As being, it is relationally structured. . . . The modes of being of God that are distinct from each other are successively related in such a way that each mode of being of God first *becomes* what it *is* together with both the other modes of being. . . . God's being is thus, as the being of God, the Father, the Son, and the Holy Spirit, a *being in becoming*.[8]

Contrary to the Western conception of God whose being is founded in substance rather than person, Gunton concludes that God's being is relational. And we know this because God revealed himself in the person of Jesus of Nazareth. Indeed, God is God for us. He acts toward the created world for the good of his creation. Through the two hands of the Father, the Son and the Spirit, God relates himself to the created world.

THE TRIUNE CREATOR AND THE CREATION: MAKER OF THE EARTH

In the previous section, the relation between the immanent and economic Trinity was examined. Gunton, understanding the being of God in light of the economic Trinity, argues that God's being is being and becoming. Hence, there is no divorce between the immanent and economic Trinity. God's trinitarian actions that are being revealed through the Son and the Spirit truly originate in the essence of his being.

In this section, the relation between the creation and the triune God will be examined in order to further explore Gunton's doctrine of God. First, we will examine what the creation is and then who the triune God is. The objective of this section is to identify the otherness that exists between God and the creation, while also identifying the relation between them.

A Biblical View of the Creation

Scripture tells us, "In the beginning, God created the heavens and the earth" (Gen 1:1).[9] The triune God is the author of creation. Several implications

---

8. Gunton, *Becoming and Being*, 143; italics in original.

9. Of course, Gen 1:1 is not the only scripture that describes God's act of creation. On the contrary, such verses are found throughout both testaments. For a comprehensive

can be drawn from this verse. First, the creation is the product of the triune God. This signifies the divine sovereignty over the creation. Gunton states that the verse shows "that the world in which we live is established firmly by the action of God."[10]

Second, the creation is *creatio ex nihilo*. An ontological distinction exists between the Creator and the creation. Gunton argues, "There is other reality than God and . . . it is really other than he."[11] Unlike in Hellenistic thought, God is not part of the cosmos; He stands distinct from his creation. This distinction, Gunton argues, signifies that "creation is an act of God, based in his very being: but it is not an extension of his being."[12] God, in fact, created the world out of nothing.

Third, God created the heavens and earth in the beginning. This denotes a distinction of the order of time and eternity. God who is eternal created a world that has a beginning and an end. In short, the world exists in time. There is a past, present and future. Unlike the eternal God, the world is moving progressively to the future. Nonetheless, as Scripture attests, the triune Creator does not leave the world alone like a deistic machine maker. On the contrary, the eternal God involves himself in the temporal world through the Son and the Spirit: God acts to preserve the creation and guide it according to his purpose.[13] Gunton contends, "Creation is not a timeless whole, as it was made in Augustine, but has a temporality and directedness to an end which is greater than its beginnings, and that they belong to its nature as creation."[14] The creation is not the result of an arbitrary decision of God but the "ordered expression of love."[15] It has a purpose and goal.

In fact, Gunton points out, "The NT teaching that the creation was formed 'in Christ', is that it is created to be the realm of one who holds it together as a unity."[16] This denotes the purposiveness and significance of creation. Creation is a place for human flourishing. Gunton writes, "Is the

---

list of verses, see the following: http://incolor.inetnebr.com/gaskell/creation_verses.pdf. Nonetheless, Gen 1:1 is perhaps the most quoted verse when God's act of creation is discussed.

10. Gunton, *Triune Creator*, 15.
11. Gunton, *Christian Faith*, 11.
12. Gunton, *Triune Creator*, 66.
13. Pss 33, 104, etc.
14. Gunton, *Promise of Trinitarian Theology*, 180–81.
15. Gunton, "Doctrine of Creation," 150.
16. Gunton, *Christian Faith*, 12.

world, or is it not, a place in which human beings may live, love, flourish and find redemption? Indeed, is it a realm *along with which* we may seek the perfection of our being?"[17] Not only that, this realm of Christ is also a place where God and humanity meet. Gunton contends,

> The place where the relation between God and the world is both realized and understood is the person of him who is the externalization in the world of the one who mediates all the Father's creating and redeeming action. This, it must be stressed, is . . . a matter of . . . attempting to ensure that the general relation between God and the world is focused in the particular place where their relation takes paradigmatic and determinative form.[18]

Creation, therefore, is a place where humanity grows and flourishes, but also a place where God and humankind relate through Christ.[19]

---

17. Gunton, *Promise of Trinitarian Theology*, 28; italics in original.

18. Gunton, "Creation and Mediation in the Theology of Robert W. Jenson," 91–92. Accordingly, Gunton, in referring to Col 1:16, concludes that the creation takes place in the Christ because Christ is the "externalization in the world of the one who mediates all the Father's creating and redeeming action." Gunton, "Creation and Mediation in the Theology of Robert W. Jenson," 92. Gunton continues, "There is a great deal of difference between saying that all things were created in God, *simpliciter*, and that it happened and happens in Christ. The reason is . . . the Son is the principle of the distinction between God and the world. It follows that to create in the Son means to create by the mediation of the one who is the way of God out into that which is not himself." Gunton, *Triune Creator*, 142–43. Hence, Gunton appeals to the Son to couch the relation between God and the creation: The world is truly outside of God because it is created in Christ, the otherness of God. Yet, such relation does not completely negate relation between them. Rather, it signifies the mediation of the Son in the world. This point will be further elaborated in chapter 4 in regard to the solidarity with Christ.

19. Gunton further describes the realm of Christ as follows: "We are not here simply dealing with two perspectives, the divine and human, but with two interrelated realms of being which bring with them two complementary perspectives, two ways of understanding the world as both the creation of the eternal God and a genuinely created reality." Gunton, *Triune Creator*, 92. The reason for the emphasis on two interrelated realms can perhaps be explained by Gunton's claim that "God is indispensable as providing a transcendent and eschatological framework for human social relationships." Gunton, *Promise of Trinitarian Theology*, 170. All things depend on God, including the social order. Nonetheless, God does not make human moral response irrelevant to the redemption and perfection of the world. On the contrary, he expects our participation. This notion of creation provides the foundation for Gunton's conception of how the triune God works together to bring the world to its perfection and redemption. God does not work alone, but invites human's participation in his eschatological work.

The Triune Creator: Father, Son and Holy Spirit

In this section, the triune Creator will be examined. The creation is the work of this triune Creator. If so, the creation reflects its Creator.[20] Gunton argues, "If the triune God is the source of all being, meaning and truth we must suppose that all being will in some way reflect the being of the one who made it and holds it in being."[21] The focus of this section is, therefore, relatedness. Given that otherness exists between the Creator and creation, relatedness between the Creator and the creation must be examined. This relatedness is the prerogative of God: Unless God chooses to relate to the world, the world cannot relate itself to God.

Gunton argues, "God is the sole creator, and indeed, sole lord of what happens within that creation's history subsequent to its creation."[22] He continues, "As the creator and redeemer he is at the same time the one who gives to that creation its proper *Selbständigkeit* or relative independence, a subsistence that it receives from its relation to God."[23] God's action toward the creation is derived from his love for creation. It is not because the triune Creator needs the creation. On the contrary, he does not lack anything because he is self-sufficient. Nonetheless, this Creator extends his hands to the world to preserve its life and bring redemption and perfection. In other words, God chooses to be God for us.

And this action of God is revealed trinitarianly. The Father reaches out to the world through his two hands, the Son and the Spirit: The creation is created and upheld by the Son, while the Spirit transforms and perfects the world to its ultimate end. Such action of the triune God, therefore, enables us to perceive that "Trinitarian theology is based on the belief that God the Father is related to the world through the creating and redeeming action of Son and Spirit who are, in Irenaeus' expression, his two hands. The doctrine of the Trinity . . . is derived from the involvement of God in creation, reconciliation, redemption."[24] The triune Creator is therefore dynamic. He freely relates to the world because he is relational.

But, how can God relate to the world since there is an ontological difference between them? That is, how can God overcome the divide that

---

20. Ps 19:1–6; Rom 1:20; Matt 5:45.
21. Gunton, *One, the Three and the Many*, 145.
22. Gunton, "Creation and Mediation," 82.
23. Gunton, "Creation and Mediation," 82.
24. Gunton, *Promise of Trinitarian Theology*, 142.

seems to preclude him being in relation to the world? Gunton points out that it is *because of* God's otherness that he is able to relate to the world. Gunton delineates this concept in terms of the relation between the immanent and economic Trinity.

> Over against such a separation [immanence and transcendence], it can be argued that otherness and relation are superior terms for performing the function that transcendence and immanence are usually given. The reason is that they are not alternatives or contraries as the latter tend to be, but correlatives which require and interpret each other. Only that which is other than something else can be related to it. Otherness and relation can therefore be conceived as correlatives rather than rivals.[25]

Gunton thus concludes that otherness and relation are not "contraries," but "correlatives which require and interpret each other." Similarly, within the Trinity, the same concept applies. God consists of three persons in communion, and each person of the Trinity is distinct from the other: The Father is not the Son and the Son is not the Father, and so on. And the distinctions that exist among them are indispensable in the Trinity. Otherness must be present when there is relation.

Further, this otherness is not only necessary for relation, but also for fostering a healthy relation between God and the world. Gunton states,

> Otherness—the ontological distinction or infinite qualitative difference between God and that which is not God—is important both for the contingency of the created order and for the freedom of the human person. In a trinitarian understanding, because God has otherness—personal freedom and "spaced"—within the dynamics of his being, he is able to grant to the world space to be itself.[26]

---

25. Gunton, *Promise of Trinitarian Theology*, 202.

26. Gunton, *Promise of Trinitarian Theology*, 202. Gunton further elaborates: "A distinction between God and the world is necessary not only to preserve the autonomy of God's action—its character as authentically divine action—but also for the sake of the world. If the world is too closely tied to the being of God, its own proper reality is endangered, for it is too easily swallowed up into the being of God, and so deprived of its own proper existence." Gunton, *Triune Creator*, 66. If no real distinction exists between them, the independence of the world cannot be preserved. God is for us, but not part of us. Yet, this independence of the world from God is not total autonomy. It is relative independence since the creation depends on God for its existence.

He adds, "All forms of monism which rule out the otherness of God to humankind or the world violate, by incorporating it into the being of God, the freedom of the world to be itself."[27] Hence, "Otherness without relation is as destructive as relation without otherness."[28] To preserve one's identity is an important key to a healthy relationship.[29] And it is by otherness that this difference can be preserved. Otherness does not signify un-relatedness. On the contrary, otherness is required for relation.

Furthermore, this ontological otherness not only preserves the freedom of the creation, but gives significance to the created world. The material world's ontological difference has been perceived to signify its inferiority. But Gunton argues that this is contrary to God's plan in creating the world in such a way. He argues, "The world is itself, not God, but worldly according to its own measure of being. Yet it is so by gift of the God who creates and sustains it in such a way that it is itself."[30] Because the world was created in this particular way, there is relation between God and the world. Therefore, it is not a sign of inferiority or un-relatedness. Rather, God made it in such a way so that the relation between God and the world would be possible.

THE TRIUNE CREATOR'S RELATION TO THE CREATION: NOT CONSTRAINED, YET INVOLVED

In the previous section, the Creator and the creation were examined in order to identify the otherness and relation that exist between them. Despite the otherness, relation exists. Otherness and relation are not contraries

---

27. Gunton, *Promise of Trinitarian Theology*, 202. Gunton argues, "This is undoubtedly true of pantheisms of all kinds, for if God is ontologically too close to the world, the world becomes simply a function of his being and so unable to be itself." Gunton, *Promise of Trinitarian Theology*, 202. The opposite case is deism, which is otherness without relation.

28. Gunton, *Promise of Trinitarian Theology*, 203.

29. Gunton states, "Otherness is a concept important for finite relationships also." Gunton, *Promise of Trinitarian Theology*, 202. In this, Gunton's concept of analogy between the triune God and humanity is clearly reflected.

30. Gunton, *Promise of Trinitarian Theology*, 143.

but correlatives. In this section, the triune Creator and the creation will be examined again. However, the focus is not on otherness and relation, but rather on the nature and character of this relation. In order to accomplish these ends, we will examine Gunton's theology of mediation to delineate the action of the triune God. Then, we will examine the nature and character of the divine love which is the catalyst of God's action toward the creation to determine how it is grounded in God's self-sufficiency.

Freedom of God and Freedom of Creation: Theology of Mediation

The creation is a product of the triune Creator. There is therefore an ontological difference between God and the creation. Yet, God overcomes this ontological difference in his relation to the creation. Hence, there is relation between them. Nonetheless, how this relation should be conceived is an important question to be examined.

Gunton observes, "If God and the world are ontologically other, some account of their relation—some theology of *mediation*—is indispensable."[31] The ontological distinction between the triune Creator and the creation requires some type of mediation: "God creates means that there is other reality than God and that it is really other than he."[32] Gunton therefore argues for mediation that is construed trinitarianly. That is, the divine action of God toward the creation must be interpreted by the actions of the two hands of the Father, namely the Son and the Spirit. Gunton states, "Irenaeus frequently says that God creates by means of his two hands, the Son and the Spirit. This enables him to give a clear account of how God related to that which is not God: of how the creator interacts with his creation."[33]

However, the relation between God and the creation has been historically interpreted as "unmediated" rather than "mediated." As a result, the trinitarian action of God toward the creation has been neglected.[34] Gunton

---

31. Gunton, "Creation and Mediation," 80.
32. Jenson, *Systematic Theology*, 2:5.
33. Gunton, *Triune Creator*, 54.
34. Gunton points to "[t]he deficiencies of the theologies . . . shown in part by a concentration on the concept of causality at the expense of a more personally conceived relation between God and the world." Gunton, *Triune Creator*, 147. He traces the doctrine of creation through the history of Christianity and delineates how the relation between God and the world had often been misconstrued through the influence of dualism (e.g., Hellenism, Platonism, rationalism) until the Reformers. Although Gunton acknowledges some early attempts to construe the relation more trinitarianly (e.g, Irenaeus) before the

notes, "What was lacking was a satisfactory conception of mediation . . . a trinitarian one."[35] The will of the Father was mediated by the actions of the Son and the Spirit. If so, a theology of mediation that is trinitarianly construed is indispensable in interpreting the relation of God to the world.

In this light, Gunton argues, "A stronger Christology forms the basis for a more satisfactory account of mediation."[36] He continues,

> The incarnation—the act of free divine interrelation with the created world—provides the model of mediation that we need. Christology, not the ontologically intermediate being represented by some (Origenistic) conception of the Logos, but the Son of God in free personal relation to the world, indeed identification with part of that world, is the basis for an understanding of God the Father's relations with his creation.[37]

Christ's incarnation signifies that God is able to relate to that which is other than himself. It is the distinctiveness of the Christ that makes mediated relation possible.[38] In short, the mediated relation is relation in otherness.

Furthermore, the incarnation of Christ signifies God's eternal plan for mediation. By sending his Son, the Father chose to mediate his will through the actions of his two hands, the Son and the Spirit. The incarnated Son, Christ, is the otherness of God. Thus, the Son is the otherness that God employs to relate himself to the created world.[39]

The mediated relation that is trinitarianly construed between God and the creation enables us to see how God relates to the world which is other than himself. With a strong emphasis on Christology, this approach reveals

---

Reformation, he concludes that theologians in the past misunderstood the relation and consequently God's true plan for the creation. See Gunton, *Triune Creator* for further details.

35. Gunton, *Triune Creator*, 182.
36. Gunton, *Triune Creator*, 183.
37. Gunton, *Triune Creator*, 183.
38. The humanity of Christ has a significant place in Gunton's theology. Gunton laments that the importance of the humanity of Christ tends to be overshadowed by the divinity of Christ. As a result, the theological significance of the humanity of Christ has not been fully appreciated. Likewise in the theology of mediation, the relation between creation and creature has often been misinterpreted due to a neglect of the humanity of Christ. Without a proper balance of the divinity and humanity of Christ, Gunton contends that the theology of mediation cannot be fully appreciated. For additional details, see Gunton, "Creation and Mediation in the Theology of Robert W. Jenson."
39. Cf. Gunton, "Creation and Mediation." 91.

how God can relate to the world in his otherness, Jesus Christ, who is the mediator of creation and redemption. In so doing, this view also reflects the dynamic nature of the triune Creator: God's being is being and becoming. He works together to achieve the ultimate perfection for the good of the world. If so, the theology of mediation is a theology that is fitting for the relation between God and the creation.

Creation and God's Aseity: Divine Love and Freedom

If trinitarian mediation is a way for God to relate to the world, then what can we suppose about the source of such outward movement towards the world? The triune Creator acts toward the creation by mediation of the Son and the Spirit. Yet, what moves him to act outwardly has not been examined. Hence, in this section, the source of God's outward movement towards the world will be examined. In this light, special attention is given to God's freedom. The main point to be examined is whether and how Gunton's argument for the source of God's outward movement to the world can preserve God's aseity.

Gunton states, "The relation of God to the creation, which is expressed in creation, reconciliation and redemption, is grounded in the other-related love of the Father, Son and Spirit in eternity."[40] It is not God's arbitrary will to create the world, but his love that is the basis of his relation to the creation. God's love, Gunton continues, is

> [l]ove that is "complete" because of the unbroken communion that is the perichoresis of the Father, Son and Spirit. The Father begets the Son as his other in an eternal act of pure love—apageistic in orienting itself entirely to the other—while the Spirit is sent to complete "the divine and blessed Trinity".[41]

Indeed, the being of God is love. Because God is love, says Gunton, "God is constituted, made up without remainder, of a personal structure of giving and receiving. Internally, God is a fellowship of *persons* whose orientation is entirely to the other."[42] And this orientation to the other is characterized by love that is *agapeistic* in orientation.

---

40. Gunton, *Theology through the Theologians*, 128.
41. Gunton, *Act and Being*, 119–20.
42. Gunton, *Christian Faith*, 186.

The divine love is thus perfect because of the communion of the Father, Son, and Spirit. Yet, despite the perfection, the divine love does not remain in the eternal being, but rather moves outward to the creation. In fact, Gunton contends,

> Love is that form of divine action which creates the world, maintains it in the face of sin and the Fall, acts for its recreation in his Son and brings it finally to perfection through the Spirit. The Father's action, mediated by the Son and the Spirit, is love in action, bearing witness as it does to the fact that God is *therefore* eternally love, love in himself eternally, so that when God is eschatologically all in all, love will be the final reality.[43]

Gunton continues, "The orientation of this God, his inner drive, we might say, is not to remain content with his eternal ordering as eternal love, but to move outwards to create a world which he loves and wishes to bring into relation with himself."[44] Because this orientation to outwardness is an "orientation to the other within the eternal structure of God's being,"[45] it seeks to reach out to what is other than himself—just as within the Trinity the three persons who are unique and distinct from each other reach out to the One who is other than himself.

This indicates that although God is self-sufficient and independent, he is not satisfied to remain within himself. Whether it is his personal structure or inner drive, God is oriented outwardly. "To be God is to be intrinsically related to the other in communion,"[46] and "because God is not in himself a closed circle but is essentially the relatedness of community, there is within his eternal being that which freely and in love creates, reconciles and redeems that which is not himself."[47] And what the divine love—the orientation of God—accomplishes is to bring into relation what is other than himself. Indeed, the divine love is eschatological in orientation.

In this light, Gunton argues that the Spirit is the eschatological Spirit. Therefore, we can infer, "In eternity the Spirit is the one who . . . perfects the being of God, so as first to enable the relation between the Father and

---

43. Gunton, *Act and Being*, 140; italics in original. For more information on Gunton's concept of the mediated divine love through the Son and the Spirit and its purpose and outcome, see Gunton, "God, Grace and Freedom."

44. Gunton, *Christian Faith*, 187.

45. Gunton, *Christian Faith*, 187.

46. Gunton, *Theology through the Theologians*, 127.

47. Gunton, *Theology through the Theologians*, 128.

the Son to be properly described as one of love: and second to provide the basis for God's movement out into the world in his Son to create and redeem."[48] Therefore, the Spirit enables "God's perfection, the perfection of personal love in relation, a perfection which takes shape in all of God's acts *ad extra*."[49] The Spirit perfects love first "in God himself and then in the world"[50] because the orientation of divine love is to move outwardly.

Further, perfect love is God's perfection which includes "notions of completeness and communion."[51] And perfect communion exists because of unity and harmony in community that comes from the perfection of particularity, "the product of mutually constitutive relations."[52] Therefore, the Spirit achieves the perfection of particularity. As the Spirit perfects love among people, he also particularizes them. Perfect love is possible only in relations that allow each person to become whom they are intended to become. Again, this perfection of particularity is realized first in God and then in the world.

Hence, a new characterization of the divine love—in fact, a new identity of the being of God—is conceived. Gunton argues that the divine love that moves outwardly to the world does not undermine God's self-sufficiency. On the contrary, it is "the basis of a movement outwards."[53] Gunton writes,

> The love of Father, Son and Spirit is a form of love which does not remain content with its eternal self-sufficiency because that self-sufficiency is the basis of a movement outwards to create and perfect a world whose otherness from God—of being distinctly itself—is based in the otherness-in-relation of Father, Son and Spirit in eternity.[54]

Expressed differently, "To say that God is already and eternally an order of love prevents us from having to say that it is in some way necessary for God to create a world, to have another being alongside himself without which he is not truly himself."[55] This indicates that it is not by necessity that

---

48. Gunton, *Christian Faith*, 185–86.
49. Gunton, *Act and Being*, 121.
50. Gunton, *Act and Being*, 121.
51. Gunton, *Act and Being*, 121.
52. Höhne, *Spirit and Sonship*, 1.
53. Gunton, *Act and Being*, 146.
54. Gunton, *Act and Being*, 146. Cf. *Theology through the Theologians*, 128.
55. Gunton, *Christian Faith*, 187.

God creates. The divine love lacks nothing, but gives life freely because it is an expression or disposition of this love. Divine love is thereby the source of God's movement toward the creation.

Freedom of God: A Function of Divine Love

What more can we say about God's freedom? If the source of this outward movement of God is the divine love that is self-sufficient and therefore not constrained, what can we say about the function of divine love? Gunton argues that freedom is a function of love.[56] He states, "Divine freedom is that which consists at once in the Father's breathing of the Spirit through the Son, and the Spirit's reciprocal perfecting of the love which God is through the Son. On such an account, freedom is indeed a function of that holy love, of that love which is the essence of God."[57] If the divine love is the essence of the divine being that enables outward movement of God to the world, the divine freedom is the function of that action that expresses the disposition of divine love.

Gunton argues, "Freedom is [thereby] to be conceived as a relation between beings."[58] Relation does not denote losing freedom. On the contrary, it signifies freedom when it is understood in light of the Trinity.[59] Gunton contends, "Otherness is an essential feature of the trinitarian freedom, because without otherness the distinctness, particularity of a person

---

56. Gunton, *Act and Being*, 107.

57. Gunton, *Act and Being*, 107. Gunton does not define freedom in individualistic term, such as being free from others. Rather, he defines it in light of the relation within the communion of the triune God. He argues, "In trinitarian terms, the otherness is not the freedom of the *individual*—a freedom *from* others, as we so often make it in the West—because it is a freedom that is a function of relatedness: it is given and received, because personal being is constituted by relatedness." Gunton, *Promise of Trinitarian Theology*, 128. Gunton argues further, "Freedom . . . is not an immediate but a mediated relation to other people." Gunton, "God, Grace and Freedom," 121. Therefore, freedom should be defined as freedom in relation.

58. Gunton, *Promise of Trinitarian Theology*, 196.

59. Gunton emphasizes the importance of the doctrine of the Trinity. He contends, "The doctrine of the Trinity is essential to the maintenance of such a teaching, showing that God is both self-sufficient in himself—the doctrine of *aseity*—and creates and remains in relationship with the world that is other than he. Thus we need a doctrine of divine freedom which corresponds to what we might consider to be a 'natural' understanding of freedom: God creates, but is not bound to." Gunton, *Act and Being*, 104–5.

is lost."[60] Each person of the Trinity is distinct from each other because of the relation: The Father begets the Son and the Spirit is breathed by the Father through the Son and the Spirit perfects the reciprocal love of the Father and the Son.[61] There is no freedom without relation; rather, freedom is a "function of relatedness."[62]

Moreover, each person of the Trinity is particular because of their perfect love for each other. Divine love allows the creaturely other to become what they are made to be. Divine love does not compel others to become someone other than themselves. On the contrary, divine love frees them to realize the identity that is true to them. Gunton asserts, "To be free is to realize what one distinctively and particularly is."[63] Therefore, freedom is a function of divine love.

If the orientation of the divine love is the eternal structure of God's being, so is the divine freedom: Freedom is eternally structured in the communion of three persons since they are distinct/particular from each other. There is freedom in the being of God. God's love moves toward the creation to invite the world into relation with God. Yet, this love does not bind the creation nor deprive it of its autonomy. Rather, this love enables the other to become truly what they are made to be because the function of the divine love is freedom—freedom to become who they are intended to be.

DOCTRINE OF PROVIDENCE: THE TRIUNE GOD WHO WORKS TOWARD THE ONE GOAL

In previous sections, we have seen that God is a relational being: God's being is "self-related being."[64] In fact, God chooses to be God for us. He is therefore neither static nor aloof from his creation. Rather, from the time of creation, God is involved in the world. God's action is indeed mediated action through his two hands of the Father, the Son and the Spirit. Despite

---

60. Gunton, *Promise of Trinitarian Theology*, 128.

61. Gunton contends that personal particularity is a result of freedom: "Freedom is that which I do with my own particularity, that which enables me to be and do what is truly and distinctively myself. Freedom is that which others do to and with my particular being, in enabling me to be and do, or preventing me from being and doing, that which is particularly myself." Gunton, "God, Grace and Freedom," 122.

62. Gunton, *Promise of the Trinitarian Theology*, 128.

63. Gunton, *Promise of the Trinitarian Theology*, 128.

64. Gunton, *Becoming and Being*, 143.

the ontological difference, he reaches out to the world so that the world will be transformed to become what it was first intended to be.

In this section, this mediated action of God toward the creation will be examined more specifically. Whereas we have examined the nature of the relation between Creator and the creation, we have not examined how such a relation actually works to bring ultimate transformation to the world. The objective of this section is therefore to delineate the mediatory work of God in preservation, transformation and perfection. In this light, the doctrine of providence seems to be the proper arena to accomplish this end.[65]

Further, along with the doctrine of providence, attention is given to the two hands of the Father, the Son and the Spirit, in hopes of showing their providential work to achieve the divine purpose for the world.[66]

The Doctrine of Providence: Two Sides of One Coin

In regard to the divine providence, Gunton contends, "God does not merely uphold but actively directs and involves himself in the day to day life of his

---

65. William B. Whitney relates that "Mediation is the term Gunton uses to describe *how* God interacts with his creation, while providence is described as God's action through the Son and Spirit to uphold and sustain the created order. However, both terms are related since both describe aspects of God's relation with that which he has created." Whitney, *Problem and Promise in Colin E. Gunton's Doctrine of Creation*, 82; italics in original. Further, Charles M. Wood explains that providence and creation have traditionally been understood as the two main actions of God in the economy. In fact, they presuppose each other. He states, "If the doctrine of creation has to do with understanding God as the author or source of the world as such, the doctrine of providence has to do with understanding God as working in and with the world." Therefore, Wood argues, "This doctrinal locus . . . houses the consideration of how God may be said to act in and with the world, insofar as Christian faith and reflection have to deal with that issue." Wood, "How Does God Act?," 138. Terry J. Wright correctly observes, "Any approach, then, to the doctrine of providence needs to clarify its understanding of God's relationship with creation." Wright, "Reconsidering *Concursus*," 210.

66. Gunton wrote little about the doctrine of providence, despite the fact that the doctrine closely relates to the areas in which Gunton had theological interest. Wright also states, "It is surprising that Colin Gunton wrote little that is explicitly concerned with divine providence. Nonetheless, what he did write is fertile." Wright, "Colin Gunton on Providence," 146. Regardless of the dearth of Gunton's writing on this topic, it is my view that Gunton's treatment of providence makes a significant contribution to the doctrine since Gunton's doctrine of providence opens the door for new possibilities of how we can understand the divine provision in relation to God's eschatological plan for his entire creation.

creatures."[67] This indicates that the triune Creator does not make a world only to leave it to function on its own. Rather, he created the world in such a way that the world needs God's active involvement for preservation and transformation.[68] Hence, "providence must be understood eschatologically, from the end."[69]

Yet, God's provision takes place in the fallen world, and requires redirecting the world along with conservation and transformation. And this redemption is not only for the human world, but also for all of creation. Gunton contends accordingly that general and special providence are "both aspects of the same divine activity bringing the world to its intended destiny."[70] Gunton defines general and special providence as follows: "General providence is a name for that activity by which God is conceived to hold in being the order of creation: maintaining the order and teleology of the human and non-human realms. By contrast, particular and special providence are ways of speaking of saving or redemptive acts directed to restoring the right order or better, directedness, of creation."[71] Because the destiny of humankind and creation are inextricably bound up, God's providence, whether it is general or special providence, must achieve the same goal: the transformation and perfection of the whole creation.

This view primarily derives from how the doctrine of providence is conceived in trinitarian terms in Gunton's theology. God is the triune God who works together to accomplish one goal: the perfection of the creation. Hence, there is one goal, not two. Despite the distinction of forms of providence—general and special—the divine providential action shows that they constitute a unity of activity.[72]

---

67. Gunton, *Christian Faith*, 21.

68. Like Wood, regarding the relation between the doctrine of creation and providence, Gunton contends, "The doctrine of creation affirms that 'in the beginning' a reality other than God was established as truly itself by triune divine action. The doctrine of providence presupposes that, but adds that the kind of God with whom we have to do is also actively concerned for the continuing life of that world." Gunton, *Christian Faith*, 37.

69. Gunton, *Christian Faith*, 36. Accordingly, this denotes that creation is a project. The created world was made very good, "yet remains to be perfected: perfect and to be perfected." Gunton, "Reformation Accounts of the Church's Response to Human Culture," 79.

70. Gunton, *Triune Creator*, 177.

71. Gunton, *Triune Creator*, 176.

72. Gunton, *Triune Creator*, 176.

The Work of the Two Hands: The Son and the Spirit

Having examined Gunton's doctrine of providence that is trinitarianly construed, we now turn to see the providential action of the two hands of the Father, the Son and the Spirit. We will explore how the two hands constitute the unity of activity in providential action.[73]

Gunton states, "We conceive providence chiefly in terms of two models: the Son as the giver of structure, and the Holy Spirit as the one who gives the world space to become within but not apart from that structuring."[74] He continues, "The Spirit's action is eschatological action, enabling things to be themselves. . . . Providential action is thus that which enables particular human actions and worldly events to become what they will be."[75] Hence, providence is "activity, mediated by the two hands of God, which at once upholds the creation against its utter dissolution and provides for its redemption by the election of Israel and incarnation of the one through whom all things were made and upheld, and to whom, as the head of the church (Col 1:18), in the Spirit all things move."[76]

The significance of the conceptual framework defined above is that Christ is identified as the mediator of the creation, not solely the redeemer of the creation. Christ interacts with the world as one of the two hands of the Father, acting as the mediator and redeemer. And Christ as the mediator of the creation identifies himself with the world by the incarnation so that he can redirect the fallen creation to what it was first intended to be.[77] Gunton thus concludes, "The incarnation of the Son of God in Jesus of Nazareth provides a way of showing that the distinction of forms of providence is yet embraced within a unity of activity. . . . 'General' providence

---

73. A more detailed examination of the relation between Christ and the Spirit in the perfection of the world will follow in chapter 4. Nonetheless, a brief examination of the relation is necessary for the purpose of this section. Thus, the following is a brief discussion of the relation between the Son and the Spirit in preserving, redeeming and transforming the world.

74. Gunton, *Triune Creator*, 192.

75. Gunton, *Triune Creator*, 192.

76. Gunton, *Triune Creator*, 192.

77. Gunton explains, "In the theology of creation, therefore, language of mediation by God's Word enables us to speak both of God's free involvement within his creation and, ultimately, in Christ of his equally free and sovereign identification with a part of it. The theology of the creating Word indicates that God can become 'worldly' while remaining truly God." Gunton, *Christian Faith*, 10.

is maintained by a new and unique—'special'—form of divine interaction with the world."[78]

On the other hand, Gunton holds that the Spirit, the other hand of the Father, is the eschatological Spirit. He explains, "The Spirit's work is best considered to be eschatological: as perfecting that which was created in the beginning, in the many and various particular ways in which that can take place, both ordinary and extraordinary."[79] Hence, the Spirit is the Father's agent to enable the created order to become what it was first intended to be.

Yet, this Spirit does not work apart from Christ. On the contrary, the Spirit perfects what Christ holds together. As Gunton observes, "The Spirit is the perfecting cause of the whole creation. . . . The Spirit is thus the agent of the Father's determination to bring all things into relation to himself through Christ: the agent of God's perfecting of the creation."[80] The Spirit perfects the whole creation as he relates it to the Father through the Son.

Therefore, by conceiving of God's providence in terms of this trinitarian action, it is plausible to say that general and special providence are "both aspects of the same divine activity bringing the world to [its] intended destiny."[81] The Father sent the Son and the Spirit who are his two hands to uphold, maintain, and perfect the world. Yet, these are not distinct actions of the triune God, but one. The work of the Son and the Spirit cannot be separated, but is unified to achieve the one goal: the perfection of the world.

Providence, trinitarianly conceived, is the mediated *activity* of God who is three persons in communion and works toward one goal: the transformation of the world. God who is the triune Creator did not make the world only to leave it alone like a deistic machine maker. On the contrary, the world needs the divine providential action to achieve its ultimate purpose. This indicates that God is God for us: He is a relational being. He reaches out to the world so that his love will free the creation to achieve its ultimate end. In short, the mediatorial work of the Son and the Spirit is where God's providential action is being revealed.

---

78. Gunton, *Triune Creator*, 176.
79. Gunton, *Christian Faith*, 185.
80. Gunton, *Theology through the Theologians*, 120.
81. Gunton, *Triune Creator*, 176.

THE TRIUNE GOD AND THE MISSIO DEI

As we have seen, the doctrine of providence reveals the action of the triune Creator. The Father is the fountainhead of the Trinity. He sends the Son who is the mediator of creation and redemption to perfect and redeem creation. Likewise, the Father sends the Spirit through the Son as the agent of perfection so that the Spirit will perfect what Christ has accomplished.

While all these points are important and necessary to understand the providential action of the triune God in upholding and transforming the world, the question remains how these mediated actions can actually be redemptive to deal with the problems and distortions of our fallen world.

Hence, in this last section, we will examine once again the triune Creator and creation in hopes of clarifying how these mediated actions can be redemptive for the fallen world. We will explore the meanings of salvation, sin and justification in order to show how the work of Christ and the Spirit enables the world to realize its proper *telos*.[82]

Sin as Social Reality

As the story of Genesis tells us, humankind is fallen due to their disobedience to God. Because of their rebellion, Adam and Eve lost intimacy with God as well as with each other. Furthermore, they lost their relationship to creation. Indeed, sin is a dysfunction or disorder in relation. Gunton contends, "Christian theology diagnoses the ill as the disruption or distortion of the relation of personal being with the personal creator God, a disruption that in mysterious fashion incorporates the whole created world in its structures. The technical term for this is sin."[83] Sin not only affects humankind, but also the environment. If so, sin not only influences individual human beings, but also impacts the structures of society.

However, as Gunton argues, the emphasis has traditionally been placed on individuals rather than on society. As a result, the influence of

---

82. Gunton is in agreement with Karl Barth that "God's perfections constitute the utter consistency of his being and act . . . God's act, rooted in his being, serves to redirect human being to its proper end." Gunton, *Intellect and Action*, 110.

83. Gunton, *Christian Faith*, 59. Gunton further elaborates the definition of sin: "The essence of sin is to attempt to be like God in ways other than that laid down for those who, because they are finite in time and space, are also limited in their capacity for knowledge and achievement. Sin is for the creature to think and act as if it were the creator." Gunton, *Christian Faith*, 60.

sin on society has often been overlooked. Gunton observes, "Individualistic conceptions of sin, encouraged by a certain kind of evangelistic strategy which seeks to impress upon individuals at almost any cost their need of salvation, underrate the fact that human evil takes essentially social form." He continues, "Sin is a social reality because that inheritance is mediated to us by our history and by the social setting in which our lives take shape."[84] The evil that manifests itself in social form should not be overlooked.

In the context of humankind's social setting, Gunton finds a two-way relation between humankind and the created world. In Genesis, there is a distinct correlation between humankind and the created world: The sin of Adam and Eve somehow brought disorder to the creation by bringing divine judgement.[85] This correlation goes in one direction—from humankind to the environment, not vice versa. However, Gunton suggests another type of correlation that goes in the other direction: the created world influences humankind.

As Gunton points out, "Our social world shapes us."[86] Because the sin that retards the transformation/perfection of humankind is transmitted socially and historically, society plays a significant role in molding human characteristics. Gunton continues, "Our social being is the compost within

---

84. Gunton, *Christian Faith*, 61. As stated above, Gunton holds that "human evil takes essentially social form." This is his attempt to regain the balance that was lost between human distortion and that of the created world. Yet, a caveat is in order. Gunton states, "To be sure, this must never be expressed in such a way as to absolve individuals from their fault and responsibility. We are individually responsible for what we do, unless so constrained physically or by sickness that our actions are no longer our own. The plight of the individual is that he or she—he *and* she, and all of the rest of us—adopt, inevitably but voluntarily, the inheritance that we have received." Gunton, *Christian Faith*, 61. Gunton acknowledges the depraved nature of humankind, yet does not neglect to take account of its influence over the environment. Applying Gunton's conception of relational ontology of being to this matter may further enhance the importance of this point. According to Gunton, the trinitarian God is a being consisting of communion. Likewise, human beings are social beings who exist in society. A human being cannot exist apart from society because we are oriented relationally. In short, "*Homo sapiens* is always, and in the same measure, *homo socius*." Berger and Luckmann, *Social Construction of Reality*, 51. Human *being* consists of relations to other human persons in communion. If so, sin affects society as well as individuals because society (communion) is part of what constitutes human existence.

85. Gunton notes the importance of reading Rom 8:20 in light of Gen 3:17, which reveals divine judgment as the ultimate source of the disorder in creation. Gunton states, "Apart... from the Spirit's act of eschatological renewal, the destiny of the whole creation, man and nature alike, is futility and death." See Gunton, *Father, Son and Holy Spirit*, 111.

86. Gunton, *Christian Faith*, 61.

which our historically transmitted fallenness is nourished and grows."[87] If so, the perfection of the created world plays an indispensable role in the salvation of humankind. The created world is thus not something to be left behind for destruction, but rather is an essential aspect of human salvation.

Salvation: A Being in Communion

Gunton defines salvation as follows: "In eschatological perspective salvation means arriving safely at one's destination, and all other symptoms and manifestations are but greater or lesser stations upon the way."[88] Gunton does not deny that the central object of salvation is humankind. He states, "Why should it not for we are the problem?"[89] But, he rightly adds, "We still have to ask the questions of, first, what is the nature of that salvation, and second, how it involves us in the material world."[90] The nature of this salvation is, as stated above, eschatological: It is the transformation of the whole creation while redeeming what has gone wrong. And, how it involves us in the material world is related to the fact that we are a relational being, a being in communion.

Gunton argues that person is an eschatological concept.[91] "To say that is to say that personhood is being that is to be realized, and whose final realization will come only when God is all in all."[92] A human person is not

---

87. Gunton, *Christian Faith*, 61. Gunton is critical of Augustine's doctrine of original sin. He states, "If the doctrine of original sin is taken to mean that sin is that which is transmitted by direct sexual begetting from the historical ancestors of the race to us today, the diagnosis is oversimplified." Gunton, *Christian Faith*, 61. Accordingly, Gunton undermines the significance of Adam in the doctrine of sin. He argues, "We do not need to believe in a historical Adam, because the biblical story is itself too subtle to require such naïve and literal reading ... there must have been a first couple or first social order, which was distinguished from all its predecessors by both the distinctiveness of its relation to God and the unique character of its relation to the world." Gunton, *Christian Faith*, 61.

88. Gunton, *Christian Faith*, 63. Gunton further elaborates, "Because evil spreads its cancer throughout the body, embracing both its temporal and spatial dimensions, so salvation can take shape only over time and through space, social time and space especially, because it is with those who are made in the image of God that both the ill and its healing take shape." Gunton, *Christian Faith*, 63.

89. Gunton, *Triune Creator*, 168.

90. Gunton, *Triune Creator*, 168.

91. Gunton agrees with John Zizioulas on this point.

92. Gunton, *Promise of Trinitarian Theology*, 115.

yet fully realized because there is sin in humankind as well as society. Pollution must be removed and wrongness must be restored. Otherwise, the true personal reality—the image of God—will not be realized.

And as the true personal reality is being realized, the created world will be also restored and transformed to its own destiny. Our relation to each other as well as the created world shapes who we are because we are an ontologically relational being. If so, although sin was born in the human heart, unless the sin that is transmitted socially and historically is dealt with, salvation cannot be completed. Put differently, to bring perfection to the world, the whole world, humankind and the created world must be restored. Our relation to God must be made right, as well as our relation to each other and the created world. When this is accomplished, we will arrive at our destination: a being in communion.

The Two Hands of the Father: On the Way to a New Relationship

The task to restore this disruption in relation is given to none other than Jesus Christ, who is the mediator of creation and redemption. Sin has polluted the whole creation, humankind and the created world, through a network of sin. Gunton contends, "What is it to be born a human being under the condition in which human births universally take place? It is to share in a network of corruption, in which a disseminated pollution . . . infects the matter from which human being is formed."[93] Gunton continues, "The inescapable conclusion is that any human being will be constituted by a diffused corruption."[94] If Adam's disobedience to God has caused the pollution and corruption of the whole created world, a new Adam, Jesus Christ, by his perfect obedience to God will restore the disruptions in relation and redirect the created world to the right direction.

In this way, Christ institutes a new beginning for fallen humanity. His obedience is "transferable because Christ is priest as well as sacrifice."[95] However, Gunton argues that the death of Christ should not primarily be understood as divine wrath or punishment upon him. Rather, "The emphasis must be on the events as a new beginning for humanity deriving from the redemptive way in which this human life was lived, a new beginning

---

93. Gunton, *Actuality of Atonement*, 130.
94. Gunton, *Actuality of Atonement*, 131.
95. Gunton, *Actuality of Atonement*, 134.

willed from eternity by the love of the Father."⁹⁶ Hence, Christ is our representative and example of how humankind should live.

Christ is our Lord because he offered perfect obedience to God when we could not. And this Christ is the second Adam who lived as a man on this earth and set an example for the rest of humankind. Gunton contends, "Thus, Christ's life is the prototype of the Spirit's work and, by virtue of the power of the same Spirit which maintained him in sinless obedience and was the agent of his resurrection, is now the means of being able to 'take up humanity into Himself.'"⁹⁷ Christ is the model of the Spirit's work of perfection: to enable a person to realize true personhood. As the Spirit guided Christ in the gospels, he will also guide us. As Christ was made perfect through his earthly ministry, the Spirit will perfect humankind by enabling us to realize true personhood.⁹⁸

Christ' sacrifice is therefore "the rightful ordering of life in the world."⁹⁹ Accordingly, "Justification is not a legal fiction but a new relationship."¹⁰⁰ It

---

96. Gunton, *Actuality of Atonement*, 132. Gunton is critical of penal substitution. Although Gunton sees Christ's death as substitutionary, he does not affirm its penal aspect. Justyn Terry explains, "He . . . affirms a substitutionary view of Christ's work, not in order to endorse a form of penal substitution, but because 'he does for us what we cannot do for ourselves'. The victory, sacrifice and judgment were his work for sinners. They were not, however, only the work of a substitute, but also of a representative." Terry, "Colin Gunton's Doctrine of Atonement," 139. I am in agreement with Terry that Gunton negates the penal aspect of Christ's substitutionary death, but also views his death as a representative or model of what humanity ought to be. Terry adds, "Substitute and representative are, then, not to be seen as alternative explanations of Christ's work, but rather as different sides of the one work." Terry, "Colin Gunton's Doctrine of Atonement," 139. This point will be further discussed in chapter 4 when we examine Christology.

97. Gunton, *Actuality of Atonement*, 135.

98. Gunton's Christology primarily focuses on Christ's humanity rather than his divinity. Gunton argues that Christ's divinity is derived from his relation with the Holy Spirit (e.g., Luke 4). Gunton's Christology provides a basis for his argument of Christ as representative. As Christ, the second Adam, lived as a perfect man by the power of the Spirit, so humankind will also be empowered by the Spirit so that we will follow the pattern of Christ's earthly life. This point is further examined in chapter 4.

99. Gunton, *Actuality of Atonement*, 137.

100. Gunton, *Actuality of Atonement*, 104. Gunton argues, "Justice has for scripture a wider embrace than fairness and the proper punishment of offence. Comprehensively, divine justice refers to the realization of God's rule over the creation, and that means the fulfillment of his project that all creation should be perfected and therefore praise him." Gunton, *Christian Faith*, 74. This is consistent with Gunton's definition of sin and salvation. For Gunton, the problem of the world is our disrupted relation with God, each other and creation. Hence, to restore the problem requires restoration of rightful relations rather than paying a penalty of sin. This point is further examined in chapter 4.

was not legal standing given to humankind that brings perfection to the world. Rather, it is through a right relationship to God, each other and the created world that true healing and transformation of the whole world takes place. It is the eschatological Spirit who is "enabling the world to relate its dynamic interrelatedness. Thus is God the Spirit conceived as the perfecting cause, the true source of the dynamic of the forward movement of the cosmos."[101] And when God is all in all, our true personhood, our particular *telos*, will be realized.[102]

BRADLEY GREEN'S CRITIQUE REVISITED

The triune God is the foundation of Gunton's theology. Gunton argues that God is necessarily trinitarian. To perceive God as he truly is requires trinitarian thinking. Accordingly, God is to be construed primarily as action rather than intellect if God is the triune God who acts toward one goal. God is being and becoming. Therefore, there is "no breach between God's action and his being."[103] Indeed, God is a relational being. He reached out to the world through the two hands of the Father, the Son and the Spirit. Moreover, the source of this outward movement is none other than the divine love.

Nonetheless, the divine love that Gunton argues for seems to create a tension for some theologians. If the divine love moves outwardly toward creation, this seems to imply that God needs creation to satisfy his love. Gunton states, "The orientation of this God, his inner drive, we might say, is *not to remain content* with his eternal ordering as eternal love, but to move outwards to create a world which he loves and wishes to bring into relation with himself."[104] Hence, further examination of this matter is necessary in order to clarify Gunton's argument for divine love as the source of the outward movement of the trinitarian God.[105]

---

101. Gunton, *Promise of Trinitarian Theology*, 153.

102. The relation between a re-formed person and community in light of transformation of the whole creation will be further examined in chapter 5.

103. Gunton, *Act and Being*, 97.

104. Gunton, *Christian Faith*, 187; italics mine.

105. Gunton's theological commitment to God's freedom is clear. Reacting to the claim that God *must* create, Gunton responds, "The claim must be rejected, because if God *must* create there is a loss of freedom both for God and for the created world, because its being is then bound up with his so closely as to call into question its distinctive reality." Gunton, *Theology through the Theologians*, 127. Gunton strongly disagrees with

This is an attempt to revisit the earlier statement by Green: "There *are* no eschatological activities apart from creation and redemption."[106] The eschatological nature of the divine love raises questions for divine self-sufficiency, which may weaken Gunton's argument for the eschatological Spirit. Green argues, "The thrust of Gunton's logic is that at the heart of what it means for the Spirit to be the Spirit is the whole realm of the Spirit's eschatological activities, but there *are* no eschatological activities apart from creation and redemption."[107] This is a serious criticism as it suggests that Gunton's approach entails that God must necessarily create.

Perhaps the best place to start is the nature of God's being. Western theology seems to infer that since God is self-sufficient, he does not require anything other than himself. In other words, self-sufficiency means that "God is in himself a closed circle."[108] Contrary to this, Gunton argues that self-sufficiency means that God is in himself "essentially the relatedness of community."[109] Accordingly, there is a fundamental philosophical difference between Gunton and Western theology.

This is where the ontology of God makes a remarkable difference. For Gunton, God is a relational being. Therefore, the nature of such a being is to move outward towards someone or something that is other than himself. On the other hand, for Western theology, God is construed as a static substance. On this conception God is often portrayed to be a solitary monad whose orientation is directed towards himself alone.

Green's criticism of the plausibility of the eschatological Spirit seems to reflect how Western theology perceives God. I am in agreement with Gunton that to perceive God as he truly is requires trinitarian thinking. In other words, conceptualizing the being of God apart from the economic Trinity is a grave mistake. Scripture attests to the eschatological Spirit.[110]

---

any claim that may undermine the freedom of God and his distinction from the world. God is not bound to creation because He is not dependent on anything. Yet, Gunton's concept of God manifests an apparent tension with the perception of God as wholly free and sufficient within himself.

106. Green, *Colin Gunton and the Failure of Augustine*, 57n126; italics in original. As I argued in chapter 2, Gunton's pneumatology has significant emphasis on the eschatological function of the Spirit. To some degree, Gunton's pneumatology is about eschatology. See my chapter 2, n53.

107. Green, *Colin Gunton and the Failure of Augustine*, 57n126.

108. Gunton, *Theology through the Theologians*, 128.

109. Gunton, *Theology through the Theologians*, 128.

110. Gen 1:2, 2:7; Ezek 37, etc.

The real issue here may be one of theological method: How we should resolve theologically what Scripture attests.

Hence, I would argue that Green's criticism of the plausibility of the eschatological Spirit is not cogent since, first and fundamentally, Scripture attests to the eschatological Spirit. Furthermore, if we perceive God as a relational being as he has revealed himself in the economy, it seems plausible that the nature of such a being is oriented outwardly for relation. Nonetheless, I am sympathetic with Green's concern that such an outward movement by the Spirit involves the necessity of creation, which would have the effect of undermining God's freedom.

Indeed, this concern derives from the core of Gunton's theology: God's act originates in his being. The theological axiom of the unity of God's act and being has much to commend it. Yet, unless one treats the axiom with caution, it can quickly turn into a theological dilemma, as we see in the present case.

Although the eschatological Spirit is scripturally and theologically attested, we must not forget the necessity of approaching God's nature apophatically. We should beware of making definite pronouncements about God's essence. Doing so can pit, or elevate, one attribute of God against another. To identify the being of God with his action without leaving room for his freedom is an unbalanced approach and ultimately causes a theological dilemma. Hence, although I commend Gunton for uncovering the eschatological Spirit, a careful examination of how Gunton uses this theological axiom is necessary in order to determine whether the concept of the eschatological Spirit falls victim, to some extent, to an unwarranted conflation of the imminent and economic Trinities.[111] We will explore this issue in greater detail in chapters 4 and 5 when we examine the Spirit's relation with Christ, humankind and the church.

CONCLUSION

In light of the preceding discussions, we can conclude that Gunton's doctrine of God that is construed trinitarianly provides strong evidence for the

---

111. Gunton defends his pneumatological conclusions, stating, "Part of the importance of the exercise is not that we may speculate about the character of the innertrinitarian relations, but that our pneumatology may play a full place in the development of a doctrine of God." Gunton, "Spirit in the Trinity," loc. 4836–39. We will examine Gunton's pneumatology in the context of his doctrine of God further in the following chapter.

eschatological Spirit. If the action of God originates in the being of God, this denotes that God is for us. God does not remain in himself. Rather, he moves outwardly to his creation for our perfection's sake.

Gunton argues that God is necessarily trinitarian. God who is revealed to us in the action of the incarnate Son is a triune God who works together to achieve one goal: the perfection of the world. Thereby, we cannot properly understand God apart from the economic Trinity. God is being and becoming. And by this, we are able to see that God is a relational being. Indeed, God relates to the world through his otherness. Thereby, the action of God is mediated through the two hands of the Father, the Son and the Spirit.

The triune God is relational. He moves outwardly to reach out to the world so that he will bring his people into relationship with himself. Put differently, the providential action of God shows that the world is created in such a way that it depends upon God's active involvement in order to realize its own destiny.

And the source of this outward movement is the divine love that is the being of God. And the function of the divine love is freedom. The divine love does not deprive each person of their uniqueness. Rather, the divine love frees us and enables us to become the person whom God first intended us to be. Sin has enslaved us to be someone other than what God intended. Salvation means being free to become who we are intended to be so that we realize our personhood in the image of God. Christ who is the mediator of creation and redemption is a prototype of the work of the Spirit. And the Spirit perfects the world as we relate ourselves to Christ by worship and communion.

The triune God is relational and eschatological. God is essentially active rather than passive. Furthermore, the triune God has a mission to accomplish: to perfect and rescue the whole created world. If God's action originates in his being, it would be logical to conclude that such action of God would reflect his essence that is relational. The bond of love, the Spirit, who perfects the love of the Father and the Son does not move inwardly only, but also outwardly. He is eschatological since the triune God is eschatological in character: "because God is not in himself a closed circle but is essentially the relatedness of community, there is within his eternal being that which freely and in love creates, reconciles and redeems that which is not himself."[112] That is to say that the Spirit's action is teleological:

---

112. Gunton, *Theology through the Theologians*, 128.

It redirects the creation to its original destiny. In this light, Gunton attempts to establish a solid foundation for the eschatological Spirit. Nonetheless, for some theologians, the eschatological Spirit raises a concern regarding God's need to create. This presents a plausible challenge to Gunton's conception. But, the concept of the eschatological Spirit is both scripturally attested and theologically supported. Hence, this concern by no means discredits Gunton's contribution in conceptualizing the Spirit relationally as well as eschatologically. Still, God's freedom must be respected, and God's otherness and relationality must be kept in balance in order to be faithful to what God has revealed of himself in the economy.

Chapter 4

THE TRINITARIAN GOD
THE TWO HANDS OF THE FATHER, THE SON AND THE SPIRIT

In chapter 3, we examined the dynamic nature of the triune God whose being is being and becoming. He is the Creator of the universe. He reaches out to the world in relation, albeit relation in otherness. Hence, God is God for us because the divine love compels him to move outwardly to reach out to what is other than himself. Yet, there is a distinction between God and the world that requires mediation. The Son, having overcome the barrier between God and the creation, becomes the mediation that is necessary for relation between God and the world. But, the Son does not work alone. He works along with the Spirit who is the eschatological Spirit. Hence, the two hands of the Father, the Son and the Spirit, work together to accomplish the will of the Father who sent them.

In this chapter, the work of the two hands will be examined. In the previous chapter, we briefly examined the work of the two hands in light of the doctrine of providence. In this chapter, we will further explore this mediatory work of the Son and the Spirit, although from slightly different perspectives. The purpose of the previous chapter was to briefly delineate how the mediatory work of the two hands of the Father, the Son and the Spirit, achieves the one goal of the ultimate transformation of the world, whereas this section aims to identify at a deeper level the inner-workings and inner-relations of the Son and the Spirit in the light of incarnation, atonement and particularity.

To accomplish this end, we will first examine the triune God once more. This is an attempt to show the continuity between the immanent and economic Trinity: How the triune God whose love moves outwardly to reach out to what is other than himself is actualized in the incarnate Son who is the second person of the Trinity. Second, we will examine the doctrine of the atonement. The primary focus of this section is the actuality of the atonement: What Christ's work represents (e.g., victory, justice, sacrifice) and how it brings atonement to the whole creation. Third, we will examine the mediatory work of the Son and the Spirit. We will attempt to unfold the essential aspects that Christ shares with humanity and how they relate to the Spirit's perfecting work of the creation.

This section is divided into two subsections: The scope of the first section is Christ, while that of the second is the Holy Spirit. These sections are designed to show not only the essential aspects that the incarnate Son shares with humanity to make the atonement possible, but also to reveal the mutual relation between the Son and the Spirit in bringing about the ultimate purpose for the created world.

DIVINE LOVE: UNIVERSALITY AND PARTICULARITY

Gunton argues that there should be no schism between the being of God and act of God.[1] Rather, there must be continuity since God's action originates in his being. Yet, how to bridge the gap that may exist between God's being and action is a question to be answered. Gunton finds a solution in the Son who is the mediator of creation and redemption. In the previous chapter, we saw that Gunton argues for the dynamic nature of God: God is not static, but rather he is being and becoming. In fact, the divine love compels him to reach out what is other than himself. This results in creating and interacting with the creation despite the ontological differences that exist between Creator and creation. And the divine love was manifested in the created world in the person of Christ.

---

1. As the chapter gets under way, the concepts of universality and particularity become clear. Gunton casts God's being and action in the form of this dyad: Universality refers to God's being, while particularity refers to God's action. Gunton's major works *The Promise of Trinitarian Theology* and *The One, the Three and the Many* both elaborate on his concepts of universality and particularity.

Divine Love: The Son

Gunton argues that Christ is the actualization of the divine love.[2] The eternal love of the triune God is revealed in the incarnate Son. Hence, "The Son is the basis of God's movement out into the creation to bring that which is not God into covenant relation with him."[3] The eternal love of God for the world was revealed by the action of the Son who lived in time and space. Indeed, Gunton calls Christ the "logic of the divine love": "Jesus of Nazareth is the logic of divine love, logic in the sense of spelling out and making present in earthly actuality its eternal reality."[4] Through the incarnate Son, God actualized his eternal love for the world.

In this light, the being and act of God are not contradictory. The divine love took the form of man and lived among us as the person of Jesus Christ. The incarnate Son, Jesus, transcended eternity to reveal the love of the eternal God in time and space. Gunton states, "At the center of things is the self-actualization of God in time, the self-differentiation through love of the eternal to become temporal for us."[5] God's love is revealed in creation in that he took the form of a creature upon himself so that he could bring his eternal love to its fruition.

In this light, one can argue that the divine love is an "initiative from the side of eternity."[6] God the Son came to identify himself with our humanity so that he would manifest the love of the Father for the world. And through this identification, he is able to re-direct the fallen creation to its perfection. Yet, Gunton warns that this divine initiative should not be considered an "unprecedented irruption or intervention of God upon the stage of history."[7] Rather, he argues that the love of God is continuous, whether it is for creation or redemption. God's action originates in his being, and

---

2. Gunton contends, "For the sake of the gospel of salvation, anything which confuses the being of creator and creation must be resisted. Yet, equally and for the same reason, the two must come together in Jesus." Gunton, *Theology through the Theologians*, 157. It is important to remember that Gunton argues that God's being is love, the divine love. From this perspective, it is plausible to conclude that what Gunton argues here is the actualization of God's inner being through the incarnate Son.

3. Gunton, *Theology through the Theologians* 127.
4. Gunton, *Yesterday and Today*, 133.
5. Gunton, *Yesterday and Today*, 134.
6. Gunton, *Yesterday and Today*, 129.
7. Gunton, *Yesterday and Today*, 133.

God's being is love. Therefore, no discontinuity exists between his action and being.

Hence, the incarnate Son, Jesus of Nazareth, is the divine love. And this gives universal significance to Jesus's presence. Gunton argues, "Because Jesus Christ takes form in the here and now, in part of mankind and on behalf of others, we are able to bring to expression the universality of his significance."[8] Because the basis of the divine love that Jesus actualizes on the earth is eternity, it has universal significance. Gunton continues, "Put simply, it is that as the love of the eternal, Jesus is also universal in his significance. Because God's love embraces those who have been called into association with Jesus, then, by implication, it embraces *all* mankind."[9] God's love does not exclude anyone, but includes all of us. Jesus, who is the logic of the divine love, therefore, has universal significance by divine intention.

Divine Love: Holy Spirit

However, Jesus is not the only one who manifests the divine love. The Holy Spirit is also the divine love whose dynamic force transforms and perfects the creation, as we examined in the previous chapter. Thus, the Son and the Spirit are the two hands of the Father: They are distinct, yet inseparable. If Jesus is "the basis of God's movement out into the creation to bring that which is not God into covenant relation with him," the Spirit is the one who brings perfection to the world based on what Christ has achieved on the cross.[10]

Gunton states, "To be God is to be intrinsically related to the other in communion and the Spirit is the one who enables this communion to be."[11] Just as the Holy Spirit perfects the love of the Father and the Son, he will "perfect creation by realizing the communion of persons and the

---

8. Gunton, *Yesterday and Today*, 177.

9. Gunton, *Yesterday and Today*, 177; italics in original.

10. Gunton reminds us of the significance of the work of the Spirit in the atoning work of Christ. The Spirit is the one who applies salvation to the world, rather than the resurrected Christ. He argues, "It is the Spirit that is the source of Jesus' self-giving humanity, and that same Spirit which enables believers to share in the one reordering sacrifice." Gunton, "Christ the Sacrifice," 238. The Spirit's work in relation to the atoning work of Christ will be further examined below.

11. Gunton, *Theology through the Theologians*, 127.

transformation of matter."[12] To perceive both the Son and the Spirit as the divine love helps us to draw a clear demarcation of the two hands, yet acknowledge the mutuality between them in order to accomplish the will of the Father. Hence, the mission of the triune God can be described as follows: The Father is the fountainhead of the Son and the Spirit. And the Son and the Spirit are sent by the Father in order to do his will for the world. Yet, the mission is the mission of the triune God: The three persons of the Trinity are present and involved in every work of God in the world. The mission of the triune God therefore reflects the eternal being of God whose being is a communion of love.[13]

THE ACTUALITY OF ATONEMENT: THE UNIVERSALITY AND PARTICULARITY OF CHRIST

As we have seen above, the divine love is actualized in both hands of the Father, the Son and the Spirit. God's love—that is, his being—that reaches out to what is other than himself is fully manifested in the actions of these two hands of the Father. In this section, having established the fact that the Son and the Spirit are the divine love, we need to turn to see *how* this divine love is actualized in the atonement. To be more specific, we need to examine how Gunton moves from universality (God) to particularity (Christ). The focus of this section, therefore, is on the incarnate Son rather than the Spirit.

We do not wish to diminish the unity of the two hands, but rather to delineate how the Son lays the foundation so that the Spirit can accomplish his divine purpose. Thus, we must first understand the Son's work as the mediator of creation and redemption. Otherwise, we are unable to understand the Spirit's work—how the Spirit builds on the foundation laid by the Son for the consummation of the world. We will give attention to

---

12. Gunton, *Theology through the Theologians*, 127.

13. Toward the end of his life, Gunton made a significant change in regard to the *taxis* of God. Before the shift, Gunton held that the priority of the Father was economical rather than ontological in nature. However, Gunton later sided with John Zizoulas and contended, "Ontologically speaking . . . the Father is prior." Gunton, *Triune God*, Preface.5.1. This previously unpublished material is found in Cumin, "Taste of Cake," 77. Cf. Gunton, "Persons and Particularity," 100. Hence, Gunton opts for the "causative particularity of the Father." Cumin, "Taste of Cake," 78. But, it is the Spirit "who is finally responsible for God's aseity." Cumin, "Taste of Cake," 79. In other words, the Father causes, while the Spirit completes.

how Christ is universal, yet particular, in relation to the world and how the universality and particularity of Christ give shape to the atonement. In so doing, we hope to delineate how Christ mediates between God (the Father) and the world.

Universal Atonement: Salvation for All

Gunton states, "Atonement is, an act of God directed to the redemption and completion of the creation, universal in being concerned with the reconciliation of all things."[14] As Paul says in 2 Cor 5:19, "God was reconciling the world to himself in Christ." In Gunton's view, atonement "implies universality, but not that universal reconciliation has already taken place."[15] Yet, "The divine purpose is for universal salvation."[16]

Universal salvation is necessary, says Gunton, because all creation is interconnected and sin has spread through the whole web of creation. Contrary to Augustine's view of original sin, sin was not passed on to humanity through procreation, but rather through our relation to each other and things. In short, sin is a universal phenomenon, and not limited to humanity. Every aspect of God's creation has been tainted by sin. As Romans 8 attests, the creation "waits in eager expectation for the sons of God to be revealed." If so, the savior must bear universal significance because redemption is not only for humanity, but the whole creation.[17]

Yet, as much as the universality of Christ is an important aspect of atonement, unfortunately, the universality by itself cannot bring redemption to the world. It must be accompanied by the relationality/particularity of Christ.[18] As noted above, just as sin spread through the web of relations

---

14. Gunton, "Universal and Particular Atonement in Atonement Theology," 458.
15. Gunton, *Christian Faith*, 163.
16. Gunton, *Christian Faith*, 163.
17. In addition to the universal significance of Christ, Gunton seems to argue for universal salvation. He argues extensively from Genesis 18 for this possibility. As God would have spared the wicked Lot because of Abraham's plea, God will spare the whole creation for the sake of a few saints. Likewise, Gunton makes the assumption that the missionary journeys of Paul might have been motivated by the fact that "Once representative samples of all nations could be brought into the people of God, God could bring time and history to an end in the eschatological kingdom, to universal blessing." Gunton, *Christian Faith*, 166. Yet, Gunton concludes, "We cannot rule out the possibility that some may finally exclude themselves from the kingdom." Gunton, *Christian Faith*, 164.
18. Gunton argues that universal significance is also given to Christ because he is the mediator of creation. See Gunton, "Atonement and the Project of Creation," 38.

in creation, so does redemption. Although the universality of Christ is absolutely necessary to cover the sin of the whole creation, the relational aspect in atonement cannot be underestimated because of the structure of the world.

Gunton states, "One is not saved first of all by learning a teaching or assimilating a philosophy, but by being brought into relation with a particular person as the route to or mediate of reconciliation with God."[19] And to be particular, universality must be embodied. In other words, Christ the eternal Son had to become like one of us so that he could enter time and space. "Particularity thus aids identification, specification and distinctiveness."[20]

Yet, particularity and universality should not be perceived as if they are two different steps to take. Rather, they should be perceived as particularity being "in some way universal."[21] Gunton explains, "God is by definition universal, so that if the work of Jesus is understood to be in some direct way the work of God, it is rendered by that very connection also in some way universal."[22] The particularity of Christ must be found in universality. When we see Jesus on the cross, we must also see the love of the Father for the world. And this is because God's being is the action of God. There should not be a division between them.[23]

The concept of the universality and particularity of Christ is also reflected in the images and metaphors of the atonement. But, this reflection is not identical with the relation between the divine love and the incarnate Son, but from a different perspective. Gunton states,

> The Christian theology of the atonement draws upon at least three families of metaphors by means of which it gives rational account of its view of human life in relation to God. These three clusters of metaphors appear elsewhere than simply in Christian theology,

19. Gunton, "Universal and Particular Atonement," 453.
20. Gunton, "Universal and Particular Atonement," 453.
21. Gunton, "Universal and Particular Atonement," 453.
22. Gunton, "Universal and Particular Atonement," 454.
23. Yet, this is a difficult concept to grasp: how eternity and temporality can co-exist within the human realm. Gunton calls this a "perichoresis, a simultaneous interaction, of the temporal and the eternal." Gunton, *Yesterday and Today*, 130. He continues, "The eternal is here conceived as a time-embracing and not a time-denying reality." Gunton, *Yesterday and Today*, 130. Hence, things below (the human realm in time and history) can be perceived by things above (eternity). This speaks to Gunton's theological methodology in regard to the doctrine of God. There is an intricate relation between the immanent and economic Trinity in Gunton's theology. The self-actualization of God in time is essential since the economic Trinity reveals the immanent Trinity.

and it is precisely there that we come upon elements of universality, because the Christian usages in some way or other share in a widespread human analysis of its condition that might almost be claimed to be transcendental. In this context, that is to say that they reflect a universal human orientation on and habitation of reality.[24]

Hence, in this case, the concept of universality and particularity is not between God and the world. It is between the world and the world. And these transcendental images that inform a "widespread human analysis of its condition" are victory, justice and sacrifice.[25]

Metaphors of Atonement: Victory, Justice, Sacrifice

First, the metaphors of victory convey that the rule of God over the world is re-inaugurated by the victory of Christ. Christ, having given perfect obedience to the Father on the cross, was given victory over the evils of this world. Gunton explains, "Metaphors of victory show that the atonement is a battle against evil, fought by God as a man, and with the weapons only of defenseless human action."[26] Thus, victory signifies the perfect obedience that was rendered to God by the incarnate Son.

Gunton contends that the metaphors of victory also unfold significant meanings in relation to our salvation. First, this victory delineates a new way to live on earth. Contrary to common images of worldly victory (violence,

---

24. Gunton, *Yesterday and Today*, 130. Gunton's tendency to look for biblical imagery in the universal human condition (e.g., sin) comes from his lack of faith in foundationalism. Gunton denies that foundationalism succeeded in providing universal foundations for thought. Hence, to make "the particular to be in some way universal," Gunton attempts to find transcendentals that provide a universal structure for his theology. Cf., *Father, Son and Holy Spirit*, 192.

25. Justyn Terry states that whereas Gunton's work is known for the doctrine of the Trinity and creation, his contribution to the doctrine of atonement cannot be overlooked. Terry states that one of Gunton's contributions to the doctrine is his use of metaphors. Metaphors enable the various facets of the atonement to be further explored. Gunton is convinced that to understand the biblical images of the atonement as theories confines the meaning(s) of those images. "Metaphor or family of metaphors takes its shape from the divine and human story it seeks to narrate, and so enables aspects of the meaning of unfathomable mystery to be expressed in language." Gunton, *Actuality of Atonement*, 113. Hence, the biblical images of the atonement—victory, justice and sacrifice—should be treated as metaphors. For additional details, see Terry, "Colin Gunton's Doctrine of Atonement."

26. Gunton, "Atonement and the Project of Creation," 38.

destruction, etc.), Christ's victory is not associated with forceful action, but rather perseverance. "To be victorious does not mean butchering your opponent with weapons, but refusing to exercise power demonically in order to overcome evil with good."[27] Christ's obedience which comes from his perseverance and patience is the example for those who are in Christ.

Second, the metaphors of victory teach us a "new vision of the world."[28] It is a reordering/redirecting of life to its intended end. This signifies that salvation does not mean only the renewal of human morality, but also the renewal of the world—"the extension of the benefits of the divine victory to all parts of the created world."[29] The world that we live in is an integral part of the redemption of mankind. The world needs to be healed as we are healed because of our mutual relation with the world.

The metaphor of justice shows that the divine justice is by nature transformational and relational, rather than penal and individualistic.[30] Gunton laments that the metaphor of justice is often perceived primarily as penal due to an excessive focus on individualism. As a result, the cosmic and social dimensions of divine justice are overlooked. If the divine justice is to reinstitute the rule of God in the world, thereby to realize God's rule over the creation, the significance of the created world cannot be underestimated.

If the divine justice is to restore God's rule over the world, then relation is a significant aspect in accomplishing this end. Gunton argues, "The

27. Gunton, *Actuality of Atonement*, 77.
28. Gunton, *Actuality of Atonement*, 79.
29. Gunton, *Actuality of Atonement*, 79.
30. Gunton's view of penal substitution has been criticized by a number of theologians (e.g., Jeffery et al., *Pierced for Our Transgressions*, 250; Letham, *Work of Christ*, 137; Vanhoozer, "Atonement in Postmodernity"; Gaffin, "Atonement in the Pauline Corpus," 161). Gunton's dislike of penal views is well known. He argues that God's justice is not "punitive in making punishment an end in itself rather than a means to the greater end of the redemption of the sinner." Gunton, *Christian Faith*, 76. But, to minimize the penal view is to risk neglecting the biblical metaphors of sin and atonement that reflect sin's gravity. Vanhoozer asks, "How can God restore right covenantal relationships without imposing covenantal sanctions? Is it possible *justly* to forgive an infraction of the law?" Vanhoozer, "Atonement in Postmodernity," 381; italics in original. Graham Cole argues, "'Can there be Christian maturity without grasping penal substitution?' To fail to incorporate the argument of Hebrews [Heb 6–10] concerning the nature of Christ's priesthood and substitutionary sacrifice into one's theology risks locking oneself into an arrested theological development." Cole, *God the Peacemaker*, 238. Gunton's diminishing of penal substitution thus marks a lack of engagement with key biblical texts relating to soteriology.

point about justice being a relational concept is very important . . . for it emphasizes that justice is not a *state* but something that takes place between God and the world or between people."[31] To be a creature is to be in relation with God. Transformation comes only from relation with God first, and then relation with others and the created world. And this is what Christ accomplished on the cross—restoring our distorted relationship with God.

Similarly, the divine justice is not static, but dynamic. That is, the divine justice refers to the realization of God's rule over his creation over time. Hence, it does not take place at one point of history, but will be achieved over a period of time. Since the divine justice is transformational and relational, as humanity relate to God, transformation takes place.[32]

The third metaphor, sacrifice, is on Gunton's view the most significant of the three. It shows how the redemptive work of the incarnate Son is relevant for the creation— humanity as well as the world. As discussed above, sin is a "disruption and distortion of the relation of personal being with the personal creator God."[33] Hence, sin should be perceived relationally. Accordingly, a sacrifice requires two parties: God and humanity—specifically, God and the incarnate Son. Gunton argues, "Because what is happening is not a transaction outside the human sphere, but is a divine action from within the heart of the human condition, it does signal a real change in the human relationship to God."[34] Thereby, Gunton concludes, "The claim that Christ is a sacrifice implies that he is now the source of the relationship with God."[35] God's redemptive action took place within the person of Jesus. The work of Jesus is the work of God: Jesus offered himself to God and God accepted his offering within the person of Jesus Christ. Jesus, the incarnate Son, is therefore a mediator between God and humanity.

---

31. Gunton, *Actuality of Atonement*, 104; italics in original.

32. William Baltmanis Whitney argues that Gunton's concept of justification is not consistent with the classical legal metaphors of justification. He states, "Gunton retains the Reformed categories of justification and sanctification, but his eschatological emphasis shapes them in a way that is relatively un-Reformed—seen especially in his non-forensic understanding of justification. Gunton approaches both creation and salvation with a wide-angle lens, choosing the broad picture of perfection over time rather than focusing on specific points *in* time. Thus, Gunton reappraises justification so that justification and sanctification are not necessarily separate concepts but *both* talk about the process of one being perfected." Whitney, *Problem and Promise in Colin E. Gunton's Doctrine of Creation*, 108; italics in original.

33. Gunton, *Christian Faith*, 59.

34. Gunton, *Actuality of Atonement*, 127.

35. Gunton, "Christ the Sacrifice," 237.

Yet, one may ask what enables Jesus to be a substitute and representative for us. Gunton answers that it is because of the fallen flesh that he took. He writes, "What is it to be born a human being under the condition in which human births universally take place? It is to share in a network of corruption, in which a disseminated pollution . . . infects the matter from which human being is formed."[36] Jesus is our substitution because of the fallen flesh that he shares with us.

Further, Jesus is not only our substitute, but also our representative. The fallen flesh that the eternal Son took is a "random but also representative sample of the infected whole."[37] Moreover, Jesus offered God a perfect obedience, "the first fruits of a true, recapitulated human life to the Father."[38] It was not the mere death of Jesus that brought redemption to the world, but a perfect obedience that was demonstrated through his death in which he became the first fruits—the sacrifice—that enabled the much-anticipated reordering of the world.

And Jesus did this so that we can follow him in order to have a right relationship with God. Gunton states, "He brings us to the Father as one of us, but does so as one who, because he is God incarnate, is able to do so."[39] This is a mediatory work of the Son between the Creator and creation. Jesus, the incarnate Son, is our substitute and representative because he not only did what we could not do, but also became the first fruits to restore what had been broken since the fall of our first couple.

CHRIST: THE MEDIATOR OF CREATION

In this section, we will examine the essential attributes of Jesus that made atonement possible. As briefly discussed above, the humanity of Christ is one of the essential attributes that Jesus shared with humanity to make atonement possible. This allowed Jesus to become the mediator of redemption, our substitute and representative who rectifies our dysfunctional relation with God.

Yet, what has often been neglected is that Christ is also the mediator of creation. And this is a crucial point. Without being the mediator of creation, Christ could not have been the mediator of redemption since the

---

36. Gunton, *Actuality of Atonement*, 131.
37. Gunton, *Actuality of Atonement*, 132.
38. Gunton, *Actuality of Atonement*, 161.
39. Gunton, *Actuality of Atonement*, 166.

former provides a necessary foundation for the latter to be realized. Hence, we will first examine Christ as the mediator of creation.

In contrast to what we have examined above, our scope in this section is the *particularity* of Christ. Now that we have observed the relation of universality and particularity in Gunton's theology, it is necessary to shift our focus to Christ the incarnate Son. We will therefore endeavor to unfold the attributes of Christ that enabled him to actualize God's eternal love in time and space.

Christ as the Lord of Creation

As Scripture reveals, there is a significant relation between Christ and creation. Col 1:16 proclaims that creation was created in the Son. Gunton explains, "To create in the Son means to create by the mediation of the one who is the way of God out into that which is not himself."[40] Hence, the Son is the co-agent of creation (1 Cor 8:6). All things were created by Him (John 1:2; Heb 1:2) and all things were created for Him (Col 1:16). Indeed, creation belongs to Christ. Furthermore, he calms and rebukes creation and creation obeys his commands (Mark 4:39–41; Matt 8:27). This signifies the authority and lordship of Christ over creation.

Christ is also the cosmic Savior. Gunton rightly frames the question, "How far may it be said that the whole creation, and not merely the human race, is to be saved through Christ's work?"[41] As we have previously noted, redemption cannot be complete without the created world (Romans 8; Revelation 21; Ephesians 1). Hence, Christ is the cosmic Savior. In explaining the meaning of Col 1:17, "In him all things hold together," Gunton contends that if all things are held together in Christ, Christ is the "'container' of all the universe."[42] This signifies a necessary precursor for the perfection of the world, in the sense that "already provision is made for a conception of God's continuing interaction with it [creation]."[43]

---

40. Gunton, *Triune Creator*, 143.

41. Gunton, *Christ and Creation*, 32.

42. Gunton, *Triune Creator*, 21.

43. Gunton, *Triune Creator*, 22. Gunton appeals to H. H. Schmid for the basis of this argument. Gunton summarizing Schmid argues that surveying many ancient cultures shows that a "conception of creations serves as a framework for cosmic, political and social order. Conceptions of salvation—of true human life on earth and in society—are framed within beliefs about the creation of the world." Gunton, *Christ and Creation*, 20.

Accordingly, Gunton concludes that the fact that creation was created by God is not insignificant, but "the fundamental theme."[44] He continues, "The theologies of the cosmic Christ are not pieces of independent speculation but are designed to bring out the meaning of Christ for the completion of that which was in the beginning."[45] Creation is not a mere stage for the salvation of humanity that will decay in the end. On the contrary, creation is a "fundamental theme" of what will take place according to the eternal will of God for the world. And for this reason, Christ is the cosmic Savior. He redeems not only humanity, but the entire universe. Everything that God created through Christ, he will redeem for the glory of God.

Christ as the Restructurer of the World

If creation is a "fundamental theme"[46] of God's will, it is also a necessary aspect of redemption. Indeed, creation prepares the way for redemption. Hence, for Christ to be the mediator of creation is also for him to be the mediator of redemption. Because creation was created through Christ, the incarnation was possible for him. Gunton observes, "His relation to the whole of creation is not incidental to it, but an essential dimension."[47] There is significance in Christ being the mediator of creation.

Nevertheless, says Gunton, this significance is often overlooked in comparison to Christ as the mediator of redemption. Christ's redemptive work is perceived apart from his work as the mediator of creation. Consequently, his relation to creation as a whole has not been satisfactorily explored. Yet this relational aspect allows Christ to achieve the goal of the perfection of the creation, which he does by restructuring the world that was tainted by sin.

In this light, one can say that Christ is the *restructurer of the world*, in the sense that he is the framework of all things and encompasses the "cosmic, social, political order."[48] Gunton contends, "A christological structuring of divine providential action understands it in the light of the one who became human, identifying with the world's structures in order to reshape

---

44. Gunton, *Christ and Creation*, 20.
45. Gunton, *Christ and Creation*, 23–24.
46. Gunton, *Christ and Creation*, 20
47. Gunton, *Christ and Creation*, 20.
48. Gunton, *Christ and Creation*, 20.

them to their eschatological destiny."[49] Gunton states, "Jesus Christ is the Son of God, the mediator of God's creation, returning to his own realm to reclaim it from threatened dissolution."[50] Hence, it seems plausible that because Christ is the mediator of creation, he is enabled to restructure the world that is perverted by sin.

Three significant points need to be noted in the light of the redemptive work of Christ. First, the incarnation of Christ was made plausible because he is the mediator of creation. Second, as a result, we can argue that it was the will of the Father from the beginning that the Son would come and reclaim what belongs to him. Third, and perhaps the most important point, is that God is concerned with the whole creation—not only humanity, but also the created world. His salvation does not exclude the created world. On the contrary, it will be perfected along with humanity. Therefore, Christ is the mediator of both creation and redemption.

CHRIST: THE MEDIATOR OF REDEMPTION

Having seen that Christ is the mediator of creation, we now turn to examine Christ as the mediator of redemption. This section demonstrates the second step in God actualizing his love for the world, redemption, following the first step of God bringing about creation through Christ. In our exploration of the implications of Christ as the mediator of creation, we examined the aspects of Christ that laid the foundation for the incarnation. Accordingly, our aim in this section is to examine the incarnate Son. More specifically, we will focus on the incarnation and humanity of Christ to see how these aspects might have enabled him to become a certain man. The aim therefore is to investigate the various aspects of what Gunton terms the particularity of Christ.[51]

---

49. Gunton, *Triune Creator*, 192.

50. Gunton, *Christian Faith*, 65.

51. Certainly, the incarnation and humanity of Christ are not the only two aspects that enabled the particularity of Christ. Christ's personhood and relationality are also very relevant to this section. However, for the sake of the structure of the book, these will be examined in the next chapter where anthropology, ecclesiology and pneumatology are discussed.

The Incarnation of Christ: God and Man

The incarnation refers to the event in which "the Word became flesh, and lived among us" (John 1:14). As Athanasius expressed, the incarnation signifies God's entrance into the world and his dealing with the human condition to bring a change to the world.[52] In fact, the incarnation is the climax of God's continuous involvement with the world. As argued above, God had prepared this entrance by his eternal Son, who is the mediator of creation, that the Son might renew creation. If so, the incarnation not only signifies God's entrance into the world, but also his divine initiative to intervene in the fallen world to redirect it to its original intention.

We should perhaps start by asking, Who is the incarnate Son? Gunton responds, "This historical human being, 'despised and rejected of man', is identical with—the same person as—the eternal Son of God through whom God created the world."[53] Hence, the incarnate Son is fully God and fully man. Without doubt, the two natures of the incarnate Son are difficult to grasp with our finite minds. It is indeed a divine mystery. But, one nature should not be emphasized at the expense of the other. A perfect unity of the divine and human natures exists in the person of Christ. Gunton observes, "Jesus is the eternal Word of God in person, yet without being in any way less human than we are; in fact, being more truly human."[54] Therefore, Gunton continues, "His earthly career... must be understood as God's personal action in his world to renew and complete the plan of creation once begun but since disrupted."[55] Thus, the incarnation conveys God's personal presence and action in the world.

Accordingly, Gunton describes the incarnation as a way for universality (God) to realize/actualize in particularity (the incarnate Son). He writes, "Simply, the incarnation achieves its redemptive end by a form of divine immanence in the world."[56] Further, "The incarnation of the Word in Jesus of Nazareth is the realization of a relationship that is eternal in being rooted in God's continuing relation with the world."[57] Moreover, "Attention to the New Testament's presentation of the life, death and resurrection of Jesus

---

52. McGrath, *Christian Theology*, 276.
53. Gunton, *Christian Faith*, 79.
54. Gunton, *Christian Faith*, 87.
55. Gunton, *Christian Faith*, 87.
56. Gunton, *Christ and Creation*, 90.
57. Gunton, *Christian Faith*, 98.

compels us to affirm that in him the eternal love of God becomes datable."[58] In short, universality was manifested in particularity.[59] In this light, writes Gunton, "The life of Jesus is the way by which the eternal God takes himself out of alienated time and re-creates it as that in which there is construction and not destruction."[60] Thus, the incarnation manifests in a concrete form the relation between the Creator and creation. Through the incarnation, God embodies himself to "enable the time of human and universal life to be a time of fulfillment."[61] Hence, Christ the incarnate Son is truly the mediator between God and creation.

If the incarnation was a vehicle to reveal God's personal presence and action in the person of Jesus Christ, it was also a means to bring about a perfect Savior, who had to be a man, as well as God. Gunton explains, "What is needed is one who is . . . a mediator: while only man ought to do what is needed, only God is able to do it. Therefore salvation can be achieved only by one who is both God and man."[62] He continues, "Jesus is what he is . . . because his suffering is God's suffering, that by which God acts in the humanity of Jesus to save the world. . . . There is real reconciliation of man to God because Jesus Christ is both fully man and fully God."[63] Unless Jesus is God and man, he could not achieve what only God could do. In Jesus, the unity of God and humanity exists and makes reconciliation possible. The Word became flesh. And this is the Savior that the world needs for its redemption.

The incarnation also reveals the divine orientation toward the creation. Gunton affirms, "God's being is in some way oriented to the world

58. Gunton, "Time, Eternity and Doctrine of the Incarnation," 267.

59. Gunton laments the failure of modern kenotic theory to understand the unity of divinity and humanity in one person. Gunton agrees that kenosis is an "appropriate concept to use in Christology insofar as it enables us to show something of how it is that everything that Jesus of Nazareth is and does is the act of God while not ceasing to be the act of one who is truly human." Gunton, *Christ and Creation*, 85–86. Nonetheless, modern kenotic theory falls short in that it renders "Jesus a depotentiated deity rather than the Son of God in action." Gunton, *Christian Faith*, 94. Following P. T. Forsyth, Gunton suggests that the self-emptying should be understood as an act of fulfillment, of plerosis. Gunton states, "In the incarnation the being of the Son expresses itself, is laid out in all its fullness, because in his self-emptying the Son is most fully divine." Gunton, *Christ and Creation*, 84.

60. Gunton, "Time, Eternity and Doctrine of the Incarnation," 267.

61. Gunton, "Time, Eternity and Doctrine of the Incarnation," 267.

62. Gunton, "Time, Eternity and Doctrine of the Incarnation," 269.

63. Gunton, *Yesterday and Today*, 181.

of time and space that he takes to himself in the incarnation."[64] Christ, the Son of God, is the mediator of creation. Having been the mediator, Christ is enabled to become incarnated as man.[65] If so, the incarnation is not a breach of the distinction between the Creator and creation. Rather, it is "the Father's good pleasure to come into personal relation with us through the incarnation of his Son."[66] It is God's perfect plan to see his love for his creation completed.

Furthermore, Gunton argues that if we understand "the initial christological and eschatological thrust of creation,"[67] we would see the necessity of incarnation.[68]

> If creation is to an end, namely that all that is should within the structures of time and space come to be perfected in praise of the creator, what we call redemption is not a new end, but the achievement of the original purpose of creation. . . . What is realized in the incarnate involvement of the Son in time and space is the redirection of the creation to its original destiny, a destiny that was

---

64. Gunton, *Father, Son and Holy Spirit*, 140.

65. Gunton elaborates, "Because the Father created and upholds the world in being through the Son, it is ontologically appropriate, so to speak, for the Son to be the one who takes flesh." Gunton, *Christ and Creation*, 84.

66. Gunton, *Christ and Creation*, 96.

67. Gunton, *Christ and Creation*, 94.

68. The question of whether there would have been an incarnation had there been no sin has been debated in the history of the church. Aquinas argued that the incarnation would not have taken place if there had been no fall. On the other hand, Duns Scotus saw Christ's incarnation as "predestined independently of man's sin." Laurence William Grensted, *Short History of the Doctrine of Atonement*, 162. Gunton commends Scotus for this view, yet argues that it does not account for the cross because it does not give a clear reason why God should have chosen the cross. As a result, the cross appears to be incidental. In this light, Gunton commends Anselm and Aquinas for holding to the absolute necessity of the cross for the redemption of the world. However, not fully satisfied with either of them, Gunton suggests a third way to perceive the incarnation that is more Christ-centered. Following Edward Irving, Gunton argues, "The ways of God for his creation involve Christ, the one through whom he created and continues to uphold the universe *in any case*, and therefore he would have come—even had sin not dictated the *form* of his coming." Gunton, *Christian Faith*, 67; italics in original. In other words, Christ would have come regardless of sin and evil because the primary impetus of the incarnation is God's love for the world. Yet, sin and evil may have determined the manner of his coming. In short, as Cole argues, "the incarnation is no afterthought." Cole, *God Who Became Human*, 46.

from the beginning *in Christ*, for all creation is through and for the Son."[69]

Incarnation was a means of enabling God's continuous involvement with humanity. Hence, we should not perceive the incarnation of Christ as if it were a contingency plan brought about by the appearance of sin—though sin may have determined the form of Christ's coming to the world. God created the world in such a way that it will be perfected over time and in space. And this was his chosen way to be God with us: The Son whom the creation was created through and for become incarnated to achieve the original purpose of the creation.

The Humanity of Christ: Fallen and Marred

If the incarnation is the form that the Word took to become man, what Christ assumed in the incarnation is humanity. As previously noted, humanity is a necessary condition for effective atonement. Unless Christ assumed humanity, he could not have atoned for our sins. Indeed, Christ's humanity reveals the unity of the Son and the Spirit in shaping humanity.

For example, declares Gunton, "The renewal of the creation can begin only by a new and miraculous act of God, the making new of our humanity, which had become soiled and tired."[70] To make our humanity new, Christ had to be born as man. Thus, the birth of Jesus was the climax of God's involvement with the world because his birth was a pivotal point for the redemption of the world. Christ had to assume our humanity in order to renew our humanity. Further, Christ had to assume humanity because through humanity he established solidarity with all mankind: It is "the corporate nature of humanity: that we stand or fall together."[71] This relational aspect is indispensable in atonement. As discussed above, sin is a "disruption and distortion of the relation of personal being with the personal creator God."[72] Hence, sin cannot be conceived in external, abstract terms, but rather relationally.

Further, the divine justice is in its nature transformative and relational. Thus, the sacrifice of Christ makes it possible for others to approach God

---

69. Gunton, *Christ and Creation*, 94; italics in original.
70. Gunton, *Christian Faith*, 100.
71. Gunton, *Theology through Theologians*, 160.
72. Gunton, *Christian Faith*, 59.

relationally. Indeed, "The sacrifice is the basis and enabler of sacrifices."[73] Yet, "What is offered is not Christ, but that which he came to realize, the gift to God in worship and life of the perfected creation."[74] Christ's humanity is therefore what was offered to God for the renewal of the creation. Gunton contends,

> The Christian gospel bears upon the whole embodied person, and along with that the whole created world which is the context of that embodied life. The Spirit's redemptive action is similarly eschatological in that it brings about the perfection of this particular sector of the created order—the humanity of Jesus Christ—as the guarantee and first fruits of the reconciliation of all things.[75]

The Spirit transformed and perfected Christ's humanity—the true humanity which was realized despite our fallenness. Hence, we stand together with Christ who is our representative and first fruits of sacrifices.

The humanity that Jesus shared with mankind is fallen humanity.[76] Gunton explains, "The material for Jesus' body comes from the common stock from which ours and that of other living creatures is constructed. The Word becomes *flesh*."[77] Scripture tells us that Jesus's body was formed in the womb of Mary by the Holy Spirit. And historically, it has been understood that this signifies the divinity of Christ. Christ's conception was immaculate. But, Gunton argues against this interpretation. He contends, "Jesus is

---

73. Gunton, *Father, Son and Holy Spirit*, 198.

74. Gunton, *Father, Son and Holy Spirit*, 198.

75. Gunton, *Triune Creator*, 171. Further, "At the centre of the disorientation of relations is the human creature, which, because of the personal and culpable form of its sin, involves all other reality in its fallenness.... It is therefore appropriate that the first fruits of redemption should be the free, obedient and loving self-offering of this true human life to God the Father." Gunton, *Christ and Creation*, 58. Finally, "But his obedience is salvific because here we have a representative sample of fallen flesh purified and presented to God the Father." Gunton, *Christ and Creation*, 59.

76. Gunton is indebted to Edward Irving in his view of the fallen nature of Christ. See Gunton, *Theology through the Theologians*, 151–68. The issue of the fallenness of Christ's human nature has been debated among contemporary theologians (e.g., Karl Barth, T. F. Torrance, etc.) For those who argue for a fallen human nature of Christ, their pressing concern is to affirm that Jesus was "made like his brothers in every respect" (Heb 2:17). Yet, this view faces some difficulties, especially in relation to a traditional understanding of original sin, that those who possess a fallen nature are guilty before God. See Crisp, "Did Christ Have a *Fallen* Human Nature?," 270–88; Paget, "Christology and Original Sin," 229–48.

77. Gunton, *Christian Faith*, 102; italics in original.

formed in the womb of Mary by the Holy Spirit to show that he is indeed part of the network of creation, in all its fallenness."[78] Jesus thus shares in a humanity that is fallen and tainted.

Moreover, Gunton argues that if Christ's humanity was not fallen, he could not have brought atonement to the world because "what is unassumed is unhealed." So Christ had to share the fallenness of man. Otherwise, real change could not be made in the human relationship to God. Gunton argues, "But, it is asked, in what sense does such a transaction [remission of penalty] transform the moral agent? Is it not merely an external transaction? . . . If Jesus Christ is not fully man, the human condition is not restored *from within*."[79] Consequently, it was necessary for Christ to assume our fallen nature to be a sacrifice for our sin.

However, if the humanity of Christ is fallen and tainted, how could Christ bring atonement for our sins?[80] Moreover, if Christ is the God-man, how could one say that his humanity was tainted without this also undermining his holiness? On the one hand it seems reasonable to argue for the fallenness of Christ's humanity, but on the other this seems to create an inconsistency between Christ's humanity and divinity. The key to understanding this mystery is the work of the Holy Spirit. Gunton contends,

> Jesus, a man in need of divine support and guidance like all human beings, shares in human flesh in all its weakness and need. . . . However . . . the Spirit's action is a renewing action, and therefore makes perfect that which enters the process marked by the accumulated corruption of the ages. The recreation of the world is begun, but first only as the renewal of a representative sample of that which is fallen. The Spirit is the one who makes Jesus of Nazareth to be the particular human being that he is.[81]

It is therefore the Spirit who transforms/perfects Jesus. To bring change within the heart of the human condition, Christ had to share the

---

78. Gunton, *Christ and Creation*, 52.

79. Gunton, *Yesterday and Today*, 180–181; italics in original.

80. This point is also argued in Paget, "Christology and Original Sin," 242.

81. Gunton, *Christian Faith*, 102. Gunton argues that one should not say that Jesus was able not to sin because this is contradictory to our fallen human condition. He declares, "Our situation being what it is, we therefore need, if this man is truly to be the author and pioneer of our faith, a stronger sense of the fact that the incarnate Word is like us in requiring divine enabling if he is to remain faithfully human. . . . 'He *was enabled* not to sin', enabled, that is, by the Spirit, the mediator of all God's perfecting action." Gunton, *Christian Faith*, 105–6; italics in original.

fallen nature of man. Otherwise, the change would be merely superficial. A genuine change takes place when the evil is uprooted. As a result, Christ offered a perfect sacrifice—the first portion of perfect humanity—to God.

Accordingly, it is the Spirit who authenticated the humanity of Christ. Gunton states, "The Spirit is the one who enabled Jesus to be the true human being, the one who as the second Adam—another Adam of flesh and blood—recapitulated our human life in the way it was meant to be."[82] The Spirit empowered Jesus so that he would accomplish what the Father willed for him. In this sense, "The whole of Jesus' authentically human life is made what it uniquely is through the action of the Spirit."[83] Jesus remained sinless because of the Spirit's presence in his life. And Jesus is the authentic and true human being because of his total obedience to the Spirit's guidance.

THE HOLY SPIRIT: RELATION TO JESUS OF NAZARETH

The Holy Spirit is the other hand of the Father whom God has sent to bring perfection to the world. Since he is the other hand of the Father, the work of the Spirit is accordingly different from that of the Son. Although the two hands work together to accomplish the one end, the perfection of the world, the work of either should not be reduced to the other. The divine love of the Son and the Spirit are therefore manifested in distinct, but inseprable ways.

Yet, the unity of the Son and the Spirit in perfecting the world should not be undermined either. The divine love of the Son and the Spirit are manifested in inseparable ways. What the Son has accomplished as the mediator of creation and redemption has an intrinsic relation to the Spirit's eschatological work. The Son and the Spirit are mutually essential in accomplishing the ultimate goal: the redemption of the world. Hence, in this section, the unity of the Son and the Spirit will be examined. While the section above focused on the preparatory work of the Son for the Spirit, this section illustrates how the Spirit builds upon the foundation laid by Christ for the perfection of the world.

---

82. Gunton, *Father, Son and Holy Spirit*, 179.
83. Gunton, *Father, Son and Holy Spirit*, 157.

The Holy Spirit: Transcendental Spirit

As noted above, the Spirit is deeply involved in the Son's earthly ministry. If Christ was the one who became part of the world by the incarnation, the Spirit is the one who transformed the humanity of the Son. Gunton writes, "To speak of the Spirit in the economy, in his relation to the world, then, is to speak of one of the modes of the transcendence of God."[84] The Spirit's work is to be perceived as transcendent, while Christ's work is immanent because he is the one who became incarnate as man.[85]

Gunton further elaborates, "The Son is the *content* of God's redemptive movement into the world, [while] the Spirit is its *form*, and that form is its freedom."[86] The divine love is manifested in the Son and through the Spirit to show God's relentless love for the world. Yet, the manner of the manifestation is different. Gunton continues, "The Spirit is God's eschatological transcendence, his futurity, as it is sometimes expressed. He is God present to the world as its liberating order, bringing it to the destiny determined by the Father, made actual, realized, in the Son."[87] The Spirit is the eschatological Spirit whose goal is to bring the world to its intended end.

Yet, Gunton argues that this eschatological Spirit is not "as appears to be implied by Augustine . . . the immanent possession of Jesus, but . . . God's free and life-giving activity towards the world as he maintains and empowers the human activity of the incarnate Son."[88] In short, the Spirit is a person, the third person of the Trinity. Since he is a person, not an endowment, he guided Jesus through his personal presence. It was indeed

---

84. Gunton, "Spirit in the Trinity," 130.

85. Gunton acknowledges that to perceive the Spirit transcendentally goes against the tendency to perceive the Spirit immanently (1 Cor 3:16–17; Rom 8:8–9; etc.). Yet he argues, "In the Old Testament the Spirit of the Lord is often characterised as a mysterious power, blowing unpredictably on parts of the created order. It is never identified with any part of the created order." Likewise in the New Testament, the Spirit is perceived based upon "this conviction of freedom and otherness" (John 3, 1 Cor 2:10, Rom 8). Gunton, *Transcendent Lord*, 6. However, Gunton by no means denies that the Spirit works immanently. Perhaps the best way to understand the otherness/transcendence of the Spirit is to see the Spirit's work as "relation in otherness." Because the Spirit is the otherness of God, he can relate to the world. And since he is not part of the creation, he can transform the whole of creation.

86. Gunton, "Spirit in the Trinity," 130; italics in original.

87. Gunton, "Spirit in the Trinity," 130.

88. Gunton, *Theology through the Theologians*, 115–16.

the Spirit who stood beside Jesus to overcome temptation, and the Spirit who raised Christ from the dead. Gunton contends,

> The Spirit is thus revealed ("manifested") in "subduing, restraining, conquering, the evil propensities of the fallen manhood, and making it an apt organ for expressing the will of the Father; a fit and holy substance to enter into personal union with the untempted and untemptable Godhead." God the Spirit opens, frees, the humanity of the Son so that it may be the vehicle of the Father's will in the world.[89]

Christ is our perfect example and the first fruits—the renewal of the first sample of the tainted creation. And this is the work of the eschatological Spirit: The Spirit makes new the humanity that was stained and corrupted. By freeing Jesus to be an authentic human, the Spirit brings about the *eschaton*, the last days of human history.

The Holy Spirit and Jesus of Nazareth: The Gospel Story

As discussed above, two hands of the Father, the Son and the Spirit, work together as the divine love. Although their work is inseparable, it is distinct. The Son is immanent in the world, while the Spirit is transcendent and otherness. In order to accomplish the will of the Father, the Son had to become part of the world. Unless the Son identified himself with the world, he could not become the atoning sacrifice for the world. On the other hand, the Spirit had to work transcendently because he is "the Father's otherness, realizing in our present the life of the age to come."[90] And, indeed, the immanent work of the Son and the transcendent work of the Spirit are manifested in the gospel story.

In the gospel story, four stages of the Son's life can be discerned: birth, mission, resurrection and ascension. At each stage, the Spirit is present. In the incarnation, Gunton notes that the Spirit forms a body in the womb of Mary: "When the Spirit shapes him a body from the flesh of Mary, what we see is . . . the renewing of the whole of creation, the redirecting of the world to its end."[91] The Spirit's work in the incarnation of Christ thus indicates the beginning of the renewing of the creation more so than a miraculous birth.

---

89. Gunton, "Spirit in the Trinity," 127.
90. Gunton, "Spirit as Lord," 85.
91. Gunton, *Christ and Creation*, 97.

Consequently, it can be argued that "the incarnation represents among other things a particular use of the created order by the Father through the Spirit, in forming a body of flesh for his eternal Son."[92] Through the incarnation, Jesus becomes a link between God and the world: the one and the many. And this particular child is none other than the Savior of the world. The one through whom all things were created becomes a child so that he can enter the world immanently to bring change. In addition, Gunton argues that the incarnation indicates particularity. He affirms, "It is in this way [the incarnation and the humanity of Christ] that the Spirit particularises: brings it about by his action in relation to the creation that this Jewish humanity is able to be distinctively what it is as the bearer of God's salvation."[93] To form a body for Jesus in the womb of Mary is the beginning of the Spirit's work of particularization. As the Spirit frees Jesus to become a certain man, he will also free those who will come to God through Jesus.

Likewise, in Jesus' life and ministry, the presence of the Spirit is indispensable. The Spirit empowers Jesus to accomplish the will of the Father. For example, in Luke 4, the Spirit enables Jesus to overcome various temptations.[94] It is the Spirit who led Jesus into the desert (Luke 4:1). Yet, it is the same Spirit who empowers him so that he will not fall into temptation. Gunton explains, "His relation to the Spirit is the means whereby Jesus is enabled to be both truly human and, so to speak, prototypically human."[95] Jesus offered a perfect sacrifice to God through the power of the Spirit. The sinless life of Jesus was indeed made possible by the Spirit. The Spirit empowered Jesus to be free to become who he was intended to be.

It was the Spirit who raised Jesus from the dead. The eschatological Spirit who is the life-giving power of God brought Jesus back from the dead. Hence, the Spirit liberated the Son from bondage so that he conquered death and became a prototype of humanity. Consequently, the Spirit brought about a new age by raising Jesus from the dead. Gunton states, "The Lord, the giver of life, transforms the body of Jesus so that it may partake of the life of the age to come, the first-born of the new creation."[96] The old has gone and the new has come.

---

92. Gunton, *Father, Son and Holy Spirit*, 116.

93. Gunton, *Theology through the Theologians*, 114.

94. Healings and exorcisms are other examples of Jesus' work by the Spirit (Matt 12:28, Luke 13:16, etc.)

95. Gunton, *Theology through the Theologians*, 163.

96. Gunton, *Theology through the Theologians*, 118.

After the ascension, Jesus sends the Spirit from the Father (John 15:26). Gunton writes, "He [Jesus] become[s] the *giver* of that Spirit who during his earthly life *gave* him to the world."[97] Having fulfilled the will of the Father, Jesus is now given authority to send the Spirit from the Father. Just as the Spirit empowered Jesus and freed him to be obedient to the Father's will, the Spirit will enable those who come to the Father through Jesus to freely offer a sacrifice of praise to God.

The Holy Spirit: Particularity

What we described above concerning the relation between Jesus and the Spirit in the gospel narratives is the Spirit's work of particularization. From the time of his birth to the cross, the Spirit was present in Jesus' life to make him a particular person. The Spirit formed a body for the Son in the womb of Mary. He filled Jesus with the knowledge of God to speak the truth. The Spirit empowered him so that he would not fall when he was tempted. And, the Spirit strengthened him in the garden of Gethsemane to be faithful to the point of death. Jesus offered a perfect sacrifice to God on the cross according to the will of the Father.

Therefore, the Spirit's work of particularization is to ensure Jesus to be a particular person. The Spirit's action in the life of Jesus was clearly to direct him to a certain destiny, and no other. Hence, to perfect Jesus is to particularize him into a certain man. In other words, the concept of perfection is not one of moral achievement. Rather, it is being conformed to the way that is intended. For the Spirit to bring about the last days of the world, the particularization of the whole creation is thus indispensable. Jesus is the archetype of the Spirit's work of particularization so that those who will come to the Father through him will also be particularized by the Spirit.[98]

---

97. Gunton, *Theology through the Theologians*, 164; italics in original.

98. There is a clear parallel between Jesus and humanity in relation to the Spirit. As the Spirit particularized Jesus to be a specific Messiah, the Spirit will particularize those who come to the Father through Jesus. David A. Höhne adds, "The perfection of this sonship remains the heuristic for discerning the perfection of particularity in the rest of creation." Höhne, *Spirit and Sonship*, 176.

The Holy Spirit: Constitution of Hypostases

The Spirit's work of particularization has scriptural warrant, as we examined above.[99] But, where does the theological warrant of such work come from?[100] Gunton argues that the economic Trinity reveals the inner life of the immanent Trinity, as previously discussed. The incarnate Son is identical with the eternal Son: "His earthly career . . . must be understood as God's personal action in his world."[101] Likewise, the work of the Spirit, Gunton argues, should be understood in light of the same parallel between the immanent and economic Trinity. "If the Spirit works in a particular way in the economy as the one who perfects the creation, it is reasonable to suppose that he has a similar kind of function to perform in relation to the being of God, to the communion that is the life of God."[102] Hence, the eschatological Spirit who perfects the creation is also the perfecter of the communion of the Godhead.

Gunton appeals to St Victor to further elaborate the concept of the Spirit's particularization.[103] Gunton states, "Richard of St Victor argued that the third person of the Trinity is essential if there is to be true otherness in the Godhead. There must be three if there is to be a true outwardgoingness and diversity in God."[104] The Spirit signifies the otherness in the Godhead

---

99. Gunton affirms, "It is in terms of particularities that we can understand many of the ways in which the New Testament characterizes the relation of Jesus and the Spirit." Gunton, *One, the Three and the Many*, 182. This is the thrust of David Höhne's volume *Spirit and Sonship*. Responding to John Webster's criticism of the historical and scriptural foundations of the concept of particularity, Höhne shows scriptural warrant for the Spirit's work of particularity. For details of Webster's criticism, see "Systematic Theology after Barth," 249-263.

100. I am not questioning the sufficiency of scripture for constructing theology. On the contrary, my attempt is to bring attention to this point so that we may further unfold Gunton's concept of particularity.

101. Gunton, *Christian Faith*, 79.

102. Gunton, *One, the Three and the Many*, 190. Gunton explicates, "The chief implication of this methodological dogma is that the exposition of the triune economic and temporal action must form the basis of an appropriate conception of the place of the Spirit in the eternal Trinity." Gunton, "Spirit in the Trinity," 131.

103. Gunton also appeals to St Basil (see *One, the Three and the Many*, 189-91). Höhne, however, questions whether Basil can be cited to support Gunton's argument: "It cannot be denied that *De Spiritu Sancto* is replete with the language of perfection but to suggest that this includes concrete substantiality is a matter of inference rather than observation." Höhne, *Spirit and Sonship*, 13.

104. Gunton, *One, the Three and the Many*, 190.

because he makes the Son to be distinct from the Father and the Father from the Son. Gunton continues, "In that sense, we may say that the Spirit's function in the Godhead is to particularize the hypostases . . . or persons of Father and Son: to liberate them to be themselves, to be particular persons in community and as communion."[105] Gunton equates otherness with particularization of the hypostases. If the Spirit functions to bring otherness between the Son and the Father, this otherness is formulated by particularization—The Spirit particularizes the hypostases of the immanent Trinity. Therefore, Gunton concludes, "The Spirit's distinctive mode of action in both time and eternity, economy and essence, consists in the constituting and realization of particularity."[106] In this way, Gunton draws a parallel between the Spirit's work in the immanent and economic Trinity.

Further, in the Spirit's work of particularization, Gunton argues that "a notion of transcendentality" should be acknowledged.[107] Put differently, Gunton sees the echo of the divine being in humanity.[108] He argues, "The *substantiality* of God resides not in his abstract being, but in the concrete particulars that we call the divine persons and in the relations by which they mutually constitute each other."[109] He continues, "God is what he is only as a communion of persons, the particularity of whom remains at the centre of all he is, for each has his own distinctive way of being or τρόπος ὑπάρξεως."[110] Likewise, our substantiality resides in a person that is a concrete particular. And we are constituted by our relations to God, others, and things. We are also, after all, beings in communion.

Gunton continues, "*Therefore*—and here we move from our understanding of the creator to a notion of transcendentality—the particularity of created beings is established by the particularity at the heart of the being

---

105. Gunton, *One, the Three and the Many*, 190.

106. Gunton, *One, the Three and the Many*, 190.

107. Gunton, *One, the Three and the Many*, 191. Gunton defines transcendentality as follows: "By transcendental I mean those notions which we may suppose to embody 'the necessary notes of being', in the pre-Kantian sense of notions which give some way of conceiving what reality truly is, everywhere and always." Gunton, *One, the Three and the Many*, 136.

108. The nature of this echo between the Creator and creatures, whether it is univocal or not, will be examined in chapter 5. Accordingly, Gunton's concept of person will be examined as well.

109. Gunton, *One the Three and the Many*, 191; italics in original.

110. Gunton, *One, the Three and the Many*, 191.

of the creator."[111] As the particularity of the persons of the Godhead is essential to the being of God, it is also crucial to the creatures because there is an "echo" between God and humanity. And this echo, which is substantial particularity, is the mark of our being of God. If God is the Creator, we must bear his imprint.

But, the question arises, Why is particularity essential to the creatures? Besides the fact that particularity is necessary for the uniqueness and individuality of a person, why is particularity necessary for the perfection of the world? Gunton answers, "My suggestion is that something is real—what it is and not another thing—by virtue of the way it is held in being not only by God also by other things in the particular configurations in space and time in which its being is constituted; that is to say, in its createdness."[112] Gunton continues, "It is thus that *hypostasis*, meaning substantial particular, variously taking shape as person and thing and constituted relationally, acquires the status of a kind of transcendental. Everyone and everything is what it uniquely is as hypostatic being; as we are often told, no two blades of grass are alike."[113]

The same holds true with Jesus of Nazareth. He is a particular hypostasis whose being is constituted relationally to God, others and things. Yet, in the case of Jesus, what differs from the rest of humankind is that he is an example of true humanity, "the heuristic for discerning the perfection of particularity in the rest of creation."[114] Therefore, for Jesus, the Spirit constitutes a hypostasis not only of the divine being, but also of the creation. He was particularized by the Spirit to be a certain man, a bearer of salvation. He did what we could not do by offering a perfect obedience to God. Therefore, he became a true example of humanity, the one that the rest of mankind should look to for the perfection of particularity.

And in this light, it is plausible to argue that it was not the penalty of death that Christ suffered on the cross so that God's wrath would be appeased. Rather, Christ suffered so that he would become our first fruits and true humanity so that the rest of humanity would look to his example. Jesus made our participation in the atonement possible through his death.

The two hands of the Father, the Son and the Spirit, work together in order to accomplish the one ultimate goal: the perfection of the world. The

---

111. Gunton, *One, the Three and the Many*, 191; italics in original.
112. Gunton, *One, the Three and the Many*, 200.
113. Gunton, *One, the Three and the Many*, 203.
114. Höhne, *Spirit and Sonship*, 176.

Son was incarnated so that he would become part of the creation. On the other hand, the Spirit particularized his humanity to bring about the last days of the world. Humanity is constituted relationally to God, each other and things. By planting our first fruits, Jesus of Nazareth, in this network of humanity, the Spirit has begun the restoration of our relationship with God. As sin has spread like cancer, Jesus of Nazareth, whose being is constituted relationally to God, others and things has brought a new day by the Spirit. The Spirit's particularizing has begun with Jesus to bring restoration to the world.

CRITIQUE

As Gunton argues, God's being and act should not be divorced. What God reveals about himself in the economic Trinity is what he is in the immanent Trinity. Because his action originates in his being, there should be no inconsistency between the act and being of God. Suffice it to say that Gunton is a champion of this axiom.[115] The core of Gunton's theology is firmly grounded upon it. Although this is an important theological axiom, it also requires extreme caution. Hence, it is appropriate to examine Gunton's use of this axiom.

Further, the ultimate goal of this examination is to determine whether Gunton has satisfactorily met the charge that God, on his view, needs creation. As those who are familiar with Gunton's writings can attest, he relentlessly argues for the importance of the distinction between the Creator and creation in order to safeguard the freedom of God and humanity. In speaking of Barth and Rahner, Gunton asserts, "Barth's and more ambiguously, Rahner's proposal is that while economy betokens being—what God does reveals who he is—being is by no means reduced to it. The point of affirming an immanent Trinity in *relative* distinction from the economic is to allow for personal space between God and the world."[116] Gunton thus

---

115. Whitney also agrees: "Who God is in his movement and relations towards the created order is who God is in his eternal being. Therefore the being and action of God are inseparable for Gunton. This is a point that Gunton emphasized consistently throughout his career." Whitney, *Problem and Promise*, 197.

116. Gunton, *Intellect and Action*, 103; italics in original. Fred Sanders praises Gunton as one of the few theologians, like Christoph Schwöbel, "who urges qualifications of Rahner's Rule, has written some of the finest manifestoes for a thoroughly trinitarian theology." *Image of the Immanent Trinity*, 161n3. Cf. Sanders, "Entangled in the Trinity, 182n31.

seems aware of the danger of collapsing the distinction between the immanent and the economic Trinity.

Yet, it must be acknowledged that there is a hint of conflating these two, especially in the work of the Spirit (particularity). It seems that Gunton falls under the spell of Rahner's Rule in this particular area of the Spirit's work, namely, that the economic Trinity is the immanent Trinity and vice versa. For example, as we have examined above, Gunton seems to conflate the immanent and economic work of the Spirit. He states, "We are, however, to say that if the Spirit works in a particular way in the economy as the one who perfects the creation, it is reasonable to suppose that he has a *similar* kind of function to perform in relation to the being of God, to the communion that is the life of God."[117] At the same time, Gunton is cautious with his language, and stipulates a "similar kind of function," not an "identical function."

This issue is significant for constructing a doctrine of God. We can only know God by what he reveals to us in the economy. Thus, epistemologically, the economic Trinity reveals the immanent Trinity.[118] Yet, the challenge is to determine the right balance in the relation between these two: While keeping enough distance between the economic and immanent Trinity to safeguard the freedom of God and humanity, the corresponding nature of the relation between the immanent and economic Trinity must not be undermined.[119]

Nevertheless, it seems to me that Gunton, contrary to what he argues in regard to the relation between the two aspects of the Trinity, appears to make a rather quick move from the economic Trinity to the immanent Trinity and ends up blurring the distinction between them. As we saw above, Gunton looks to St Victor who argues that there must be a third person if

---

117. Gunton, *One, the Three and the Many*, 190; italics mine.

118. For a helpful guide to navigating how to determine the right balance of the relationship between the economic and the immanent Trinity, see Johnson, *Rethinking the Trinity and Religious Pluralism*, 78. Johnson summarizes Augustine's account and lists four criteria for assessing the relation between the immanent and economic Trinity.

119. Sanders argues, "The instability of Rahner's Rule demands that its interpreters develop their systems in one of the two general directions outlined in previous chapters [radicalizers or restricters]." Sanders, *Image of the Immanent Trinity*, 167. Radicalizers interpret Rahner's Rule in a literal sense: The immanent Trinity *is* the economic Trinity and vice versa. On the other hand, restricters argue for qualifications of Rahner's Rule in order to avoid the collapse of the two Trinities into each other. Gunton is a restricter according to Sanders. For a more detailed definition of restricters, see Harrower, *Trinitarian Self and Salvation*, 3–4.

there is to be true otherness in the Godhead. Gunton proposes, "In that sense, we may say that the Spirit's function in the Godhead is to particularize the *hypostases* . . . or person of Father and Son: to liberate them to be themselves, to be particular *persons* in community and as communion."[120] This seems to be speculation about the inner life of the immanent Trinity. Further, it is uncertain whether "the otherness" that St Victor refers to should be understood as "particularity."

As a result, this reduces the immanent Trinity to the economic Trinity. Gunton continues, "Accordingly, the Spirit's distinctive mode of action in both time and eternity, economy and essence consists in the constituting and realization of particularity. There is, then, and it is crucial for the argument, a form of particularity at the very heart of the being of God."[121] Gunton seems to say that particularity is the essential part of who God is.

It seems clear that Gunton's intention behind this close correspondence is providing an ontological ground for the economic Trinity. Nonetheless, it appears to me that Gunton has overstepped an important line of demarcation. It is speculative for him to argue that the nature of the particularity of the divine persons and human persons is in some sense identical, given the mysterious nature of the Trinity.[122] Although Gunton qualifies such statements to avoid suggesting a *direct* correspondence, he still appears to be overlooking the vast ontological difference between God and humanity. God is three persons in one being. But, at the same time, they perichoretically exist in each other. Karen Kilby observes, "There is among the three divine persons, it is said, a kind of mutual interpenetration which is not to be found among human persons, and it is because of this perfect interpenetration that the three persons are one God."[123] Therefore, it

---

120. Gunton, *One, the Three and the Many*, 190; italics in original.

121. Gunton, *One, the Three and the Many*, 190.

122. I am not arguing that particularity of the persons in the being of God is not significant. On the contrary, I believe this is one of Gunton's important contributions. Yet, it is problematic to state with confidence the specific nature of the being of God given the limitations of our knowledge. God revealed himself as the Father, the Son and the Spirit in the economic Trinity. Therefore, the doctrine of the Trinity sets a parameter for what can be rightly said about God. To proceed as Gunton does seems to go beyond this parameter. As a result, he falls victim to the tendency to define divine persons and human persons univocally despite their vast ontological differences.

123. Kilby, "Perichoresis and Projection," 435.

is hasty and possibly misleading to assume that the hypostases of the divine being and humanity are identical.[124]

The way Gunton defines the Spirit's work of particularization is similarly problematic. As examined above, on Gunton's view the Spirit particularizes Jesus to make him fitting for God. This certainly implies fallenness, imperfection, and corruption. Indeed, Gunton strongly affirms the fallenness of Christ's flesh as we have seen. Yet, Gunton also claims that the Spirit particularizes the Father and Son in the same way in the immanent Trinity. He asserts, " . . . the Spirit is the perfecting cause not only of the creation, but also of the being of God. . . . the Spirit perfects the divine and holy Trinity. As the one who 'completes', the Spirit does indeed establish God's aseity, his utter self-sufficiency."[125] But if these two cases are parallel (the particularizing of Jesus and the Father and Son), it seems to indicate a deficiency in the Trinity that the Spirit must correct. Therefore, this raises a question of how to interpret "God's aseity, his utter self-sufficiency" in this perspective.[126]

Perhaps the real issue in Gunton's view of the Spirit's particularizing work is the meaning of "particularity." Despite Gunton's efforts to describe this concept (e.g., freeing to be a self, constitution of self, receiving the shape of their being from the particularizing Spirit, etc.), it requires further elaboration in order to clarify several issues mentioned above. Depending on the context (e.g., the inner being of God, the humanity of Jesus, etc.), Gunton's definition of the function of particularity differs. This problem further illustrates the great difficulty in drawing direct parallels between the immanent and economic Trinity.

There is a tendency in Gunton's theology to conflate these two. Despite his efforts to keep them apart from each other, he seems, after all, to collapse the distinction. On the one hand, he earnestly argues,

---

124. This point will be further examined in the following chapter. Gunton does affirm univocity between God and humanity. See Höhne, *Spirit and Sonship*, 30.

125. Gunton, *Christian Dogmatic Theology*, 2.7.31.3 [unpublished].

126. Cumin attempts to offer an explanation of Gunton's concept of God's aseity: "But by suggesting that it is the Spirit (and not the Father) who is finally responsible for God's aseity—for 'completing' the divine life—Gunton has developed a doctrine of God that looks less like the top portion of a vertical continuum and more like an open dynamic of personal love." Cumin, "Taste of Cake," 79. Cumin appears to be saying, then, that Gunton sees aseity as a property that God possesses in degrees, which reaches its full extent through the Spirit's work. Yet, aseity does not appear to be the kind of property that can possess degrees (either one possesses it or does not—one could not be, for example, fifty percent self-existent), which makes this approach suspect.

THE TRINITARIAN GOD

> If God is what we are given in the economy, then we may rely on it that the economy is a reliable guide to what God is, eternally and in himself. This is however, an asymmetrical relationship between knowing and being, and we are not obliged to accept the apparent view of Rahner that the thesis, "the Economic Trinity is the Immanent Trinity" is also true "reciprocally" (*umgekehrt*).[127]

But, on the other hand, he seems to undermine this distinction of the two Trinities:

> What God is in his relation with the world, he is also in his eternal being, because there is no breach, as there is with fallen creatures, between what God is and what he does. Because the Father's action is mediated by the Son and the Spirit, the Son and the Spirit are correspondingly intrinsic to God's eternal being. It would follow that the relation of the Son to the Father in God's inner being is in some way mediated by the Spirit. The Son is—we might say—enabled to be the Son by virtue of the way the Spirit realizes and perfects the love between him and the Father. Only so are the three truly one God. If we apply that to our particular case, we shall see that the Spirit does here in time what he does eternally in the being of God.... The Spirit is the one who makes Jesus of Nazareth to be the particular human being that he is.[128]

At the end of the day, for Gunton, "The immanent Trinity is the economic Trinity." Hence, there is no longer an asymmetrical relationship of the immanent and the economic Trinity. Rather, Gunton is making an ontological statement: "The immanent Trinity *is* the economic Trinity," which signifies a symmetrical modus operandi whether in eternity or time.

It is uncertain how to reconcile this discrepancy in Gunton's theology. Yet, one repercussion of this stance is to limit God. Unfortunately, this seems to be the implication of some aspects of Gunton's theology. The theological axiom of the unity of God's act and being is cogent. Nonetheless, the richness of the axiom can quickly turn into unexpected poverty. The axiom

---

127. Gunton, "Spirit in the Trinity," 131.

128. Gunton, *Christian Faith*, 101–2. Whitney explicates, "For Gunton, since being and action of God are inseparable then the Trinity and doctrine of creation are also inseparably related. In sum, God in his very nature, is constantly involved in the created world through the Son and the Spirit, and this means that to speak of the Trinity means to speak of God's action towards creation. Or said another way, who God is in his movement and relations towards the created order is who God is in his eternal being. Gunton never tired of championing this point." Whitney, *Problem and Promise*, 100–101.

requires caution and balance, lest God's transcendence be diminished and his freedom curtailed.

CONCLUSION

In this chapter we have examined the nature of God's involvement in the world through the two hands of the Father, the Son and the Spirit. First, we examined how the divine love is actualized in the two hands of the Father. In this, we focused on the relation of universality and particularity to identify the continuity between the immanent and economic Trinity. Second, we examined how the atonement is actualized by the Son. The three metaphors—victory, justice and sacrifice—were examined in order to show how the Son brings atonement in order to realize God's eternal love for the world. Third, we examined the mediatory work of the Son and the Spirit to identify the various aspects of the Son and the Spirit that make their mediatory work possible. Here, the scope shifted from the relation of universality and particularity to particularity only. In this, we explored the nature of the immanent work of the Son (e.g., incarnation) and the transcendent work of the Spirit (e.g., particularity). As a result, we identified the intricate relation between the Son and the Spirit that makes the transformation and perfection of the world possible.

Hence, we discussed the actualization of the divine love, the movement from universality to particularity. God's act originates in his being. From this we can conclude that God is God for us. Accordingly, his eschatological Spirit reaches out to creation to bring a new day to the world. The Spirit particularizes those who come to God to be free as he did with Jesus of Nazareth. In so doing, the restoration of the world will take place. The Spirit is therefore the eschatological Spirit who works transcendentally to renew the creation just as he perfected/authenticated Jesus's humanity that is a representative sample of the whole to enable him to be our first fruits.

Nevertheless, concerns arise in relation to the core of Gunton's theology: that God's act originates in his being. Despite Gunton's relentless effort to keep distance between the economic and immanent Trinities, in the end he appears to conflate the two, especially in the work of the Spirit (particularity). As a result, Gunton seems to affirm, after all, that the immanent Trinity is the economic Trinity, not as a matter of identity but as positing a symmetrical relation between the Trinitarian activity ad intra and ad extra. Consequently, this binds God to his creation and diminishes his freedom because it implies that to be God means to be a creator. The theological axiom of the unity of God's act and being is cogent. Yet, unless one treats the axiom with caution and balance, it can quickly turn into a theological dilemma. Unfortunately, Gunton seems to have failed to maintain the balance by in effect fusing the economic and immanent Trinities.

CHAPTER 5

GUNTON'S DOCTRINES OF ANTHROPOLOGY, ECCLESIOLOGY, AND PNEUMATOLOGY

IN THE PREVIOUS CHAPTER, we discussed the relation of the Son and the Spirit in redeeming and transforming the created world. As a result, we concluded that the Spirit transformed the humanity of the Son by conforming him to be a particular man so that he would become our representative, and consequently an example for us to follow. In Gunton's view, perfection is conformity/particularization to the way that is intended by God. Perfection means achieving a right relation to God, each other, and the world. Perfection of the created world will come only when we are rightly related to God and others. To help accomplish this perfection, God has gathered a community of his people who are aligned with God and others.

But, to achieve this end, the Son had to become incarnate. The particularization of the whole creation began with the birth of Jesus: The Spirit created a body for Jesus in the womb of Mary.[1] As the Spirit particularized Jesus, he will particularize humanity after the example of the Son. Consequently, humanity will be placed in a right relation with God and others. If so, particularity is indispensable for the renewing of the created world. "Neither human nature in itself nor the death Christ suffered as a man can

---

1. Gunton states, "It is better to understand the incarnation of the eternal Son in the flesh as the beginning of an eschatological act of renewal, in which the true *telos*, direction, of the creation is restored from within." Gunton, *Triune Creator*, 223.

be such as the means of salvation. It is the 'hidden' . . . and 'efficacious' . . . power of the Spirit which gives significance to this particular sacrificial self-giving."[2] It is the Spirit who *constitutes* a community of believers as the agent of perfection, while Christ is the one who *institutes* such a community where his perfect humanity is the example to follow.

In this chapter, we will therefore examine how the Spirit works to particularize humanity after the example of the Son in order to restore a right relationship with God, each other, and the created world. The primary place of particularization will be in the church. Other institutions such as schools, workplaces, and community centers are by no means excluded, though the Spirit works in such elusively. Yet, it remains true that among all the places where the Spirit may work to particularize humanity, the church is the place where the Spirit's work of particularization will most clearly be manifested. Hence, in this section, the relation between the church and the Spirit will be explored.

Accordingly, we will examine the concept of human personhood, especially focusing on the image of God and humanity's relation with the Spirit. By identifying the relational aspect of humanity, we hope to answer questions about the nature of the church—the community of the people of God. We will end the chapter by looking at culture and the eschatological Spirit to delineate how humanity participates in the perfecting of the created order.

THE CHURCH: TRINITARIAN COMMUNITY

The church is a community where reconciliation takes place. As the eschatological Spirit brings people to God through the Son, he creates a community of people. Because sin destroyed the relationship between humanity and God, and between each other and the created world, a communion which echoes the communion of the three persons of the Trinity must be restored for the reconciliation of the world. As noted, the church is the center of this reconciliation. The eschatological Spirit works within the church to bring reconciliation to the world. Consequently, it is imperative to understand the church: First, we must understand what the church is in relation to the Spirit's eschatological work. Second, we must grasp where the church is located in the broad picture of God's redemptive activity for the world.

2. Gunton, *Actuality of Atonement*, 130.

The Relation of the Son, the Spirit and the Church

What is the church? The church is a community of the people of God who are brought into that community by the Holy Spirit and gathers around the resurrected Christ. In much of traditional ecclesiology, however, Gunton argues that the church has been misrepresented or misconstrued. For example, the church has been presented as if it were an impeccable institution or as wielding the absolute authority of God. The outcome of such a misrepresentation is losing the eschatological nature of the church. Consequently, the church becomes a static rather than dynamic community in the scheme of God's redemptive plan for the world.

Perhaps the main reason for such misconceptions can be traced back to misconstruing the work and person of the Spirit. Gunton argues, "The key to ecclesiology as to eschatology is pneumatology, and in this connection, that means the role of the Spirit in enabling the Church to be the Church at once in worship and in the obedience that is definitive of its being."[3] The Spirit's work has been misconstrued due to a failure to see the Spirit as a person and distinct from the Father and the Son. Gunton argues that he is "the transcendent and free Lord who creates community by bringing men and women to the Father through Jesus Christ and so in relation with one another."[4] But, when the Spirit's work is misconstrued, the eschatological nature as well as the redemptive purpose of the church fails to be understood. The church fails to be rightly located within the divine plan of the redemption of the world. Gunton contends,

> The problem derives, I believe, from the failure to give to the Holy Spirit the kind of personal identity or particularity that is required if we are to speak of him and identify his action in the world. If we do not find adequate means of identification, the danger remains that we shall identify his work apart from the work of the Father and the Son, and in terms of what we happen to find attractive or appealing at the present time.[5]

Hence, the relation of the church and the Spirit must be understood according to God's saving action toward the world. And this saving action is the free personal action of the triune God. The Spirit is the transcendent Lord who brings the *eschaton* to the world.

---

3. Gunton, *Father, Son and Holy Spirit*, 203.
4. Gunton, "Transcendent Lord," 8.
5. Gunton, "Transcendent Lord," 4.

To further grasp the relation between the church and the Spirit within the context of the divine plan of redemption, one must consider the relation of the Son and the Spirit toward the church. As examined in chapter 4, the Spirit particularizes the Son so that he will become whom he is intended to be. As a result, the Son becomes the ultimate example of humanity, the one whose relation is right with God. And in so doing, the Son makes salvation possible for the created world. Indeed, the Son and the Spirit are the two hands of the Father who work together toward the redemption of the world. The Son institutes the church which is his body, while the Spirit constitutes the church by bringing people to God through the Son.

The church is therefore a place where the Spirit works to create a communion of people. He particularizes people in order to set them in right relation with God. But, the example for humanity is Christ. Gunton argues, "If the Spirit which constitutes the Church is the one who was responsible for the shape of Jesus' life, we are still free to teach that he will give the Church a christomorphic direction."[6] He continues, "Christology is . . . the starting point, because it is so closely related to the question of the status of the events from which the Church originated."[7] Yet, Christology is only the starting point because Christ is the first-fruits of what is to come. Christ alone is not the foundation or ontology of the church. Rather, the ontology of the church is grounded in the triune God.[8]

The Church as the Echo of the Triune God

The church is constituted by people who are freely brought into community by the eschatological Spirit. Therefore, the church comprises people who are united in Christ. However, Gunton laments that the church has been historically understood as a mere institution rather than a community of people.[9] He writes,

---

6. Gunton, "Church on Earth," 64.
7. Gunton, "Church on Earth," 65.
8. Gunton, *Promise of Trinitarian Theology*, 79.
9. Gunton does not deny the necessity of the church being an institution. He states, "Without doubt the Church needs to be an institution in the sense that it must—theologically must—be a historically given reality." Gunton, "Transcendent Lord," 12. Rather, what Gunton opposes is the church being conceived apart from the eschatological work of the Spirit.

> The protest against the Church as an institution is to be heard on many lips: often, of course, for simplistic and individualistic reasons, but not only that. Why is it, we may ask, that a faith at whose centre is the notion of freedom should have taken shape in the world in ways widely regarded as a threat to freedom?[10]

If the church is a community that people are freely brought into by the Spirit, an *institution* is not a proper way to describe the church since "an institution is not, as such, a community because its existence is independent and logically prior to the persons who become part of it."[11]

Perhaps the best way to understand the relationship that characterizes persons as the basis of the church is to reflect on the relation of the persons of the triune God. Gunton observes, "The doctrine of the Trinity is being used to suggest ways of allowing the eternal becoming of God—the eternally interanimating energies of the three—to provide the basis for the personal dynamics of the community."[12] He asks, "What kind of analogy between God and the Church, Trinity and community, may there then be?"[13] He continues, "The real being of the Church is to be found underlying the relations of the people rather than being a function of them."[14] Just as the triune God is the three persons who are intrinsically related to each other in communion, the church is also an entity that is constituted by the communion of people who are brought together by the eschatological Spirit. Gunton argues,

> Christian teaching about God, expressed as it is in the doctrine of the Trinity, conceives God as a community constituted, made what it is, by the relations of three persons. The one is only the one by virtue of the free giving and receiving of the three. Similarly, the three guarantee the uniqueness, otherness and particularity of each other by their mutual giving and receiving. The communion is not prior to the persons, nor the persons prior to the communion. Rather, the communion consists in what the persons are and do. There is no opposition of person and communion for they require each other.[15]

---

10. Gunton, "Transcendent Lord," 11.
11. Gunton, "Transcendent Lord," 11.
12. Gunton, *Promise of Trinitarian Theology*, 80–81.
13. Gunton, "Church on the Earth," 69.
14. Gunton, "Church on the Earth," 70.
15. Gunton, "Community of the Church in Communion with God," 40. Gunton blames Augustine for this misconstrual of the mutual relation between persons and

The church is therefore an echo of the Triune God. If God is a community constituted by the relations of the three persons, so is the church: The church is a community constituted by the relations of people who are freely brought into it by the Spirit. Therefore, the trinitarian God is the basis of the ontology of the church.

Yet, this echo is only at the finite level. "The being of the Church should echo the interrelation between the three persons who together constitute the deity. The Church is called to be the kind of reality at a finite level that God is in eternity."[16] Although the church reflects the interrelation of the triune God, which is a "perichoretic interrelation,"[17] this echo is merely at a finite level, not the exact representation of the interrelation of the triune God. Yet, the church is a church of God: "If the church is to be the church it must also have a trinitarian shape.... The church, as the body of Christ and the elect of the Spirit, is called to embody the giving and receiving in love that is life in the image of God."[18] If so, the church is still to reflect the interrelation of the divine being that is perichoretic.

The Character of the Church:
The Communion of the Eschatological Community

The church is the echo of the triune God and thus is to reflect the character and relational nature of the Trinity. As the people of God gather around the resurrected Christ, they also reflect the communal/harmonious character/nature of the triune God. Indeed, although the church has often been known for "one-sex institutions and orders,"[19] the true character of the

---

community. Gunton argues, "Corresponding to the Augustinian conception there is an ecclesiology which conceives the being of the church as in some sense *anterior* to the concrete historical relationships of the visible community." Gunton, *Promise of Trinitarian Theology*, 74; italics in original. Gunton suggests that a "platonizing" conception of the invisible church and institutional nature of the church are two recognizable outcomes of this misconception.

16. Gunton, *Promise of Trinitarian Theology*, 80.
17. Gunton, *Promise of Trinitarian Theology*, 81.
18. Gunton, "Community of the Church in Communion with God," 40.
19. Gunton, *Promise of Trinitarian Theology*, 79. It is common in some evangelical denominations, such as the Southern Baptist Convention and Presbyterian Church in America, for only men to be ordained or serve in mixed-gender leadership roles. Women often serve in roles that have no influence over the polity and teachings of the church. As a result, a harmonious relation between men and women in service is often lacking.

church should reflect harmonious relations between man and woman in serving and worshiping.

Gunton supports this harmonious relation between man and woman from the perspective of the image of God. He contends, "If the image of God is primarily or even only largely realised in terms of the unity of the sexes, a major aspect of the church's calling is to be a community of women and men."[20] Furthermore, in this communion, people are giving and receiving from each other to become what they are intended to be. If so, the church should include all people of God whether female or male, young or old, children or adults.[21] Because the triune God is constituted by the three persons who freely give and receive from each other, the church cannot fully realize herself unless all members of the church participate in giving and receiving from each other.

Nonetheless, this unity does not entail that particularity is being lost because the unity consists of relation-in-otherness. As the nature of the triune God reveals, unity does not preclude otherness. A person will not lose his or her identity because this unity does not call for assimilation. Human action manifests itself in a variety of ways. But, despite the diversity, the ultimate end of human action is to glorify God, our Creator. Hence, although our actions are diverse, God unites us all in praising and worshiping him.

Gunton further argues that "The other is central for our being."[22] He continues, "What we receive from and give to others is constitutive: not self-fulfillment but relation to the other as other is the key to human being, universally."[23] Hence, without diversity, the church cannot fully realize her true being. It is not one person or one group of people who enables the church to realize her full potentiality because the other is necessary for one to be a self. Rather, it is people of diverse backgrounds (e.g., gender, age, economic status, ethnicity, etc.) who freely relate to each other in communion and in giving and receiving from each other in sacrificial ways that enable the church to become herself.

Accordingly, Gunton writes, "The church is the body called to be the community of the last times."[24] As the being of the church is grounded

---

20. Gunton, *Promise of Trinitarian Theology*, 79.

21. Gunton emphasizes the importance of the inclusiveness of all God's people in "Baptism: Baptism and the Church Community" in *Father, Son and Holy Spirit*.

22. Gunton, *One, the Three and the Many*, 227.

23. Gunton, *One, the Three and the Many*, 227.

24. Gunton, *Promise of Trinitarian Theology*, 81.

in "the source of the being of all things, the eternal energies of the three persons of the Trinity as they are in perichoretic interrelation,"[25] the nature of the church is eschatological. As the persons of the Trinity work together to create and bring redemption to the created world, the church acts as a medium for the divine salvific plan for the world. Hence, the church is the eschatological community of people who are freely brought into communion by the eschatological Spirit who worship and praise God in a sacrificial manner. And one day, all things will be consummated in Christ for perfection (Col 1:20).[26]

The Purpose of the Church: The Community of Reconciliation

Gunton holds that the church is the community of the last days. He states, "As a remnant . . . the Church gathers in hope for the final gathering in of all people."[27] The fall of humanity has distorted its relationship with God, others, and the created world. Reconciliation is therefore a restoration of this distorted relationship, first with God and then with others. Through this, the created world will be liberated from the bondage of sin. In fact, Gunton argues that the atonement is "the *mediatorial* rather than *penal* substitution whereby God himself re-establishes the communion which was broken by human sin."[28] It is Jesus who has begun the re-establishment of the broken communion through his death. And as we follow his example, this fractured communion begins to be mended in human relationships with God and others.

If the church is called to be the community of the last days, it is also the *place* of reconciliation, and consequently communion, since communion is "the will of the creator for his people . . . the shape of their being

---

25. Gunton, *Promise of Trinitarian Theology*, 81.

26. Gunton writes that the body of Christ has been interpreted as an "organic metaphor" rather than a "personal unity of distinct but freely related persons." Gunton, *Promise of Trinitarian Theology*, 78. Accordingly, there is a tendency to perceive the concept of the church as "totalitarian or pantheistic." Gunton, *Promise of Trinitarian Theology*, 78. However, as discussed above, the concept of the church should be relation-in-otherness patterned after the trinitarian God. Gunton appeals to John 17:11 as the basis for this patterning. Further, Gunton argues that the Pauline metaphor of the church as a body should be understood in the same light (e.g., 1 Cor 12:14–31, Rom 12:4–8).

27. Gunton, "Introduction," 7.

28. Gunton, "Introduction," 2; italics in original.

in relation."[29] Gunton observes, "According to the New Testament, human community becomes concrete in the church, whose calling is to be the medium and realization of communion."[30] The purpose of the church is therefore to be the catalyst of reconciliation for the world, while the church herself is to be shaped into a perfect communion, having been reconciled with God, others and the created world.

ANTHROPOLOGY: THE TRIUNE GOD

The Spirit is the transcendent Lord who brings the *eschaton* to the world. The Spirit brings people to God through Christ and creates a community of individuals who comprise the church. The church is therefore a community in which the Spirit particularizes believers after the example of Christ for reconciliation with God, others and the creation. In so doing, he creates a perfect communion. While Christ institutes the church, the Spirit particularizes those who are brought to God through Christ.

Having understood the relation between the Spirit and the church, it is important to examine the relation between the Spirit and humanity because the church is a community of people who gather around the resurrected Christ and are being conformed to his example by the power of the eschatological Spirit. If so, it is essential to examine humanity and our relation with the Spirit in order to fully grasp how the Spirit constitutes the church.

Therefore, what follows is an exploration of the relation between the Spirit and humanity. The primary focus will be the eschatological Spirit's work of particularization in humanity. The goal is to illustrate how particularization contributes to the constitution of the church, a community of people. Also, the concept of *person* will be examined in order to identify the nature and purpose of personhood, since the church is constituted by persons. Finally, the sacraments of baptism and the Lord's Supper will be examined as examples of how the Spirit actually particularizes a person and how such actions create communion among believers.

---

29. Gunton, *One, the Three and the Many*, 217n5.
30. Gunton, *One, the Three and the Many*, 217.

The Relation of the Spirit and Humanity: Personal Constitution

The relation of the Spirit and humanity is a hotly debated topic in pneumatology. With the strong and ongoing growth of Pentecostal churches, the popular understanding of the Spirit's work tends to focus on the charismatic nature of the Spirit. It is plausible that such a trend can be traced back to the doctrine of the Trinity in the Western church. As Gunton argues, the Western church fails to recognize the personhood of the Spirit. Consequently, this has resulted in an excessive emphasis on the indwelling of the Spirit in believers.

Yet, the Holy Spirit is the third person of the Trinity. He is personally present among us. Gunton argues, "The Spirit is not some inner fuel, compulsion or qualification—in fact he is nothing impersonal at all—but the free Lord who as our other liberates us for community."[31] Indeed, when the Spirit guided Jesus into the desert, his personal presence was with Jesus. Therefore, when one thinks about the relation of the Spirit with humanity, it is important to understand that the Spirit is a person of the Trinity. He does not merely indwell us, but his personal presence is with us. And as he particularized Jesus to be a certain man, he will also particularize us after the example of the incarnate Son.

The Spirit's relation with humanity is therefore the particularization or constitution of a person. As Gunton argues, "While justification denotes the status of the faithful, their adoption through the work of the Spirit, sanctification denotes the way upon which they are set."[32] Hence, the particularization of a person is to set them in a right place with God, others and the world. But, Gunton argues, "The holiness of the community is not primarily the holiness of the individuals within it—though that is a part of it—but that of a people bound together because they shape in the life of worship, proclamation, teaching, sharing and good works."[33] Although the Spirit works upon individuals, he does not shape them to exist apart from each other. On the contrary, he conforms them so that they will be in communion.

In short, particularization is a means to restore the community which is broken by sin. Particularization is like being conformed to the shape of a piece of a puzzle in order to fit with the rest of the pieces. This is indeed the

---

31. Gunton, "Transcendent Lord," 8; italics in original.
32. Gunton, *Christian Faith*, 148.
33. Gunton, *Christian Faith*, 148.

ultimate purpose of the Spirit's work because "to be human is to be created in and for community."³⁴ Hence, as the Spirit particularizes humanity, the "human community becomes concrete in the church."³⁵ They are no longer a mere cluster of individuals, but a group of people in unity who worship and praise the resurrected Christ.³⁶

The Concept of Person: The Triune God

The eschatological Spirit particularizes humans as he particularized the incarnate Son. But, what is the locus for the Spirit's particularizing? It is indeed personhood. As we examined above, the eschatological Spirit who particularizes the incarnate Son as well as humans also particularizes the persons of the Trinity, the Father and the Son. Just as the Godhead mutually constitutes each other as persons, humans also constitute each other by giving and receiving as persons. In short, we are, ontologically, relational beings. The Spirit is able to particularize both divine and human persons in the same manner because both share a relational ontology.

Gunton therefore argues that the triune God is the basis of human personhood. He states, "One, perhaps, *the*, point of trinitarian theology is that it enables us to develop an ontology of the personal, or, better, an understanding of God as the personal creator and redeemer of the world, and so the basis of the priority of the personal elsewhere, too."³⁷ Gunton holds that the term "person" is used of God and us "univocally" but "not in exactly the same sense."³⁸ Rather, it is a qualified sameness.

---

34. Gunton, *One, the Three and the Many*, 218.

35. Gunton, *One, the Three and the Many*, 217.

36. Yet, the nature of such unity must be understood in the light of the one and the many. Gunton states, "They only become themselves in communion with others. It is in the discussion of the relation between the one and many, the community and its members, that Paul's discussion of the body of Christ takes its chief orientation." Gunton, *Christian Faith*, 150. When the one and the many are in balance, it creates a perfect community where humans become whom they were created to be.

37. Gunton, *Promise of Trinitarian Theology*, 195; italics in original. William B. Whitney has a nice summary of Gunton's argument on this point in relation to the image of God. See Whitney, *Problem and Promise in Colin E. Gunton's Doctrine of Creation*, 111–19.

38. Gunton addresses his view of univocity between God and humanity as follows: "When we speak of persons, divine and human, is 'person' being used univocally? By this is meant not in exactly the same sense, but recalling Scotus' view, that 'the concept [is] univocal which possesses sufficient unity in itself, so that to affirm and deny it of

But if the being of God lies in the relation of persons, what does this tell us about the nature of personhood? Gunton defines *person* as follows: "To be a person is to be distinct from other persons, and yet inextricably bound up with them: to be 'other' only in 'relation'. Just as God is who he is in the inextricable fellowship of Father, Son and Spirit, so for us to be personal is to be what we are in relation to other persons."[39] Personhood thus entails relationality—a person cannot be a person without relation with others because only in relation is a person constituted. Further, a person can be particular only when we are in relation with others. Indeed, the one and the many must co-exist in order for a particular being to exist.

If so, the concept of person should be understood as including the one and the many. Gunton writes, "To be creature is to be constituted, to be made what one is, by and in a network of relationships."[40] This point is significant in light of the constitution of the church because it delineates how persons are the basis of its constitution. A person is created for life in community because the nature of person—relationality—compels them to be in relation with others. In so doing, a community is formed: One will become many to constitute the community of believers. Again, community's existence is not "independent and logically prior to the persons who become part of it."[41] Hence, a communion will be shaped among persons.[42]

If the triune God is the basis of human personhood, then the taxis of the triune God is the basis of that of humans. Gunton declares, "To be in the image of God is to be structured in a manner in some way similar to

---

the same thing would be a contradiction.'" Gunton, *Act and Being*, 146. This concept reflects his reservations about negative theology. Gunton continues, "It would perhaps not be too crude to say that unless, let us say, the concept of good meant in some way the same in respect to God and to the creatures, there is no way of knowing how it is to be predicated of either." Gunton, *Act and Being*, 70. Thereby, he concludes that some concepts are univocal when they apply to God and the creature. The crux of the matter for Gunton, however, is christology. He points to Jesus and contends, "What it is to be a human person in this case is identical with what it is to be a divine person." Gunton, *Act and Being*, 147. This point will be further explored below.

39. Gunton, *Christian Faith*, 43.

40. Gunton, *Christ and Creation*, 36.

41. Gunton, "Transcendent Lord," 11.

42. The opposite case of this is how sin has spread in the world. Gunton argues, "We make or break ourselves and each other by the way we live together in the world. The horizontal aspects of what has traditionally been described as sin encompasses the way in which personal relationships are disordered, and so are in different ways destructive rather than constructive of humanity." Gunton, *Christ and Creation*, 39–40.

that in which the divine being is ordered. To the taxis of God there corresponds a human taxis, a human way of being in and with the world."[43] A person is a relational being because they are constituted by other persons. Yet, this—being in a community—requires a manner or way of being in a community. The persons are not just randomly placed, but rather placed in a certain way of being in a community.

This human structure is another significant point because sanctification "denotes the way upon which they are set."[44] To constitute the church, humans are to be in right relation with others just as they need to be in right relation with God. In short, this structure is the key to the constitution of the church. Mere or bare relation is not enough to constitute the church, but relation in right order to create communion. Gunton states, "The ecclesiological function of the Spirit . . . is the creation of communion between free and distinct—but without him, separate and so unatoned—persons."[45] The Spirit particularizes humanity in such a way that they will be placed in right relation with God and others. In so doing, the Spirit realizes a community among humans.

The Image of God

In the previous section we examined the concept of person. As we have seen, the triune God is the basis of human personhood (e.g., in relation and taxis). The human person is made in God's image. In fact, Gunton argues that the image of God distinguishes a human person from all other creatures. Because we are made in his image, we can relate to God in a special way. The image largely defines what it means to be a person.

Therefore, in this section, the concept of the image of God will be examined in order to further illuminate the concept of person. As we will see, Gunton's anthropology has a strong christological emphasis. Hence, this section examines the various aspects of the image of God in the light of christology. We will then examine the types of relations with God and others that stem from being made in God's image.

Genesis 1:26 states clearly that humans are made in the image of God. Nonetheless, beginning with Augustine, what the image of God refers to has been debated (e.g., substantial or relational or functional). Gunton

---

43. Gunton, *Triune Creator*, 205.
44. Gunton, *Christian Faith*, 148.
45. Gunton, "Spirit in the Trinity," 129.

writes, "To be a person is to be made in the image of God: that is the heart of the matter."[46] What the image of God entails thus determines what we are as persons.

Scripture communicates that Jesus is the exact representation of the being of God (Heb 1:3). Therefore, he is the true image of God. Further, he is "the source of human renewal in it [the image of God]."[47] Gunton explains, "To be in the image of God is to be created through the Son, who is the archetypal bearer of the image. To be in the image of God therefore means to be conformed to the person of Christ."[48] Hence, the image of God should be understood in relation to the person of Christ, since to be in the image is to be conformed to the person of Christ.

But, how should we understand the concept that Jesus is the true image of God and the source of human renewal? Gunton describes imaging in the case of the Son, who is our representative, as follows: "Imaging is therefore a triune act: the Son images the Father as through the Spirit he realizes a particular pattern of life on earth."[49] Gunton elaborates on that "particular pattern of life on earth" as follows: "First, that Jesus represents God to the creation in the way that the first human beings were called, but failed, to do; and second that he enables other human beings to achieve the directedness to God of which their fallenness has deprived them."[50] To restore relation with God, the image of God that has been distorted by sin has to be recovered.

If the image of God refers to being conformed to Christ, the Holy Spirit is the one who conforms/particularizes humans after Christ's example: "It is the Holy Spirit's act to *make particular*."[51] In other words, it is the Spirit who acts to shape the true human life of Jesus—the image of God—in humanity.[52] Hence, to be a person in the fullest sense is to be shaped into the exemplary life that Jesus demonstrated in the world.

---

46. Gunton, *Promise of Trinitarian Theology*, 113.
47. Gunton, *Christ and Creation*, 100.
48. Gunton, *Promise of Trinitarian Theology*, 113.
49. Gunton, *Christ and Creation*, 101.
50. Gunton, *Christ and Creation*, 100.
51. Gunton, *Christ and Creation*, 110.
52. Gunton further elaborates, "We often think of the Spirit as the one who makes universal the work of Christ. But, if he does, it is by realizing in time *particular* instantiations of the perfection that belongs to eternity." Gunton, *Christ and Creation*, 110; italics in original.

Further, the image of God signifies our relation to God and others. Our relation to God is a vital part of our constitution as persons because our whole being depends on him. Likewise, if to be a person is to be made in the image of God, our relation to God is imperative in restoring/constituting the image of God after the fall. Gunton argues, "If God upholds all the creation, and *a fortiori* the human creation, in and through Jesus Christ, then that is the primary ontology of the continuing subsistence of the image of God in human kind."[53] The image of God is indelible because it is sustained by the triune God. Gunton states, "The image of God is then that being human which takes shape by virtue of the creating and redeeming agency of the triune God."[54] The image of God therefore signifies our dependency on God for our uniquely human existence and the special relationship that we have with the triune God as those made in his image.

The image of God not only has implications for vertical relations, but also horizontal relations. To be conformed to Christ, humans also need to be related with others. Indeed, true humanity can only be found in relation with others. Gunton asserts, "To be in the image of God is at once to be created as a particular kind of being—person—and to be called to realize a certain destiny. The shape of that destiny is to be found in God-given forms of human community and of human responsibility to the universe."[55] Jesus, who is the image of God, was a particular Jewish man who lived in a particular time and place. He lived life in a way that no one else could have: His destiny was to offer the perfect sacrifice through his death for the redemption of the world. In the same way, God made each of us to be a particular person. Yet, the shape of our destiny can be found in our everyday interactions with others in society.

The image of God is sustained by God. But, to be *in* the image is to realize our certain destiny by placing ourselves in relation with others in society. Gunton argues, "We are in the image of God when, like God but dependent on his giving, we find our reality in what we give and receive from others in human community."[56] Hence, to be conformed to Christ, humanity needs to be in relation with one another. For this reason, "God-given forms of human community" are indispensable to finding the "shape of [our] destiny."

---

53. Gunton, *Triune Creator*, 207.
54. Gunton, *Promise of Trinitarian Theology*, 113.
55. Gunton, *Promise of Trinitarian Theology*, 116.
56. Gunton, *Promise of Trinitarian Theology*, 114.

Relation with God as well as others is necessary for constituting the image of God in humanity. But, the significance of relation with the non-personal world cannot be overlooked. Gunton contends, "We are not human apart from our relation with the non-personal world."[57] Yet, as much as we need the non-personal world in constituting our personhood, the non-personal world needs humanity since its destiny is bound up with ours. Naturally, this speaks to the ethics of human conduct toward our society and natural environment.

Gunton therefore argues, "Here, being in the image of God has something to do with the human responsibility to offer the creation, perfected, back to its creator as a perfect sacrifice of praise."[58] Human stewardship of the creation is certainly one of the aspects of being in the image of God. Gunton continues, "*To be in the image of God is therefore to be called to represent God to the creation and the creation to God*, so enabling it to reach its perfection."[59] To be in the image of God is thus to participate in God's mission to bring the whole created world to perfection.

THE ESCHATOLOGICAL SPIRIT, THE CHURCH AND CULTURE

In the previous sections, we have examined the concepts of the church and person. We argued that the church is not reducible to an institution, but a community of people because it is people who make up the church, not an institution. Further, we argued that if it is people who make up the church, then the driving force of the constitution of the church is the Holy Spirit. Yet, human persons are fallen and in need of being conformed to the Son who is the image of God. The re-formation and constitution of persons is necessary to comprise the church that is eschatological in nature.

In this section, the re-formation of persons in the church will be examined. This is an attempt to further elaborate how the re-formation of persons in the image of God contributes to the constitution and reconstitution of the church. Furthermore, if the church is the "community where that representative humanity becomes the form of the teleology of others,"[60] it is important to examine how this humanity becomes reshaped in the

---

57. Gunton, *Promise of Trinitarian Theology*, 115.
58. Gunton, *Promise of Trinitarian Theology*, 115.
59. Gunton, *Christ and Creation*, 102–3; italics in original.
60. Gunton, *Christ and Creation*, 111.

church. We will see that the restoration of our relation with God, others, and the created world, as examined above, is the basis of such re-formation.

The Eschatological Spirit, the Church, Worship, Word and the Sacraments

Gunton argues, "The church is the community placed by Word and sacrament under the rule of Christ and therefore in saving relation to God the creator and redeemer."[61] And it is only in this context that the church becomes a place where the restoration and constitution of the image of God takes place. Gunton contends,

> The re-formation of the image is . . . to be conceived as freedom in a double sense: as freedom *from* idolatry and freedom *for* redeemed relationships with person and world. But how does such reshaping take place? The answer to that question is that it takes place in worship and life, not, of course, as two completely separate forms of being in the world, but as two sides of the same dynamic. It is for reasons such as this that we must locate the beginning of the re-formation of the image of God in the church.[62]

Worship is therefore a means to form/re-form the image of God.

Gunton declares, "The heart of the constitution of the Church by the Spirit is to be found in worship. Every act of worship that is in the Spirit is a constituting of the Church. . . . When true worship takes place, there is a sharing in the worship of heaven and an anticipation of the life of the age to come."[63] When the Word is proclaimed, the community is called to worship the resurrected Christ. And as we worship the Lord, the church is being constituted because the Spirit particularizes us so that we will be conformed to a right relation with God, others and the created world. In other words, "a human way of being in and with the world" begins to be realized.[64] Writes Gunton, "The Spirit lifts the community to the Father through the Son: and therefore we must say that the Church is constituted

---

61. Gunton, *Christ and Creation*, 108.

62. Gunton, *Christ and Creation*, 108.

63. Gunton, "Transcendent Lord," 15. Gunton does not intend to say that the church is impeccable. Although when true worship happens "there is a sharing in the worship of heaven," he argues that it happens from "time to time [to] anticipate that of the age to come." Gunton, *Father, Son and Holy Spirit*, 232. The Church is not immune from the fallenness of the world.

64. Gunton, *Triune Creator*, 205.

as the Spirit, through the word of the gospel—the risen Christ becoming concrete in the present—calls the community into being."[65] Christ is the beginning of the re-formation of the image of God. And having become concrete in the present, he incorporates all into himself, calling the community into being.

Similarly, the sacraments are the means to constitute and re-constitute the church. Gunton states, "The sacraments of baptism and the Lord's Supper before all else operate to shape a particular pattern of community in the form of Christ. They are the way the sacrifice of Christ takes form in the world."[66] In baptism, people are brought into the community and incorporated into Christ by the Spirit. "Baptism, therefore, brings a person into relation with that community, so that he or she is now by means of a sacramental action brought within a new pattern of relationships: relationships which are what they are by virtue of their derivation from and orientation to the triune God."[67] When a person gets baptized, the dynamics of the community change. In other words, "When another becomes incorporate in Christ through the Spirit, there is a new creation."[68] The church is re-constituted according to the manner of the new human relations with God and others.

Likewise, people are also brought into the community by the Lord's Supper. As believers break bread and drink wine, we become united: The sacrifice of Christ calls for reconciliation and sacrificial acts to seek for the good of others. Furthermore, as we take the Lord's Supper, we eagerly wait for his return as a community. It shifts our eyes toward future glory. Gunton observes, "The Lord's Supper becomes the means by which the praise of God and the transformation of human life out of alienation and into the eschatological community are at once symbolized and realised."[69] The eschatological Spirit re-forms the image of God as we gather around the table in unity and wait for the glorious return of our risen Lord.

---

65. Gunton, "Transcendent Lord," 15.
66. Gunton, *Christ and Creation*, 114.
67. Gunton, *Father, Son and Holy Spirit*, 213.
68. Gunton, "Transcendent Lord," 15. Gunton interprets Paul's claim that a new creation is the new community of the church, rather than an "inner change, invisible and having no empirical results." Gunton, "Transcendent Lord," 15. By baptism, the dynamics of human relationship which constitute the community change. There is therefore a new creation.
69. Gunton, *Christ and Creation*, 115.

The Eschatological Spirit and Culture

Having examined how the image of God is being shaped/reshaped by the Spirit in the church, we must now turn to how the image witnesses to the world. Gunton contends, "The logic of our embodiedness, of our createdness in the image of God, is the presentation of a certain shape of being before the throne of God. Such logic will concern in large part our relatedness to other people, for there is no action, however apparently private, that does not have implications for our life with others."[70] Gunton holds that the notion of sacrifice is the key to grasping this concept.

To be in the image of God is to be a "priest of creation."[71] By rightly offering God the sacrifice of praise, which is an "act or form of relatedness with ourselves or with other people,"[72] one fulfills the call of being in the image of God. As we offer the sacrifice of praise, it shapes us in a certain way. Consequently, we are placed in right relation with others. As the incarnate Son gave the perfect sacrifice for our redemption, we must offer the sacrifice of praise to God for the good of others.

Yet, this sacrificial act is not directed only to humanity. Gunton insists, "A more adequate ethic of sacrifice will involve a double orientation: to what we do with our persons, with ourselves as souls and bodies, and to what we do with the rest of the world."[73] Thus, to be in the image of God involves being the shepherd of the world, as Gen 1:28 teaches.[74] Humans are expected to participate in the perfecting of the creation as the eschatological Spirit enables us to achieve the task. In so doing, we offer the sacrifice of praise to God.

---

70. Gunton, *Christ and Creation*, 117. Suffice it to say that in Gunton's theology, the redemption means the restoration of our relation with God, each other and the created world. And such restored relation arises from placing ourselves in the right place in relation to others.

71. Gunton, *Christ and Creation*, 121. In regard to the image of God, Gunton holds a relational as well as a functional view. Gunton contends that both relational and functional aspects of the image of God are indispensable for us to be conformed to the image of Christ. For additional details, see ch. 4 of *Christ and Creation*; *Triune Creator*, 206–11; ch. 6 of *Promise of Trinitarian Theology*.

72. Gunton, *Christ and Creation*, 117.

73. Gunton, *Christ and Creation*, 117.

74. Gunton explains, "Eschatologically speaking, even 'in the beginning,' before the fall, things are not yet as they are created to be, because there is a task laid upon those created in the image of God and it involves both the moral and the cultural, insofar as they can be separated." Gunton, "Reformation Accounts of the Church's Response to Human Culture," 79–80.

Nonetheless, one may wonder how it is that humans can participate in the perfecting work of the eschatological Spirit. Gunton writes, "Culture, we might say, is that set of activities in which those made in the image of God share in the divine perfecting of that which was made in the beginning."[75] Hence, culture is a means of participating in the perfecting of the creation.[76] Furthermore, the purpose of culture is to perfect "that which was created very good; completing, we might say, God's work of art—his drama or symphony."[77] Yet, we are responsible only for the particular circumstances in which we live.

Just as the Spirit particularized Jesus to be a particular Jewish man who lived in a particular time, the Spirit particularizes us so that we are empowered by him to achieve "particular instances of the good, the true and the beautiful in anticipation of the eschatological completion of all things."[78] Gunton contends, "If God the Spirit is God the Father's way of enabling truth, beauty and goodness to be realized in his creation, then culture is a matter of human agents being enabled by God to shape the creation towards what it is made to be."[79] Through culture, we are enabled by the Spirit to participate in the perfecting work of the Spirit.

Pushing the discussion further, how should we see the place of the church in cultural engagement? If the church is the community where reformation of the image of God takes place, the church must place herself in the center of cultural engagement. The redemption of the world is only possible when humanity is able to restore their relation with God and others. Gunton argues that Israel and the church are "forms of culture instituted by God."[80] He writes,

> Worship is at the heart of the calling of both Israel and the church, for in their cults human life in community and in the world is

---

75. Gunton, "Reformation Accounts of the Church's Response," 80.

76. Gunton further defines culture as follows: "By culture, I mean neither high culture—though I shall make mention of it—nor culture in the sense sometimes used by social scientists of the symbolic worlds human beings develop, but something much more general. As nature is that which comes from the hand of the Creator, so culture is all things that human beings do, with, and in that created world. It is nature in some way affected or shaped by human hands, paradigmatically represented by bread and wine." Gunton, *Father, Son and Holy Spirit*, 120.

77. Gunton, *Christian Faith*, 50.

78. Gunton, *Christian Faith*, 50.

79. Gunton, *Christian Faith*, 50.

80. Gunton, *Father, Son and Holy Spirit*, 121.

consciously ordered to God's historic acts in creation and redemption, and the creation's eschatological orientation restored. Specific forms of symbolic actions place human life in relation to God, human social order and the material world. The action of the Spirit is required if those actions and their social context are to achieve what they are designed to do.[81]

Gunton observes that in the book of Romans "Paul begins with an account of life in the Spirit—of churchly culture—and proceeds to set this form of life in the context of the whole created order."[82] Hence, this ecclesial form of culture is a God-ordained culture which every culture should emulate.

Yet, this does not mean that all culture is derived from Israel and the church.[83] Gunton acknowledges that not every aspect of culture is good or praiseworthy. In fact, many aspects exhibit fallenness. Hence, "after the Fall, the Spirit's work is achieved only against opposition."[84] But, Gunton argues, "This is why we must begin with some account of the communities of redemption.... According to biblical witness, the shape of the two communities [Israel and the church] is determined by the covenants, divine acts by which human life is reoriented to the end for which it was created."[85] Churchly culture maintains the form of culture that is ordained by God. If so, the church should place herself in the center of cultural engagement. Accordingly, Christians should engage in culture in such a way that is

---

81. Gunton, *Father, Son and Holy Spirit*, 121–22.

82. Gunton, *Father, Son and Holy Spirit*, 122.

83. Gunton holds as well that good culture can be created outside of the church. "The Spirit is free to enable those who by no means confess God's being and action to achieve the greatest of things." Gunton, *Father, Son and Holy Spirit*, 123.

84. Gunton, *Father, Son and Holy Spirit*, 121. Although the Spirit's work is affected by sin, Gunton states that the work of the Spirit is "by no means constrained or constricted by the Fall." Gunton, *Father, Son and Holy Spirit*, 121. Any good culture is the result of the work of the Spirit in perfecting the created order. Further, although some aspects of culture may become corrupted, "culture is never outside the overruling power of God, but is sometimes allowed to take its destructive course, as, for example, Revelation 6 makes clear." Gunton, *Father, Son and Holy Spirit*, 121. In terms of what makes a culture *good*, one criterion Gunton proposes is "whether it [the culture] enables the creature, human and non-human alike, to join in praise of the creator by giving him glory." Gunton, *Father, Son and Holy Spirit*, 123. More specifically, Gunton argues that modern ethical practice which "systematically fails to respect the personal life that only God may give and take away" is "the culture of death." Gunton, *Father, Son and Holy Spirit*, 125–26.

85. Gunton, *Father, Son and Holy Spirit*, 125–26.

faithful to God while relying on the power of the Spirit who enables us to create culture and participate in it.

CRITIQUE

In the previous chapter I critiqued how Gunton perceives the relation between the immanent and economic Trinity. I concluded that despite Gunton's relentless effort to maintain a distinction between the two trinities, he ultimately conflates them, especially in light of the eschatological work of the Spirit.

In this chapter, I will examine again the relation between the economic and immanent Trinity, but from a different perspective. I will critique the way Gunton moves from the immanent Trinity to the economic Trinity in order to "further illuminate the shape of God's action."[86] Clearly, the eschatological Spirit's work in the church and in persons reflects how Gunton perceives the movement from the immanent to the economic Trinity. Hence, the criticism is directed toward Gunton's ecclesiology and anthropology in relation to the eschatological Spirit.

Gunton argues that the ontology of the church is grounded in the trinitarian God. Hence, the church should echo "the interrelation between the three persons who together constitute the deity," albeit on a finite level.[87] What the church echoes in relation to the trinitarian God is "the eternally interanimating energies of the three," which is the perichoretic interrelation of the divine beings.[88] However, it is difficult to grasp what the "perichoretic interrelation of the divine beings" might look like in the temporal, created world. Nonetheless, Gunton argues that the concept of "perichoretic interrelation" in the Trinity should guide our understanding of the communal nature of the church as well as personhood.

However, "In traditional discussions . . . the doctrine of perichoresis was applied to the Trinity to affirm the *oneness* of the Godhead."[89] It is a divine mystery that three distinct persons, the Father, the Son and the Holy

---

86. Gunton, *Barth Lectures*, 91.

87. Gunton states, "The church is what it is by virtue of being called to be a temporal echo of the eternal community that God is." Gunton, *Promise of Trinitarian Theology*, 78.

88. Gunton, *Promise of Trinitarian Theology*, 81.

89. Anizor, "Spirited Humanity," 36; italics in original. Anizor adds, "Such were the perspectives of Gregory of Nyssa, Gregory Nazianzen, Pseudo-Cyril, and John of Damascus" (36). See Anizor, "Spirited Humanity," for a helpful overview of this topic.

Spirit, are one because this would certainly not make sense within human experience and understanding. Hence, the concept of perichoresis has traditionally been used to illuminate this divine mystery: It is formulated to "show that in essence and in action each person of the Godhead interpenetrates the others (and vice versa), individuating properties excluded."[90] In this light, Gunton's use of the doctrine of perichoresis in relation to temporal entities such as the church and human persons is questionable, since its proper application seems limited to the nature of the triune God.

If one accepts that there is a vast ontological difference between God and humans, certainly there will be some ontological aspects of the divine being that we cannot explain or understand. And if the doctrine of perichoresis is traditionally used to explain the divine mystery of oneness that stems from this ontological difference, it would be a significant mistake to use such a concept to hypothesize commonalities that exist between God and humans, as this undermines the Creator/creature distinction. As Keith Johnson argues,

> Substantial differences exist between divine relations and human relations that disallow *direct* imitation of God's inner life. *Perichoresis* represents an excellent case in point.... Despite contemporary references to imitating the "dance" of the Trinity, it is difficult to imagine precisely how human beings imitate divine *perichoresis*.[91]

What may be taking place in Gunton's theology on this point is a type of projectionism, as argued by Karen Kilby. She contends that Gunton's use of the doctrine of perichoresis as "a transcendental"—that is, "a concept which captures something universal about all being and which is also suggestive and fruitful for further reflection"—seems to be dictated by problems in our contemporary world (e.g., individualism) rather than the immanent Trinity itself.[92] Hence, she questions Gunton's employment of the doctrine.

90. Anizor, "Spirited Humanity," 37.

91. Johnson, "*Imitatio Trinitatis*," 322; italics in original. In addition, see Fermer, "Limits of Trinitarian Theology as a Methodological Paradigm," 173. Fermer argues that Gunton's and Zizioulas's view of the church and God that is characterized by interrelation conflates the distinction between God and the world. See also Coakley, "Why Three?," 29–56. Further, Stephen Holmes is concerned that Gunton's perception of person in the divine and human is univocal: "Towards the end of his life Colin became convinced that there needed to be univocity in reference to God and creatures; I think this is a mistake (and told him so)." Stephen Holmes, email correspondence, July 23, 2013.

92. Kilby, "Perichoresis and Projection," 438.

> In short, then, I am suggesting we have here something like a three stage process. First, a concept, perichoresis, is used to name what is not understood, to name whatever it is that makes the three Persons one. Secondly, the concept is filled out rather suggestively with notions borrowed from our own experience of relationships and relatedness. And then, finally, it is presented as an exciting resource Christian theology has to offer the wider world in its reflections upon relationships and relatedness.[93]

Although one cannot enter into the mind of another person, Kilby's criticism appears plausible, and suggests that Gunton's approach confuses the divide between Creator and creature, and that attempting to address societal issues may have caused Gunton to overlook potential problems with these ideas.

In one sense it is difficult to understand how Gunton could fall victim to projectionism. As we have seen earlier, he relentlessly argues for the importance of the ontological difference between the creator and creature for the freedom of both. Yet he appears to overlook this distinction in applying the doctrine of perichoresis to the interrelation between God and the creation (e.g., the church and persons). Paul Molnar echoes the observation of other critics in pointing to the apparent underlying issue. He writes, "In spite of the important contributions Gunton has made to our understanding of the proper relation between the immanent and economic Trinity, there remains a problem with his theological epistemology. . . . Gunton at times appears to imply that relationality is the subject while God's act becomes the predicate."[94] Molnar proposes that when Gunton looks at the immanent Trinity that is revealed by the Son to see how the triune God interacts with the world in creation and redemption, he is not guided by the immanent Trinity, but rather by human experience.

The root of the problem thus seems to lie in Gunton's christology. Molnar continues, "Ultimately, the difficulty here concerns the fact that Gunton is willing to abstract from Jesus' being as the Word in areas of his reflection and then search for transcendentals or analogies grounded in a concept of relationality that is not always dictated by the immanent Trinity."[95] Gunton looks to the incarnate Son because "the Incarnation provides the cornerstone . . . that human personality offers the decisive insight

---

93. Kilby, "Perichoresis and Projection," 442.
94. Molnar, *Divine Freedom and the Doctrine of the Immanent Trinity*, 294.
95. Molnar, *Divine Freedom and the Doctrine of the Immanent Trinity*, 310.

into the existence and nature of a personal God . . . because the Incarnation reveals the perfect being of God as the 'archetype' of humanity's potential being."[96] Yet, what he draws from the incarnate Son is not always dictated by the immanent Trinity. Consequently, in Gunton's earnest desire to make the Trinity relevant and practical to our contemporary world, he seems to start with the world to see how the Trinity can answer the problems that our contemporary world faces.

Of course, this does not discredit Gunton's contributions to the doctrine of the Trinity and pneumatology. His effort to construe the relation of the Creator and world in light of the Trinity serves as a corrective to the misconception that God is impersonal and distant from the creation. Further, Gunton's emphasis on God's free personal relation to the world through the two hands, the Son and the Spirit, has resulted in a "pneumatological model in which the Spirit is the 'perfecting cause' of the creaturely being."[97]

How then should we approach the question of the relation between God and humans?[98] If "Christian faith is irreducibly trinitarian in character"[99] and a "trinitarian approach radically affects the exposition of who is the God in whom Christians believe, and the presentation of what can be asserted about God's being and the God-world relationship,"[100] scholarly work such as Gunton's must not be dismissed. Molnar asks, "Do the relations in which we stand make known who we are, or is it God himself in his Word and Spirit who does this in and through our faith as we read scripture and live the Christian life?"[101] Molnar is surely right to say that we should not allow our worldly relations to dictate our thinking when we try to understand the God-world relation. Yet, it seems to go too far to

---

96. Schwöbel, "Introduction," 3.

97. Webster, "Systematic Theology after Barth," 261.

98. Lewis Ayers gives helpful suggestions for how to construe divine and human relationality in "(Mis)Adventures in Trinitarian Ontology," 142–45. Also see Johnson, "*Imitatio Trinitatis*," 325–31.

99. Schwöbel, "Introduction," 10.

100. Schwöbel, "Introduction," 11. Ayers also argues, "The characteristics of the divine relationships certainly should provide material that should be of immense help in shaping our vision of the world. Envisioning the shape of the divine unity and relationality should, however, be an analogical and anagogic exercise." Ayers, "(Mis)Adventures in Trinitarian Ontology," 143.

101. Molnar, *Divine Freedom and the Doctrine of the Immanent Trinity*, 295.

say that our worldly human relations have no place in understanding the God-world relation.

The triune Creator interacts with the world through personal relation as has been noted above. Therefore, it is plausible to hold that "mediation must be fundamentally an account of persons in relation."[102] Yet, the underlying issue is how to define *mediation*. Does mediation mean being particularized by the Spirit in order to place oneself in right relation with God, others, and the world, and consequently to realize a perfect communion in the world to echo the immanent Trinity? Or, should mediation be understood as more than just the particularization of persons? It seems that Gunton's misjudgment stems from his effort to see "*analogia personae et relationis*" in every area of creation and redemption so that he undermines the distinction between the divine persons and human persons.[103]

The eschatological Spirit is the perfecting agent of the creation. As Gunton argues, the eschatological Spirit realizes the eschatological community of the church by bringing people to the Father through the Son and transforms humans to be reconciled with God, others and the created world after the example of the Son who is the true image of God. Therefore, relationality of persons (divine and human) is a significant key to the restoration of the created world. But, for one to say that perichoresis is a transcendental that is a mark of all being and thereby that humans imitate God by constituting each other by giving and receiving from each other seems to go beyond what the doctrine of the Trinity allows us to say.

Schwöbel observes, "The doctrine of the Trinity determines what can theologically be said about God as well as what can be stated about the world and humankind."[104] In this light, it seems to me that Gunton fails to remain within the parameters that the doctrine of the Trinity sets. Accordingly, he makes an unjustified movement from the immanent Trinity to the economic Trinity and from the economic Trinity to the nature and relations of human persons and the created world.

CONCLUSION

In this chapter, we have examined the relation between the Spirit and the church as well as the Spirit and humanity. This was for the purpose of

102. Holmes, "Towards the *Analogia Personae et Relationis*," 41.
103. Holmes, "Towards the *Analogia Personae et Relationis*," 42.
104. Schwöbel, "Introduction," 11.

further exploring the Spirit's work of particularization for the redemption of the world. If the Spirit *constitutes* a community of believers as the agent of perfection, while Christ is the one who *institutes* such a community, it is imperative to examine the church and human personhood in light of the Spirit's work of particularization.

First, we examined how the church is a finite echo of the Trinity that is the community of reconciliation and of the new age to come. Second, we examined how the Holy Spirit is the driving force of the constitution of the church because the church is constituted by a community of people who are freely brought together by the eschatological Spirit. Third, we examined that through our relation with God, and each other in the sacraments, the eschatological Spirit enables the church to be a place for the re-formation of the image of God so that she will be a "community where that representative humanity becomes the form of the teleology of others."[105] Consequently, the Spirit enables the church to engage culture. Church culture that is oriented toward the sacraments, worship and the Word orders human life to God. Indeed, it is a form "of culture instituted by God."[106] In so doing, the church offers the sacrifice of praise to God for the restoration of the created world.

As much as relational ontology is a significant aspect of Gunton's theology in the doctrines of pneumatology, ecclesiology, and anthropology, and is indeed a key concept in Gunton's scheme of salvation, I have argued that Gunton appears to conflate the distinction between God and humanity since he argues that the church and human persons echo the perichoretic interrelation of the divine being. Given Gunton's expressly stated concerns about contemporary problems in society, especially as they relate to a breakdown in interpersonal relationships, it seems plausible that Gunton's views are the result of a kind of projectionism.

Yet, this does not discredit Gunton's contribution. On the contrary, relational ontology is an important theological concept for those who wish to understand the triune God, humans and the world since a "trinitarian approach radically affects the exposition of who is the God in whom Christians believe, and the presentation of what can be asserted about God's being and the God-world relationship."[107] But, Gunton goes beyond what the doctrine of the Trinity allows us to say. As a result, he fails to maintain the important ontological distinction between God and humans.

---

105. Gunton, *Christ and Creation*, 111.

106. Gunton, *Father, Son and Holy Spirit*, 121.

107. Schwöbel, "Introduction," 11.

In the end, although one may agree with Gunton on the significance of relational ontology, his univocal ontology of God and human persons, and his theological epistemology that appears to begin with human relations and society, raises significant concerns about theological overreach.

In addition to this concern, one also detects a lacuna in Gunton's theology of the Spirit. As mentioned above, Gunton argues,

> The problem [misconstruing the Sprit's work] derives, I believe, from the failure to give to the Holy Spirit the kind of personal identity or particularity that is required if we are to speak of him and identify his action in the world. If we do not find adequate means of identification, the danger remains that we shall identify his work apart from the work of the Father and the Son, and in terms of what we happen to find attractive or appealing at the present time.[108]

Gunton speaks of properly identifying the Spirit's action in the world. Yet, throughout his writings he does so only in the context of the Church (community). Although Gunton acknowledges the need to find "adequate means of identification" of the Spirit's work in the world, he does not propose such means beyond the Spirit's work in the Church.

Gunton states, ". . . with all human culture where it is good, it is because it is enabled to be so by the power of the God who upholds all things in Christ."[109] Gunton sees the true, the beautiful, and the good reflected in culture when human relations with God, each other, and the created world are correctly ordered, which is the goal of the eschatological Spirit. At the same time, Gunton gives little to go on in terms of determining which specific movements in culture may be the Spirit's work.

For this reason, this aspect of Gunton's theology of the Spirit leaves us without adequate criteria for determining where or in what way the Spirit is working in the world (apart from the Church). One wishes that Gunton had proposed such criteria in order to better demonstrate the practical outworking of his pneumatology in society.

---

108. Gunton, "Transcendent Lord," 4.
109. Gunton, *Father, Son and Holy Spirit*, 121.

CHAPTER 6

SEEKING THE WELFARE OF THE CITY
PUBLIC THEOLOGY FOR THE USA IN THE TWENTY-FIRST CENTURY[1]

IN THIS CHAPTER, I will discuss Colin Gunton's contribution to public theology per se. As I argued in chapter 1, in the history of public theology, pneumatology has been underexplored, especially in the area of the eschatological aspect of the Spirit's work. Due to the absence of the concept of eschatological Spirit, the relation between the trinitarian God and the public square is rarely treated. Put differently, public theology has not been approached trinitarianly. Gunton's robust pneumatology provides the necessary resources to develop a full-bodied, holistic and trinitarian public theology.

We have therefore examined in the previous chapters the distinctive function of the Spirit in the transformation of the creation in relation to the triune God. As a result, we can conclude that the eschatological Spirit is the agent of the transformation of the created world. Hence, in this section, we now turn to discuss how the Spirit works within the public square to bring the created world to the intended end in the context of modern society. We will draw upon the resources uncovered in previous chapters to outline applications for Christian engagement of the public square in the twenty-first century.

1. Part of chapter 6 was first published in "Colin E. Gunton and Public Theologians: Toward a Trinitarian Public Theology," *Evangelical Review of Theology* 41 (2017) 150–65.

To accomplish this end, we will first review the history of public theology, and I will state my definition of a trinitarian public theology. Next, six prominent public theologians and thinkers in the United States context are examined. These theologians are used as foils to discern whether pneumatology plays any significant role in their public theology. Then I discuss Gunton's contribution to public theology, followed by my suggestions of a way forward for a trinitarian public theology. Finally, I discuss criteria for discerning the Spirit's work in relation to public theology.

A BRIEF HISTORY OF PUBLIC THEOLOGY

Public theology emerged in the middle of the twentieth century in the United States. E. Harold Breitenberg writes, "It originated in discussions about civil religion and its role in the United States that began in 1967 with sociologist Robert Bellah's seminal work on American civil religion."[2] Later, the terms "public theology" and "public theologian" were coined by historian Martin Marty "to distinguish his interpretations of persons and features within the Christian tradition in the United States from the understanding of civil religion held by Bellah and others."[3] On the other hand, J. Budziszewski argues that Evangelical Christians have been active in the American public square since the founding in 1941 of the National Association of Evangelicals.[4] Public theology has taken a prominent place in the minds of many Christian thinkers as American society becomes more secularized.

Consequently, public theology has received acclaim as well as criticism. While some view it as part of "the Catholic tradition . . . [and the heir] of the Reformation,"[5] it has also been criticized as a "distortion of the church's true calling."[6] The main criticism is that public theology is contrary to the true nature of the church and theology because "theology has nothing essential to do with these publics." [7] In short, "Theology is essentially personal, not social."[8] Hence, for those who understand theology to be private in nature, public theology does not provide a welcome opportunity to

2. Breitenberg, "To Tell the Truth," 55.
3. Breitenberg, "To Tell the Truth," 55.
4. Budziszewski, "Evangelicals in the Public Square," 15.
5. Stackhouse, "Christian Social Ethics in a Global Era," 13.
6. Breitenberg, "To Tell the Truth," 15
7. Stackhouse, "Public Theology," 1132.
8. Stackhouse, "Public Theology," 1132.

fulfill the cultural mandate, but a misrepresentation of what the true church is to be.

Moreover, it is not only that scholars are divided in their attitudes toward public theology, but there is also confusion over how to define it. The term is used in a variety of ways by different writers. Nonetheless, there is broad agreement among public theologians about what public theology refers to. Breitenberg writes, "Public theology intends to provide theologically informed interpretations of and guidance for individuals, faith communities, and the institutions and interactions of civil society, in ways that are understandable, assessable, and possibly convincing to those inside the church and those outside as well."[9] In short, public theology is a theology that seeks to be relevant to our contemporary world with theological truth and ultimately to influence the world with divine guidance.

Returning to Gunton, it was only toward the end of his life that he became interested in public theology. Indeed, he contributed a chapter to a book commissioned by the British and Foreign Bible Society, *Public Theology in Cultural Engagement*.[10] Unfortunately, his argument is somewhat underdeveloped although he explores the concept of the eschatological Spirit. One cannot help thinking that had he lived longer, he might have made an even more significant contribution to public theology.

Nonetheless, Gunton's robust pneumatology can still make a significant contribution to a trinitarian public theology. As one can see above, public theology is hardly defined trinitarianly. As a result, the Spirit's eschatological work becomes invisible and is easily dismissed as simply common grace. Hence, there is a need to reformulate the definition.

As mentioned above in my first chapter, Stephen Holmes's definition of public theology seems to me to capture the most prominent features of public theology that reflect evangelical commitments. Hence, his definition is used here as a framework in order to move forward to a trinitarian public theology. On this definition, public theology is a category of theology that seeks to engage contemporary realities with theological truth and to understand how to identify the relevance of biblical texts and values for particular societal and cultural contexts. Moreover, for theological engagement with cultural realities to work effectively, theology must be able to take its place in the "marketplace of ideas." Further, public theology must be done with a view toward the transformation of the world.

9. Breitenberg, "To Tell the Truth," 66.
10. Gunton, "Reformation Accounts of the Church's Response to Human Culture."

At the same time, public theology must also be firmly grounded in the triune Creator who reaches out to the creation through his two hands, the Son and the Spirit. And it is the eschatological Spirit who transforms the world by reconciling humanity with God, each other and the creation. Thereby, the burden of public theology is ultimately reconciliation. In this way, public theology begins with sensitivity to the work of the eschatological Spirit. In other words, the divine intention to transform the world through the eschatological Spirit in relation to the Father and the Son needs to be recognized. In sum, public theology must be done under the guidance of the triune Creator who is at work for the redemption of the world. With this in view, we can move forward to a public theology that is trinitarianly informed and oriented.

SEEKING THE WELFARE OF THE CITY: THE AIM OF PUBLIC THEOLOGY

As mentioned above, while public theology has its proponents, it also has its detractors. One of the long-standing problems of public theology is the issue of how to live in the City of Man while Christians are citizens of the City of God. Surely Christians should not forsake the responsibilities we have to promote civil peace and prosperity in the City of Man. Yet, we are faced with how we should "perform [this] delicate balancing act, exercising citizenship in the earthly city but ultimately loyal to [our] higher citizenship in heaven."[11] We are called to take care of the creation, but we are not of this world. While Christians engage with society in hopes of bringing Christian influence, our ultimate loyalty lies with the City of God. Hence, we will briefly survey several principles of engagement that provide guidance for living responsibly in this present church age.[12] Through this discussion we will also discern the aim of public theology—seeking the welfare of the city.

Bruce Winter argues that Christians in the first-century Greco-Roman world were instructed to follow the tradition of Jer 29:7, "seek the welfare of the city," as a "paradigm which enabled Christians as citizens to adopt

---

11. Forster, *Contested Public Square*, 64.

12. Graham A. Cole defines responsible living as "the conduct expected by God in concrete historical settings as the divine intention is worked out in history. Responsible living is not to be viewed in a way that detaches it from the divine plan. It is the lifestyle appropriate to the particular stage which redemptive history has reached." Cole, "Responsible Lifestyle in Old Testament Perspective," 2.

and adapt the role of benefactor as they sought the city's welfare."[13] Winter argues that all Christians are called to do good regardless of their social status and wealth. "Social ethics is defined in 1 Peter as 'the doing of good works' in all spheres of life and was every Christian's calling and a central theme (2:11ff.)." [14] Surely Christians in the twenty-first century should also follow Jeremiah's injunction to "seek the welfare of the city."

Winter argues that such a principle of engagement gives a positive attitude to the city. God's virtues are revealed in "the social engagement of Christians in the everyday life of the city through good works."[15] In short, seclusion from society was not viewed as a valid option for Christians in the Greco-Roman world. Instead, Christians were called to live as citizens worthy of the gospel (Phil 1:27–2:18) and to be benefactors of the city (Rom 13:3–4; 1 Pet 2:14–15) regardless of their social status or wealth.

Accordingly, selfish ambition and strife have no place in this engagement. Winter argues that to seek the welfare of the city, one must put other's interests ahead of their own. This means giving up one's rights (1 Cor 10:22–33), seeking concord rather than discord for the sake of the community (Phil 1:27–2:18), and serving as public benefactors (Rom 13:3–4; 1 Pet 2:14–15). Winter contends, "The pursuit of one's rights on the grounds that is lawful (πάντα ἔξεστιν) cannot be undertaken at the same time as the pursuit of the 'welfare of all' (πάντα συμφέρει) or the 'building up of all.'"[16] Seen another way, the concept of seeking the welfare of the city reflects the selfless sacrifice of Christ. As Paul exhorts, all Christians must imitate Christ, and this includes Christ's selfless act in seeking the welfare of the city.

Nonetheless, although Christians are called to live as citizens worthy of the gospel, this does not mean that Christians are of this world. Indeed, Christians are resident aliens. Winter argues that for the Christians in the Greco-Roman world "the reality of the *parousia* was a motivating reason

---

13. Winter, *Seek the Welfare of the City*, 1.
14. Winter, *Seek the Welfare of the City*, 13. Cf. Rom 13:3–4.
15. Winter, *Seek the Welfare of the City*, 15.
16. Winter, *Seek the Welfare of the City*, 176. Winter argues that these parallel Greek phrases in 1 Cor 10:23, 33 "elucidate the meaning of the term 'welfare.'" Winter, *Seek the Welfare of the City*, 176. He contends that the concept of "building up" is unique to the Christian faith. "'Edification' was a unique term which Paul coined for the Christian faith which reflects the responsibility individuals should assume for the welfare of others as a matter of 'religious' obligation." Winter, *Seek the Welfare of the City*, 176.

and not an escape for seeking the welfare of the city because of the eschatological judgement."[17] He continues,

> To stand in 'the true grace of God' demanded a deep commitment to the welfare of the city within the framework of a living eschatological hope. That enabled the Christian to place personal concerns second to the needs of others in the city. This firm, eschatological hope of a secure inheritance meant that their present or impending suffering would be no ultimate catastrophe for them (1 Pet 4:12). The setting of one's hope on the grace to be revealed at the revelation of Jesus Christ (1 Pet 1:13) provided the perspective for fulfilling the Christian mandate to seek the welfare of the earthly city and not personal aggrandizement.[18]

Christians should not be discouraged by how the world responds to us. But, as the Lord sends rain to both the just and the unjust and causes his sun to rise on both, Christians should also seek the welfare of the city regardless of the mistreatment that we may experience.

In the end, to seek the welfare of the city is to seek human flourishing. Miroslav Volf argues that human flourishing "consists in love of God and neighbor and enjoyment of both."[19] Therefore, he continues, "Our concern will . . . be not just to lead life well ourselves. Instead, we will strive for life to go well for our neighbors and for them to lead their lives well, and we will acknowledge that their flourishing is tied deeply to our flourishing."[20] Hence, to seek the welfare of the city is to seek human flourishing.

As part of seeking the city's welfare, we are called to take care of God's creation—both natural and cultural. Although the world will experience God's wrath at the end, we must be faithful to our calling by taking care

---

17. Winter, *Seek the Welfare of the City*, 19.

18. Winter, *Seek the Welfare of the City*, 19. I would add that our call to the cultural mandate is also a motivation to seek the welfare of the city. Cole argues that in defining a responsible lifestyle, one must keep both testaments, Old and New, in balance: "Our hermeneutic must take into account the whole canon and in turn this canon must set the parameters of discussion." Cole, "Responsible Lifestyle," 5. Despite my admiration for Winter, his argument seems to lack a comprehensive foundation. As a result, he appears unable to provide a satisfactory answer to a question such as "Why should we care for this world when nothing in this world eternally matters?" Hence, the eschatological hope in 1 Peter should be taken into account within the divine scheme of redemption in order to provide a more robust answer—since, as Winter rightly points out, the welfare of the city is two-fold, "physical" and "spiritual." Winter, *Seek the Welfare of the City*, 201.

19. Volf, *Public Faith*, 58.

20. Volf, *Public Faith*, 71.

of his creation in seeking the welfare of the city. We must hold on to the eschatological hope that we have in Christ. Yet, we must remember that this eschatological hope does not exclude his creation. "The nations will walk by its [the city's] light, and the kings of the earth will bring their splendor into it" (Rev 21:24). Human society began in a garden (Genesis 1), but ends in a city (Revelation 22), entailing the ongoing existence of human culture.

The eschatological Spirit is working against opposition in order to bring transformation to the world in the present church age. While such a concept seems utopian to some Christians, the eschatological Spirit is actively bringing the world to its divinely appointed goal. The kings of the earth will bring splendor into the city one day. Yet in the present we live in a time of eschatological tension. Christians are, like Abraham, people who are "living in the interim period between the declaration of the divine intention and its implementation in full."[21] Like Abraham, we must be steadfast in what God calls us to do, walking by faith. Hence, to seek the welfare of the city is the foundational principle of all our engagement. And this leads ultimately to human flourishing which is the object of public theology.

HOW SHOULD WE ENGAGE IN PUBLIC THEOLOGY? PUBLIC THEOLOGIANS, THINKERS AND COLIN E. GUNTON

In this section I will examine public theologians and thinkers in the United States context. I have selected six prominent public theologians and thinkers whose work has had significant influence in public theology in the United States. In addition, they represent mainline Protestant (Niebuhr, Stackhouse, Hunter and Hauerwas), evangelical (Carson) and Roman Catholic (Neuhaus) thought. Similarly, Reformed and non-Reformed (e.g., Anabaptist) perspectives are represented by these theologians. Following this, I will evaluate Colin Gunton's contribution to public theology. My intention is to use these six theologians and thinkers as foils in evaluating whether pneumatology plays any significant role in their public theology. Finally, I will suggest a way forward drawing upon Gunton's work, particularly his pneumatology.

---

21. Cole, "Responsible Lifestyle," 5.

Public Theologians and Thinkers

H. Richard Niebuhr

H. Richard Niebuhr was the leading figure in American public theology in the mid twentieth century. His *magnum opus*, *Christ and Culture*, is considered a classic in the field of public theology.[22] Since its publication in 1951, the book has been read by theologians, students, pastors and laypeople. It continues to influence the discussion of public theology in the twenty-first century.[23] Niebuhr was ordained in the Evangelical and Reformed Church and taught at Yale Divinity School.

In *Christ and Culture*, Niebuhr begins with what he calls "the enduring problem" which "has to do with the relation of a faith community to its surroundings."[24] He argues that Jesus' Sonship to the Father involves a "double movement—with men toward God, with God toward men; from the world to the Other, from the Other to the world."[25] If Christ directs Christians to the world, what is the relationship that reflects our faithfulness and loyalty to Christ in dealing with the world? To answer this question, Niebuhr constructs his famous five typologies: Christ against culture, Christ of culture, Christ above culture, Christ and culture in paradox and Christ the transformer of culture.[26]

The Christ against culture paradigm perceives culture as sinful and non-redemptive. Hence, "the counterpart of loyalty to Christ and the brothers is the rejection of cultural society; a clear line of separation is

---

22. See Marty, "Foreword to," xiii.

23. Though some scholars dismiss the influence and relevance of Niebuhr in the twenty-first century (e.g., Craig A. Carter and Mark Nation), Richard J. Mouw argues that Niebuhr is still relevant and presents a cogent argument for the Christ transforming culture type. See Mouw, "Cultural Discipleship in a Time of God's Patience," 80–91.

24. Marty, "Foreword to," xiv.

25. Niebuhr, *Christ and Culture*, 29.

26. James M. Gustafson who was a doctoral student and colleague of Niebuhr's states the purpose and intention of these typologies in order to clarify some misunderstandings. In reply to George Marsden, Gustafson states, "Marsden notes Niebuhr's heuristic use of the types; but he also adds that they are used as explanatory devices. The latter is false; ideal types do not explain anything, as Niebuhr indicates in his 1942 paper ["Types of Christian Ethics"]. They help readers to understand, not explain the subject." Gustafson, "Preface," xxxii. Echoing Gustafson, Niebuhr states, "The typologist needs to remember that he is not constructing a value scale. His enterprise is directed toward neither explanation nor evaluation, but toward understanding and appreciation." Niebuhr, "Introduction," xxxviii–xxxix.

drawn between the brotherhood of the children of God and the world."[27] Some historical representatives of this sectarian approach include Tertullian, Tolstoy, and the Mennonites. Further, this type requires a radical lifestyle of poverty, denial, and humility. In fact, the Beatitudes (Matthew 5) are a model for an authentic Christian lifestyle since Jesus is the source of the commands. This is an extreme type since adherents completely reject culture and seek to build a new society that is not corrupted by culture.

The opposite pole of this extreme is the Christ of culture type. Reflections of this type are found in Gnosticism, cultural Protestantism, and in the work of Albrecht Ritschl. Contrary to Christ against culture, this type accepts culture. Although adherents are loyal to Christ, they "seem equally at home in the community of culture."[28] This is because Jesus is not a radical Messiah who taught his followers to deny themselves by seeking a life of poverty. Instead, Jesus is a great teacher, reformer and philosopher who promoted pursuing a good life on this earth. Hence, culture does not oppose Christ because "Christ is identified with what men conceive to be their finest ideas, their noblest institutions, and their best philosophy."[29]

Niebuhr argues that despite their differences, these two types are in fact similar to each other.[30] For example, they are unitarian instead of trinitarian in their theology: "Jesus Christ being essentially God for the former [Christ against] and the Almighty Father the single God of the latter [Christ of]."[31] Further, these two types are one worldly instead of two worldly. For Christ against culture, it considers this world to be corrupted beyond redemption. Therefore, its focus is on the next world. Similarly, with Christ of culture, it is melioristic and does not "abandon the idea of another world but makes it an extension of the best parts of this aeon."[32]

In between these two extremities, Niebuhr identifies the remaining three types: Christ above culture, Christ and culture in paradox, and Christ

---

27. Niebuhr, *Christ and Culture*, 47–48.

28. Niebuhr, *Christ and Culture*, 83.

29. Niebuhr, *Christ and Culture*, 103. Cf. Ottati, "Christ and Culture," 321.

30. Ottati argues that Niebuhr analyzes each type in terms of five polarities: "reason and revelation, nature and grace, sin and good, law and gospel, and church and world." Ottati, "Christ and Culture," 321. Depending on how each type understands these polarities, their approach to culture changes. For example, the relation between reason and revelation defines "the epistemological issue or the question of the sources of knowledge and insight for Christian theology." Ottati, "Christ and Culture," 321.

31. Niebuhr, *Christ and Culture*, xlix.

32. Niebuhr, *Christ and Culture*, xlvii.

as the transformer of culture.[33] For them, the main issue is not whether to reject or accept culture. Rather, it is how to embrace this world and the next at the same time—how to live a responsible life in the world while remaining faithful to Christ.

A further contrast is that these types are not unitarian. Niebuhr states that they are "if not trinitarian, at least bi-nitarian."[34] Unlike the extreme types, they distinguish three persons of the Trinity and their respective missions. Further, they understand the world to be two-worldly, rather than one-worldly, and they acknowledge the usefulness of culture. The divine values and imperatives can be appreciated both in Christ (Bible, church) and nature (reason, culture). Nonetheless, sin infects culture. Despite God's creating, governing and redeeming work, none can escape the effects of sin.

Christ above culture incorporates elements of Christ of culture, while maintaining the lordship of Christ over the created world. This typology is represented by Thomas Aquinas and the modern Roman Catholic Church. Matthew 22:21 and Rom 13:16 are also used to support this typology. The world was created through Christ and is upheld by him. Hence, Christ and the world cannot be opposed to each other. Indeed, "both faith and knowledge proceed from the same divine source."[35] Nonetheless, adherents do not perceive Christ as the Christ of culture. A discontinuity exists between the imperatives of nature and those of the gospel. Niebuhr observes, "We must not say, 'Both Christ and culture,' as though there were no great distinction between them; but we must say, 'Both Christ and culture,' in full awareness of the dual nature of our law, our end, and our situation."[36] The distinction must be maintained although culture is ultimately under the sovereignty of God.

The church plays a significant role in this typology. The church does not isolate herself from culture and is also not a mere social institution that helps build a better society. Rather, the church is the institution that corrects and guides fallen society. Writes Niebuhr, "the church . . . is also a double organization, the religious institution in the world and monastic

---

33. Ottati explains, "'The church of the center' [the median types] share a general field of theological agreement anchored by relatively common convictions about nature and grace, and sin and good." Ottati, "Christ and Culture," 322.
34. Niebuhr, *Christ and Culture*, xlix.
35. Ottati, "Christ and Culture," 323.
36. Niebuhr, *Christ and Culture*, 122.

order."³⁷ Thus, the church is not isolated or assimilated into culture, but places herself in the center of all human activity.

Christ and culture in paradox is represented by Marcion, Martin Luther, and Søren Kierkegaard, among others. This type is characterized by tension between God's righteousness and human righteousness. Like Christ against culture, this type sees culture as corrupted. But unlike Christ against culture, it accepts the reality that humanity is surrounded by culture and believes that it is impossible to avoid it.

This position finds scriptural support in the Pauline epistles where Paul makes dualistic contrasts—for example, between the flesh and the Spirit.³⁸ Yet, this dualism has a paradoxical aspect: "He is under law, and yet not under law but grace; he is a sinner, and yet righteous. . . . In Christ all things have become new, and yet everything remains as it was from the beginning."³⁹ Christians are expected to live in this world because "the kingdom of God and the kingdom of this world are closely related."⁴⁰ Synthesis of Christ and culture is not an option. But the paradoxical relation between Christ and culture is acknowledged in this typology.

Christ the transformer of culture argues for the transformation of humanity as well as the created world. Like Christ and culture in paradox, advocates believe that sin has corrupted the entire created world and that we are in need of God's forgiveness and mercy. Yet, this corrupted world is still under God's sovereign rule. Therefore, Christians must participate in God's creating and redeeming work. Representatives of this view include Augustine and F. D. Maurice.

Niebuhr offers several points of theological support for this typology. The first is creation. Christians must participate in the Son's creating and redeeming work. Niebuhr states, "The Word that became flesh and dwelt among us, the Son who does the work of the Father in the world of creation, has entered into a human culture that has never been without his ordering action."⁴¹ The second is the "nature of man's fall from his created

---

37. Niebuhr, *Christ and Culture*, 136.

38. Niebuhr, speaking of Gal 5:19, argues that although Paul exhorts the church to refrain from the works of the flesh, he is "far from suggesting that those who refrain from such conduct will therefore inherit the kingdom, or that training in good moral habits is a step in preparation for the gift of the spirit." Niebuhr, *Christ and Culture*, 163.

39. Niebuhr, *Christ and Culture*, 157.

40. Niebuhr, *Christ and Culture*, 172.

41. Niebuhr, *Christ and Culture*, 193.

goodness."[42] The fall has corrupted God's creation. But it did not corrupt the creation to the extent of requiring a replacement. "Man's good nature has become corrupted; it is not bad, as something that ought not to exist, but warped, twisted and misdirected."[43] Likewise, culture is "corrupted order rather than order for corruption."[44] Hence, culture needs to be transformed in order to restore its goodness even if this means a rebirth through transformation.

The third theological support is a view of history. In light of the two points described above, Niebuhr argues that it becomes clear that history is not merely a series of human events. It is rather a "dynamic interaction between God and man."[45] Niebuhr observes that on this view the triune God works together to create, forgive and redeem the world in order to bring transformation.[46] But humankind is to participate in this divine work. And in such a dynamic interaction between God and man, "the eschatological future has become for him an eschatological present."[47] Hence, Christ is the transformer of culture.[48]

---

42. Niebuhr, *Christ and Culture*, 193.

43. Niebuhr, *Christ and Culture*, 194.

44. Niebuhr, *Christ and Culture*, 194. Niebuhr continues to say, "It is perverted good, not evil; or it is evil as perversion, and not as badness of being." Niebuhr, *Christ and Culture*, 194. Richard Mouw argues that this is a crucial point when one tries to understand Niebuhr's fifth typology. Mouw argues that many critiques of Niebuhr overlook how Niebuhr perceives culture. Niebuhr defines culture as an "artificial, secondary environment which man superimposes on the natural. It comprises language, habits, ideas, beliefs, customs, social organization, inherited artifacts, technical processes, and values." Niebuhr, *Christ and Culture*, 32. Mouw contends that while Niebuhr begins at the most basic stage, many of Niebuhr's opponents "quickly focus instead on some selected features of culture, such as coercive politics, military violence, and the nature of power arrangements, proceeding to argue that any sort of attempt to 'transform' these cultural phenomena inevitably compromises the church's witness." Mouw, "Cultural Discipline," 89.

45. Niebuhr, *Christ and* Culture, 194.

46. John Howard Yoder criticizes Niebuhr's lack of criteria for transformation. He argues, "To 'transform' must mean to change the form of something according to some standard. We should have had to be shown 'before' and 'after' pictures of how the impact of Christ can be expected to modify cultural values, or how it has in fact done so in history. We would have expected to see by what criteria adequate and less adequate 'transformation' would be discerned." Yoder, "How H. Richard Niebuhr Reasoned," 40. Yoder points out that Niebuhr fails to list specific cultural achievements down through the centuries that would provide concrete examples of transformation.

47. Niebuhr, *Christ and Culture*, 195.

48. The difference between Christ against culture and Christ the transformer of

Niebuhr's five typologies cover a wide spectrum of approaches for how Christians engage culture. Three median typologies are placed between two extremes. Although it is often hard to separate the explanatory aspect of these types from the heuristic, the latter is the ultimate purpose of the typologies. Niebuhr's intention is to provide a heuristic device for exploring how Christians approach issues of Christ and culture, and scholars continue to find the typologies useful in thinking through this complex topic. One of the great weaknesses of his typology, as Yoder points out, is his failure to give concrete examples of transformation.

D. A. Carson

D. A. Carson is an Emeritus Professor of New Testament who teaches at Trinity Evangelical Divinity School. Although he is not typically described as a "public theologian," much of his work addresses issues at the intersection of Christianity and culture. In 2008, Carson published *Christ & Culture Revisited*. As the title suggests, this is a treatment of Niebuhr's five typologies seen through the eyes of a biblical theologian. In this volume Carson reshapes the typologies and offers several suggestions.

Carson criticizes Niebuhr's handling of scripture. He argues that although it is commendable that Niebuhr provides scriptural evidence, his handling of it fails to be holistic. Concerning "Christ transforming culture," Carson argues,

> Most notable, perhaps, is his reading of the Fourth Gospel in defense of his fifth pattern, "Christ the transformer of culture." When John tells us that all things were made by the Logos, and apart from him nothing was made that has been made (John 1:1–3), Niebuhr infers, "John could not say more forcefully that whatever is is good." But surely it would be more accurate to infer, "John

---

culture also hinges on how we perceive the Way of Jesus. Richard Mouw provides an insightful comment in responding to Anabaptist thinkers. He argues, "As I see things, it is important to see the Way of Jesus against the background of the purposes that shaped God's original creative activity. In that sense, what Jesus taught and did cannot be isolated from the designs of the good creation. With the necessary aid of biblical spectacles we can still discern vestiges of the original created order. No matter how perverse the processes and products of cultural formation have become, human beings still work within the structures of the good creation." Mouw, "Cultural Discipleship," 88.

could not say more forcefully that whatever the Logos *originally* made was good."[49]

"Carson acknowledges that the gospel of John is "eschatologically more realized than some other New Testament documents," but disagrees with Niebuhr's conclusions: " . . . but his [John's] ultimate hope is not in the progressive transformation of the world but in the final cataclysm: Jesus is going away to prepare a place so that his followers may join him (John 14)."[50] Carson is critical of Niebuhr's reading of scripture in other areas as well.[51]

Carson determines that Niebuhr's problem originates in how he perceives the biblical canon. He states, "Niebuhr's view, a view that is still quite common in some academic circles, is that the Bible in general, and the New Testament in particular, provides us with a number of discrete paradigms."[52] Suffice it to say that this view discourages us from reading the Bible in a holistic manner. Niebuhr's reading violates the "canon's 'rule' [which] lies in the totality of the canon's instruction."[53] Hence, Niebuhr's handling of scripture comes across as piecemeal. Carson argues that we need to listen to all the voices of the canon and integrate them systematically. To do so involves the following "non-negotiables":

> In addition to close exegesis of a wide range of biblical texts, we need to think through how they fit into the great turning points of redemptive history, into the massive movement from creation to the new heaven and the new earth, with critical stops along the way for the fall, the call of Abraham, the rise and fall and rise again of Israel, the resurrection, the gift of the Spirit and the birth of the church. Nor can we ignore great theological structures, including the Trinitarian nature of the Godhead, all that the cross achieves, and the unavoidable implications of New Testament eschatology with its underlying combination of inaugurated and future eschatology.[54]

---

49. Carson, *Christ and Culture Revisited*, 37; italics in original.

50. Carson, *Christ and Culture Revisited*, 38.

51. Carson also argues that Niebuhr's second typology, "Christ of culture," is scripturally unfounded: "Niebuhr's second pattern is certainly found in historical movements, but these movements are of doubtful Christian authenticity and have no warrant in the Bible." Carson, *Christ and Culture Revisited*, 40.

52. Carson, *Christ and Culture Revisited*, 41.

53. Carson, *Christ and Culture Revisited*, 41.

54. Carson, *Christ and Culture Revisited*, 226.

Carson contends that it is not enough to examine a wide range of biblical texts and see what each one says. We also need to listen to the voices in relation to the grand biblical and theological scheme of creation, fall, redemption and consummation. In short, it is imperative to understand the relation between Christ and culture within the *flow* of the divine drama.[55]

Carson is also concerned that whatever models we conceive should be grounded in Scripture.

> If for any reason we continue to think of different models of the relation between Christ and culture, we must insist that they are not *alternative* models, that we may choose to accept or reject. Rather, we shall ask in what sense they are grounded in the Scriptures and ponder their interrelations *within* the Scriptures, and how and when they should be emphasized under different circumstances exemplified *in* the Scriptures.[56]

Thinking about the relation between Christ and culture is thus not a matter of preference of one paradigm over another, but of discerning a holistically biblical pattern. Moreover, "As empirically useful as certain grids may be, thoughtful Christians need to adopt an extra degree of hesitation about canonizing any of them."[57] Further, Niebuhr's discrete paradigms do not accurately reflect the rich and complex nature of scripture. Scripture is like a multi-faceted diamond. It shines with multiple colors depending on how you are looking at it.

Eschatologically speaking, we are living in a time of tension. Jesus inaugurated the kingdom of God. Yet, this kingdom will not be consummated until his second coming. Hence, it is not either "Christ against culture" or "Christ transforming culture," but should be both. Carson therefore argues that Christians must live as a "people in tension."[58] He writes, "On the

---

55. The non-negotiables of biblical theology that Carson suggests should act as the framework for all approaches to Christ and culture. Indeed, some differences in approach may result from how one understands the big picture of the divine drama. For instance, as noted above, the difference between the Anabaptist (Christ against culture) and the Neo-Calvinist (Christ transforming culture) approach (see my footnote 48 in this chapter).

56. Carson, *Christ and Culture Revisited*, 62; italics in original.

57. Carson, *Christ and Culture Revisited*, 224.

58. Carson, *Christ and Culture Revisited*, 64. Carson utilizes Jesus' famous utterance, "Give back to Caesar what is Caesar's, and to God what is God's" (Matt 22:21; Mark 12:17; Luke 20:25) to explain how we should understand the tension that exists in the Christian life. He avers, "Jesus does not encourage withholding taxes. The traditional interpretation of Mark 12 is surely the obvious one and is in line with the sweeping New

one hand, we belong to the broader culture in which we find ourselves; on the other, we belong to the culture of the consummated kingdom of God, which has dawned among us."[59] This tension exists in the Christian life, but we're not free to ignore or reject the tension. Rather, Christians must embrace the tension and seek the welfare of the city while we wait for the final consummation of the creation.

Carson's effort to reshape Niebuhr's five typologies is commendable. Through the eyes of a biblical scholar, he rightly points out the weaknesses of Niebuhr's typologies and suggests helpful corrections. Although Carson does not offer his own typology, one cannot discredit his contribution to the issue of Christ and culture. Carson's modifications to Niebuhr's five typologies have made them a better heuristic device for twenty-first century Christians.

Max Stackhouse

Max L. Stackhouse was the late Emeritus Professor of Theology and Society at Princeton University and one of the leading public theologians of the twenty-first century. He has written numerous books and articles in the area of public theology and Christian ethics. His approach to public theology is apologetic rather than confessional.

Stackhouse defines public theology as theology that is grounded in dogmatic theology, yet whose function is polemical and apologetic. Stackhouse argues that systematic theology is primarily a "work of the modern academy,"[60] while public theology's main purpose is "to seek to identify those genuinely universalistic dimensions of divine reality and of human existence that are indispensable aspects of theology."[61] In other words, while systematic theology is confessional in nature and therefore not always intelligible to those outside of the Christian faith, public theology goes beyond this to identify the "transnational aspects of faith and morality, but . . . also

---

Testament tension between inaugurated eschatology and consummation: Jesus already claims that all authority in heaven and earth is his (Matthew 28) and he is presented as the mediatorial king who exercises all of God's sweeping authority (1 Corinthians 15), and yet that authority is itself mediated and frequently contested until the consummation." Carson, *Christ and Culture Revisited*, 160.

59. Carson, *Christ and Culture Revisited*, 160.
60. Stackhouse, *Shaping Public Theology*, 187.
61. Stackhouse, *God and Globalization*, 4:84.

self-consciously draws from an equally strong apologetics emphasis."[62] Although divine revelation is indispensable to public theology, its purpose is not to remain within the Christian community. Public theology is therefore apologetic rather than confessional.

In light of the transnational aspects of faith and morality in public theology, Stackhouse argues that public theology is a public discourse. Hence, pubic theology has the potential to make a significant contribution to public life. Stackhouse identifies two reasons for engaging in public theology.

> First, because that which we as Christians believe we have to offer the world for its salvation is not esoteric, privileged, irrational, or inaccessible. It is something that we believe to be both comprehensible and indispensable for all, something that we can reasonably discuss with Hindus and Buddhists, Jews and Muslims, Humanists and Marxists. Second, such a theology will give guidance to the structures and policies of public life. It is ethical in nature. The truth for which we argue must imply a viable element of justice, and its adequacy can be tested on that basis.[63]

If public theology is a public discourse, the public theologian should be able to speak to those outside the Christian faith in an intelligible manner by appealing to its universality. In so doing, Christian theology can bring significant change to society and redirect it in a way that reflects God's design for human relationships.[64]

Stackhouse argues that divine sovereignty makes such a social order possible. He contends, "Reformation Protestants depend on the basic doctrine of the sovereignty of God, a doctrine that implies that all areas of life are under God, and thus no earthly power can be sovereign over them all."[65] Stackhouse argues that despite differences in culture, traditions, and religions, there are universal laws that exist transcendentally. There are many goods (e.g., love and kindness) and wrongs (e.g., murder and theft) that

---

62. Stackhouse, *Shaping Public Theology*, 119.

63. Stackhouse, *Public Theology and Political Economy*, xi. Stackhouse argues for the Wesleyan Quadrilateral (scripture, tradition, reason, and experience) as the touchstones of authority. See chapter 1 of *Public Theology and Political Economy*.

64. Stackhouse takes the issue further. He argues that Christianity must engage natural science and the social sciences in order to "find out which kinds of faith enhance life and which lead to contempt for all that is holy to incoherence, injustice, or poverty and want." Stackhouse, *Shaping Public Theology*, 119. For details on the interface of Christianity with the social sciences, see Reese, "Social Sciences" and "Sociology," 632–34.

65. Stackhouse, *Shaping Public Theology*, 202.

humanity can come to agreement on that transcend differences in traditions, cultures and religions.[66]

Further, Stackhouse argues that religion is the basis of human community. Social science, having attempted to replace religion by understanding and controlling human behavior, has failed in its mission.[67] Stackhouse notes that "the problem was the basis or foundation for this reorganization."[68] Science attempted to appeal to moral grounds without referring to God. As a result, it failed to bring significant change to society.[69] Hence, public theology is needed since a reliable basis for religious assessment, ethical judgment, and public discourse is essential to the fabric of human community.

Stackhouse thus argues that "Christian public theology points toward a social order that is as close to how God wants us to live together as humanity has yet discerned."[70] Yet, such a social order first forms in "ecclesiology, then in civil society and through the influence of these as carried by ordinary believers into the political realm."[71] Because public theology is a "revelatory source that stands as the norm,"[72] it echoes "'top-down' reality as not having implications for the political order in the first instance, but

---

66. Some sociologists would disagree with Stackhouse on this. A sociology professor I had as an undergraduate fervently denied the universality of morality and values. He argued that in some parts of Africa a husband beating his wife is considered an expression of love. In fact, when a wife gets severely beaten by her husband, she reportedly goes to her friends and brags about how much her husband loves her. But the fact that some cultures have skewed views of human rights does not entail that such rights do not exist. The effects of sin operate both individually and culturally. The Christian faith contains the moral resources to counter such barbaric practices.

67. The fathers of sociology, Auguste Comte and Émile Durkheim, while attempting to replace religion with social science, understood that religion functions as a source of solidarity for society. In fact, Durkheim conducted studies to understand what common denominators might exist in religions in different cultures. See Reese, "Émile Durkheim," 195–96.

68. Stackhouse, *Shaping Public Theology*, 122.

69. Stackhouse argues that it is not only the sciences that failed to build a genuine foundation for human flourishing, but also other schools of thought that arose as a reaction to modernity, such as the premodernist (e.g., traditionalism) and hypermodernist (e.g., libertarian individualism, liberationist nationalism). All of these failed since they also lacked a transcendent foundation for morality. See Stackhouse, *Shaping Public Theology*, 118–28.

70. Stackhouse, *Shaping Public Theology*, 201.

71. Stackhouse, *Shaping Public Theology*, 201.

72. Stackhouse, *Shaping Public Theology*, 203.

first of all for inner personal convictions, the communities of faith, and the associations that they generate in an open society."[73] Stackhouse continues,

> With the proper cultivation and development, they [the principles and purposes of public theology] are refined as they work their way not from the bottom up, nor from the top down, but from the center out. They show up eventually in the formation of a limited constitutional political order that serves the people, protects their human rights, and allows the multiple institutions and spheres of a pluralistic society to flourish in the glory of God, and by their constantly prophetic, priestly, and princely mutual correction, serve the well-being of an unavoidably sinful, but morally and spiritually edified, community of communities.[74]

In short, since public theology is a theology which is grounded in the divine revelation, it has the power to transform society. As a result, the lives of people in society will be changed.

How then should Christians live? God calls all of us to take care of the world and participate in his salvific plan for the whole creation. Further, we are called to "form communities of mutual responsibility as we live out our vocations. People require one another to be whole, and persons in community require a shared framework of common moral obligation that provides the principles by which to structure these relationships."[75] Hence, the significance of the church should not be underestimated. As stated above, social reform takes place in the church first, then in society.

Stackhouse holds that the task of the church is to be a "theological center."[76] The church must continue to preach and teach the Scripture "so as to explore the public as well as the personal theological content of the faith."[77] Theology functions as a norm, teaching us God's will for society. In fact, Stackhouse argues, "Every vital theology evokes personal commitment to shape habits and relationships that accord with the best we can know of God's will."[78] Hence, the church must continue to preach the Word: The divine truth works in our heart to generate inner personal conviction

---

73. Stackhouse, *Shaping Public Theology*, 203.
74. Stackhouse, *Shaping Public Theology*, 203.
75. Stackhouse, *Public Theology and Political Economy*, 26.
76. Stackhouse, "Public Theology and the Future of Democratic Society," 80.
77. Stackhouse, "Public Theology and the Future of Democratic Society," 80.
78. Stackhouse, "Christian Social Ethics in a Global Era," 13.

and form the communities of faith which become the basis for engagement in public discourse.

Stackhouse observes, "We must seek the conversion of souls, bringing people to the recognition of their relation to a source beyond themselves; living in a covenanted association of people . . . will inspire and support virtuous habits and invite action toward a responsible society."[79] Public theology therefore seeks to identify the universalistic dimension of the divine reality for the purpose of inviting those outside our faith to the true source of change, God. In so doing, God enables us to create a society that accords with his will.

James Davison Hunter

James Davison Hunter is the LaBrosse-Levinson Distinguished Professor of Religion, Culture, and Social Theory at the University of Virginia. He seeks to find a new way for Christians to engage with the twenty-first century world. Hunter supports his claims using sociological and historical evidence and contends that the traditional ways of Christian engagement are based on flawed social theory and therefore ineffective in achieving their goals.[80] Hunter makes two significant arguments based on sociological evidence.

First, Hunter contends that the traditional means of engagement encourage Christians to evangelize people in order to bring change to society. This basic principle derives from a belief that the more Christians there are in society, the stronger the Christian influence will be because "cultures are shaped from the cumulative values and beliefs that reside in the hearts and minds of ordinary people. The means and ends of world-changing . . . are to change the hearts and minds of enough people that the social order will finally come to reflect the values and beliefs that they hold."[81] Yet, Hunter contends that this is a misconception since none of the evidence of history and sociology support such a theory. On the contrary, changes in society

---

79. Stackhouse, "Christian Social Ethics in a Global Era," 68.

80. Hunter defines three paradigms of engagement: "defense against," "relevance to," and "purity from." The "defense against" paradigm seeks to emphasize the differences between Christianity and secular society, while the "relevance to" paradigm seeks to be relevant to secular society. The "purity from" paradigm is a separatist approach, often represented by Anabaptists. For further information, see chapter 2 of Hunter, *To Change the World*.

81. Hunter, *To Change the World*, 274.

often take place when people in positions of power work together for a common purpose through networks of the elite.

Second, our traditional ways of cultural engagement are no longer adequate for the cultural changes that our modern society has experienced. Two such changes resulting from modern pluralism are "difference" and "dissolution."[82] Hunter argues that the prevalence of "difference" does not foster religious belief that is strong and coherent because of the lack of surrounding cultural structures to reinforce such beliefs. "Dissolution," on the other hand, creates skepticism about basic features of reality. Furthermore, "They [difference and dissolution] present conditions advantageous for the development of nihilism—genial and otherwise."[83] Hunter writes,

> The power of will first becomes nihilistic at the point at which it becomes absolute; when it submits to no authority higher than itself; that is, when impulse and desire become their own moral gauge and when it is guided by no other ends than its own exercise. The nature of pluralism . . . creates conditions in which one is required to choose. The dynamics of dissolution are that it dissolves all reality, all meaningful authority, and all meaningful moral purposes but will. In America, nihilism of this kind tends to foster a culture of banality that is manifested as self-indulgence, acquisition for its own sake, and empty spectacle that makes so much of popular culture and consumer culture trivial.[84]

Difference and dissolution not only undermine the "credibility and coherence of faith" and therefore our capacity to function as faithful witnesses of Christ, but also shifts our eyes to our own agenda rather than seeking God's will. Eventually, the basis of cultural engagement becomes coercion and force.

Therefore, Hunter argues for a new approach. But, it must be remembered that this new approach should not be taken as a means to manifest or utilize one's power to influence. God invites humanity who is made in the image of God to participate in world-making since "world-making is an

---

82. Hunter explains "difference" as various worldviews, beliefs, or cultures that surround us and make claims as to how we should perceive the world. On the other hand, Hunter defines "dissolution" to be the "deconstruction of the most basic assumptions about reality." Hunter, *To Change the World*, 205.

83. Hunter, *To Change the World*, 211. Hunter defines nihilism as "autonomous desire and unfettered will legitimated by the ideology and practice of choice" (211).

84. Hunter, *To Change the World*, 211.

expression of our divine nature."[85] Yet, Hunter qualifies that "it is also important to underscore that while the activity of culture-making has validity before God, this work is not, strictly speaking, redemptive or salvific in character. Where Christians participate in the work of world-building they are not, in any precise sense of the phrase, 'building the kingdom of God.'"[86]

Hunter argues that the concept "building the kingdom of God" is indeed a dangerous idea. It invokes the idea of "taking over" or "conquering" which leads to a type of Constantinian engagement. He contends, "The ideal is to shift to a *post*-Constantinian engagement, which means a way of engaging the world that neither seeks domination nor defines identity and witness over against domination."[87] Christians are not here to dominate or take over the culture. But, our engagement with the culture should proclaim the coming of the kingdom and be the foretaste of what is to come. Hunter states,

> *If there are benevolent consequences of our engagement with the world . . . it is precisely because it is **not** rooted in a desire to change the world for the better but rather because it is an expression of desire to honor the creator of all goodness, beauty, and truth, a manifestation of our loving obedience to God, and a fulfillment of God's command to love our neighbor.*[88]

---

85. Hunter, *To Change the World*, 232.

86. Hunter, *To Change the World*, 233.

87. Hunter, *To Change the World*, 280; italics in original. Hunter's strong words against Constantinianism echo his great concerns over the Christian traditions derived from Constantinianism. "It is essential in my view, to abandon altogether talk of 'redeeming the culture,' 'advancing the kingdom,' 'building the kingdom,' 'transforming the world,' 'reclaiming the culture,' 'reforming the culture,' and 'changing the world.' Christians need to leave such language behind them because it carries too much weight. It implies conquest, take-over, or dominion, which in my view is precisely what God does not call us to pursue." Hunter, *To Change the World*, 280. An interesting contrast to Hunter is Peter J. Leithart, who argues for Constantinianism: "Constantine provides in many respects a model for Christian political practice." Leithart, *Defending Constantine*, 11. Despite their differences, there seem to be points of agreement between these two scholars. Leithart's criticism of "Americanism," which he defines as "the fundamental theology of the American order, a quasi-Christian, biblically laced heresy." Leithart, *Between Babel and Beast*, xii and Hunter's criticism of traditional Christian cultural engagement seem to overlap in many ways. Indeed, one of Leithart's main arguments concerns how Christendom, "God's *imperium*," lost its metapolitical framework of Christian politics to secular politics over the centuries and how this contributed to the birth of "Americanism." See Leithart's *Between Babel and Beast* for further details.

88. Hunter, *To Change the World*, 234; italics and emphasis in original.

The primary goal of Christian cultural engagement, contrary to what Christians traditionally believe, is not to bring change to the world. Rather, Hunter argues that the world cannot be changed.[89] Instead, the purpose of participating in world-making is ultimately to honor God, the Creator, for his goodness and to fulfill our duty to love our neighbors as God commands us.

In addition to this, Hunter argues that this new approach needs structures that can support a coherent belief system. "Most of us . . . need the reinforcement that social institutions provide to believe coherently and live with integrity. . . . Strong and coherent beliefs require strong institutions enveloping those who aspire to believe."[90] Happily, the church is a social institution that can provide the structures that Christians need in this pluralistic world.[91] Hunter explains,

> Only within strong communities can one find the relational means to sustain the difficulties endemic to life in the modern world. Only within strong institutions can one find the resources to resist its destructive influences and pressures. . . . As a community and an institution, the church is a plausibility structure and the only one with the resources capable of offering an alternative formation to that offered by popular culture.[92]

Therefore, the church must be at the center of Christian cultural engagement. Further, the church must embody the peace of God to the world which is a "vision of order and harmony, fruitfulness and abundance, wholeness, beauty, joy, and well-being."[93] Indeed, God sent his Son to model the peace of God. Hence, all believers are to be conformed to Christ and live peacefully together.

Hunter proposes a "theology of faithful presence" as a new approach that Christians should take in order to be the light and salt of the world. He

---

89. Hunter questions, "Will engaging the world in the way discussed here change the world? This I believe is the wrong question. The question is wrong in part because it is based on the dubious assumption that the world, and thus history, can be controlled and managed." Hunter, *To Change the World*, 285.

90. Hunter, *To Change the World*, 202.

91. Peter L. Berger calls these structures "plausibility structures." Berger states, "There is a direct relation between the cohesion of institutions and the subjective cohesiveness of beliefs, values and worldviews." Berger, *Heretical Imperative*, 18. See also Berger and Luckmann, *Social Construction of Reality*.

92. Hunter, *To Change the World*, 282–83.

93. Hunter, *To Change the World*, 228.

states, "A theology of faithful presence begins with an acknowledgement of God's faithful presence to us and that his call upon us is that we be faithfully present to him in return. This is the foundation, the logic, the paradigm."[94] Faithful presence calls us to be present to others who are inside or outside the community. This presence requires sacrificial love. Further, faithful presence calls for us to be faithful to our vocational tasks, which we are to strive for excellence in. Through these tasks, Christians honor God.

However, Hunter does not overlook the tension that may result from faithful presence in the world. Although Christians are to embody the peace of God through our conduct and love, this does not mean "passive conformity to the established structures."[95] Rather, Hunter contends,

> Within the dialectic between affirmation and antithesis, faithful presence means a constructive resistance that seeks new patterns of social organization that challenge, undermine, and otherwise diminish oppression, injustice, enmity, and corruption and, in turn, encourage harmony, fruitfulness and abundance, wholeness, beauty, joy, security, and well-being.[96]

We must thus seek new patterns of social organization that promote human flourishing. Hunter relates how Christians in a pluralistic world should not attempt to subjugate society but respond with a "'bursting out' of an alternative within the proper space of the old" social structures.[97] Christians are not outsiders to society, but insiders who are given a new identity in Christ. Hence, as the Israelites in the exile were commanded by God to seek the welfare of the city (Jer 29:4–7), we must also seek the welfare of the city, and commit ourselves to contributing to human flourishing. Yet, the welfare of the city cannot be sought out by force or coercion, but by being a faithful witness through seeking the will of God. As Jesus embodied the peace of God on earth, we should follow him and conduct ourselves in

---

94. Hunter, *To Change the World*, 243.
95. Hunter, *To Change the World*, 247.
96. Hunter, *To Change the World*, 247–48.
97. Hunter, *To Change the World*, 248. Hunter borrows the concept of "bursting out" from Miraslov Volf. Volf writes, "Christian difference is . . . not an insertion of something new into the old from the outside, but a bursting out of the new *precisely within the proper space of the old.*" Volf, "Soft Difference," 19; italics in original. Volf does not see Christians as complete outsiders in society, but rather those who have been given a new identity by conversion: "They are not outsiders who either seek to become insiders or maintain strenuously the status of outsiders. Christians are the *insiders* who have diverted from their culture by being born again." Volf, "Soft Difference," 18–19; italics in original.

a way that similarly exemplifies the peace of God in the world. In so doing, Christians can truly become the salt and light of the world.

Stanley Hauerwas

Stanley Hauerwas is a United Methodist theologian and ethicist who is also Gilbert T. Rowe Professor Emeritus of Divinity and Law at Duke University. He was named "America's Best Theologian" by *Time* magazine in 2001. He has authored many books and articles, and written extensively on Christian pacifism and its place in the theology and life of the church. Hauerwas has been greatly influenced by John Howard Yoder, the Mennonite scholar known for his defense of Christian pacifism.[98]

In *Resident Aliens: A Provocative Christian Assessment of Culture and Ministry for People Who Know that Something Is Wrong*, Hauerwas offers scathing criticisms of both Christian conservatives and liberals in regard to political engagement. He contends, "Both [the conservative and liberal church] assume wrongly that the American church's primary social task is to underwrite American democracy. In so doing, they have unwittingly underwritten the moral presuppositions that destroy the church."[99] Hauerwas asserts that the church should be "something the world is not and can never be, lacking the gift of faith and vision, which is ours in Christ."[100] He insists

---

98. Hauerwas argues that Christian pacifism is not merely one of many moral options that Christians can choose. Rather, "We cannot be anything other than nonviolent . . . nonviolence is simply one of the essential practices that is intrinsic to the story of being a Christian." Hauerwas, *Dispatched from the Front*, 137. In fact, his conviction led him to resign from the editorial board of *First Things* in 2002 following a disagreement with the editors over their view of war in response to the terrorist attacks of September 11, 2001.

99. Hauerwas and Willimon, *Resident Aliens*, 32.

100. Hauerwas and Willimon, *Resident Aliens*, 46. In contrast to Niebuhr's typology in *Christ and Culture*, Hauerwas employs John Howard Yoder's typology of churches which are the activist church, conversionist church and confessing church. Not surprisingly, Hauerwas sees the ideal church to be the confessing church, which is "a radical alternative" and "finds its main political task to lie, not in the personal transformation of individual hearts [the conversionist church] or the modification of society [the activist church], but rather in the congregation's determination to worship Christ in all things." Hauerwas and Willimon, *Resident Aliens*, 45. Hauerwas is known for his criticism of Richard H. Niebuhr. In fact, he disparages Niebuhr's *Christ and Culture* as "a . . . hindrance to an accurate assessment of our situation" because "his call to Christians to accept 'culture' . . . and politics in the name of the unity of God's creating and redeeming activity had the effect of endorsing a Constantinian social strategy." Hauerwas and

that the church should not accommodate itself to the world, but should stand in opposition to the world.

Hauerwas argues that Christians are resident aliens. We are not of this world, although we are in the world. Yet, this does not mean that the church is anti-world. On the contrary, Hauerwas argues that the first social task and ethic of the church is to help the world understand what has gone wrong with the world due to the fall. In short, the task of the church is not so much doing (e.g., Christian political engagement), but showing the world what is wrong with it.

Hauerwas argues that the church can actively engage with the world by helping the world to perceive itself in the light of the gospel. He explains, "It is a call for the church to be a community which tries to develop the resources to stand within the world witnessing to the peaceable kingdom and thus rightly understanding the world."[101] The church should serve as a resource to the world because "the church gives us the interpretive skills, a truthful understanding whereby we first seek the world for what it is."[102] Faithful witness to the peaceable kingdom is how the church witnesses to the world.

Hauerwas argues that the church should embody the life of Jesus as he embodied how God rules the world. Jesus was crucified because he challenged the conventions of the world: Jesus did not use coercion to overcome evil, but overcame evil by being non-violent. In fact, Jesus' teachings and actions proclaimed to the world the "inbreaking kingdom of God, which brought an end to other kingdoms."[103] Hauerwas writes,

> The Sermon on the Mount begins as an announcement of something that God has done to change the history of the world. In the Sermon we see the end of history, an ending made most explicit and visible in the crucifixion and resurrection of Jesus. Therefore, Christians begin our ethics, not with anxious, self-serving questions of what we ought to do as individuals to make history come

---

Willimon, *Resident Aliens*, 40. Hauerwas argues that the way Niebuhr describes the typology leads many to believe that "Christians are in an all-or-nothing relationship to the culture; that we must responsibly choose to be 'all,' or irresponsibly choose to be sectarian nothing" (41).

101. Hauerwas, *Peaceable Kingdom*, 107.
102. Hauerwas and Willimon, *Resident Aliens*, 38.
103. Hauerwas and Willimon, *Resident Aliens*, 87.

out right, because in Christ God has already made history come out right.[104]

In Christ, the eschatological kingdom of God is already being realized. However, this Kingdom is a glimpse of what is to come in the end. In the meantime, the church and Christians learn the way of God's rule in the world: As Christ suffered and sacrificed himself, Christians should also suffer. Hauerwas contends, "What the Christian has to give to the world is his very life."[105]

Consequently, violence does not belong to the kingdom of God. Power must be actively resisted in order for the world to see the kingdom of God, which is radically different from the kingdoms of the world.[106] This may mean death and suffering for us. But the Christian life is characterized by joy and peaceableness. Hauerwas asserts, "It cannot be our task to transform the violence of this world into God's peace, for in fact that has been done through the cross and resurrection of Jesus. Our joy is the simple willingness to live with the assurance of God's redemption."[107] The church is not expected to change the world because we are not called to transform the world, but rather to embody the life of Christ as a faithful witness to the world.

Hauerwas suggests that the church is not only a representative of the kingdom of God, but also a place where those who are faithful to their witness will be sustained and strengthened. He states, "Through the teaching, support, sacrifice, worship, and commitment of the church, utterly ordinary people are enabled to do some rather extraordinary, even heroic acts, not on the basis of their own gifts or abilities, but rather by having a

---

104. Hauerwas and Willimon, *Resident Aliens*, 87.

105. Hauerwas, *Dispatches from the Front*, 113.

106. Although Hauerwas is a committed pacifist, he expresses sympathy for those who employ coercive efforts to accomplish just ends. He states, "Although I have sympathy with this position and though it certainly cannot be discounted as a possibility for Christians, the problem with these attempts to commit the Christian to limited use of violence is that they too often distort the character of our alternatives. Violence used in the name of justice, or freedom, or equality is seldom simply a matter of justice—it is a matter of the power of some over others. Moreover, when violence is justified in principle as a necessary strategy for securing justice, it stills the imaginative search for nonviolent ways of resistance to injustice." Hauerwas, *Peaceable Kingdom*, 114.

107. Hauerwas, *Peaceable Kingdom*, 147.

community capable of sustaining Christian virtue." [108] Indeed, Christian ethics cannot exist outside the church.

Hauerwas continues, "If we offer ourselves to a truthful story and the community formed by listening to and enacting that story in the church, we will be transformed into people more significant than we could ever have been on our own."[109] Any political or cultural engagement outside the church risks Christian ethics being abstracted from the church. Outside the church, there is no resource for determining what Christian virtues may look like.[110] Consequently, apart from the church, Christians are unable to be sustained and strengthened in order to embody the life of Christ to the world.

For Hauerwas, the church plays an essential role for faithful Christians. But, fundamentally, the church is significant because "the Kingdom is inherently communal."[111] As Christians remember the life, death, and resurrection of Christ and take communion together, we will be united as one in Christ. And through such communal acts, the "church's life [becomes] part of God's Trinitarian life."[112] Indeed, one's Christian life cannot be sustained apart from the church. And as we become one in Christ, we experience a foretaste of the kingdom of God. For this reason, Christian ethics are not possible outside of the church because we can only experience the eschatological Kingdom when we are united with each other as the church.

Hauerwas thus challenges us to reconsider the methods we employ for Christian political engagement. The church should not remove itself from the world, but the world must come to see the radically different ways of the church in order to realize its own fallenness. Therefore, sectarianism is necessary. Despite appearances, this approach is an active engagement with the world in which the church displays Christian ethics, which only function within the context of the church. This is the only legitimate means of Christian political engagement.

---

108. Hauerwas and Willimon, *Resident Aliens*, 81.

109. Hauerwas and Willimon, *Resident Aliens*, 83.

110. Hauerwas criticizes both conservative and liberal churches in this context: "Both groups imply that one can practice Christian ethics without being in the Christian community. Both begin with the Constantinian assumption that there is no way for the gospel to be present in our world without asking the world to support our conviction through its own social and political institutionalization. The result is the gospel transformed into civil religion." Hauerwas and Willimon, *Resident Aliens*, 80–81.

111. Gingerich, "Church as Kingdom," 141.

112. Hauerwas, *Performing the Faith*, 160.

Richard John Neuhaus

With Richard John Neuhaus we turn from Protestant public theologians to an eminent Roman Catholic one. Neuhaus was a Lutheran pastor who later converted to Catholicism. He is a cultural icon and was one of the main activists for Christian political engagement, along with Jerry Falwell, in the 1980s. He was active in the American civil rights movement and protested against Vietnam War policy. He served as a pastor at a large parish in Brooklyn where the majority of the parishioners were economically depressed African Americans. He was also editor of the journal *First Things*.

In 1984, Neuhaus published his *magnum opus*, *The Naked Public Square: Religion and Democracy in America*. The book appealed to many conservative Christians who were seeking to establish a Christian presence in the public square, and it has become one of the most influential books in the area of Christianity and politics. In the book, Neuhaus argues that the "naked public square" is the result of the exclusion of religion and religiously grounded values from public discourse. He observes that it is "political doctrine and practice"[113] to enforce secularism in the public square since America is viewed as a secular society.

But, Neuhaus disagrees that America is a secular society since the majority of Americans still resonate with the values and morality of the Judeo-Christian tradition.[114] Further, Neuhaus contends, "The naked public square cannot remain naked. When the value-bearing institutions of religion and culture are excluded, the value-laden concerns of human life flow back into the square under the banner of politics."[115]

---

113. Neuhaus, *Naked Public Square*, ix.

114. The book was written in the first term of the presidency of Ronald Reagan. Prior to Reagan, Jimmy Carter had captured the attention of the American people by professing to be a born-again Christian. Hence, despite the predictions of many social scientists, Christianity was on the rise again. However, Neuhaus argues that despite the resurgence of Christianity in the 1980s, the values and morality of Americans have always been rooted in the Judeo-Christian tradition. America is indeed a religious society.

115. Neuhaus, *Naked Public Square*, 156. Some critics (e.g., Robert L. Maddox, Barry W. Lynn, and Oliver S. Thomas) argue that no naked public square exists. On the contrary, the presence of Christianity in the public square is visible and its influence is strong. However, Neuhaus debunks such criticism by pointing out that the government is not neutral toward religion. For example, the government may provide a grant for a religious organization that helps the poor. But, as soon as the government perceives anything distinctively religious about the program, it will withdraw the grant in the name of secularism. Neuhaus contends that "an alternative principle is that the government should be truly neutral toward religion. If a government program advances a legitimate

Yet, it is problematic that secularism teaches that religion has no role in the public square since religion is nothing more than privatized conscience. Writes Neuhaus, "Religion as a mediating structure—a community that generates and transmits moral values—is no longer available as a countervailing force to the ambitions of the state."[116] The ultimate consequence of the exclusion of religion is the possibility of totalitarianism by the state that destroys liberal democracy.[117]

Nonetheless, Neuhaus laments that in the past Christians' behavior in the public square has been either triumphalism/Constantinianism or sectarianism. Suffice it to say that neither approach fosters liberal democracy. Hence, in order to revive or maintain liberal democracy, a fresh approach is needed. Neuhaus argues that we need to "devise forms for that interaction [religion and politics] which can revive rather than destroy the liberal democracy that is required by a society that would be pluralistic and free."[118] Neuhaus contends that such forms must foster a democratic government which is "premised upon the acknowledgement of transcendent truth to which the political order is held accountable."[119] Further, "democracy assumes the lively interaction among people who are acting from values that are, in most instances, grounded in specific religious belief."[120] Hence, Neuhaus argues that we need a system that is neither triumphalist nor sectarian. That is, the relation between the church and the state should not be perceived as either domination or separation, but cooperation and complementarity, though tensions remain.[121]

Neuhaus proposes a theonomous culture as ideal for a liberal democratic society. He explains, "A theonomous culture . . . is one in which

---

public purpose, as democratically determined, it is a matter of indifference as to whether it also aids religion." Neuhaus, "Public Square," 80.

116. Neuhaus, *Naked Public Square*, 82.

117. Neuhaus further adds, "When particularist religious values and the institutions that bear them are excluded, the inescapable need to make public moral judgments will result in an elite construction of a normative morality from sources and principles not democratically recognized by the society." Neuhaus, *Naked Public Square*, 86. Liberal democracy, Neuhaus argues, is "the appropriate form of governance in a fallen creation in which no person or institution, including the church, can infallibly speak for God." Neuhaus, *Naked Public Square*, 116.

118. Neuhaus, *Naked Public Square*, 9.

119. Neuhaus, *Naked Public Square*, 120.

120. Neuhaus, *Naked Public Square*, 120.

121. Neuhaus, *Naked Public Square*, 170.

religious and cultural aspirations toward the transcendent are given public expression."[122] Yet, he is careful not to identify theonomy with theocracy. He states, "Theocracy is in fact a form of heteronomy in which an institution, namely religion, claims to embody and authoritatively articulate absolute truth. Theocracy is an act of historical closure, and therefore a form of idolatry."[123] A theonomous culture not only promotes liberal democracy, but also "suggests a 'sacred canopy' that legitimates a social order."[124]

Neuhaus states that the task of forming this new way for democratic society is difficult, but not impossible. He calls for religious leaders to "liberate themselves from their captivity to political partisanship. It [the public role of religion] will be decided by religion's ability to help construct a 'sacred canopy' for the American experiment."[125] He continues,

---

122. Neuhaus, *Naked Public Square*, 188. The logic behind Neuhaus's proposal here is that "politics is most importantly a function of culture, and at the heart of culture is religion, whether or not it is called by that name." Neuhaus, *Naked Public Square*, 190. As a result, religion must function as a resource in public life for revealing transcendent meaning. Neuhaus was greatly influenced by Paul Tillich on the idea of a theonomous culture. For details see Hauerwas, "Naked Public Square Now: A Symposium," 12.

123. Neuhaus, *Naked Public Square*, 188. Neuhaus is ambiguous on the meaning of *transcendent*, as Stanley Hauerwas points out Hauerwas, "The Naked Public Square Now: A Symposium," 12. Neuhaus responds to Hauerwas: "Today I would make the appeal more explicitly and insistently to the human capacity for reason, including moral reason. Natural law enters here, but somebody has to come up with a better term than natural law, which is too easily seen as a peculiarly Catholic thing." Neuhaus, "Naked Public Square Now: A Symposium," 24. Stanley J. Grenz sees Robert Bellah's influence in Neuhaus's work, especially in the idea of the "transcendent." Grenz states, "His concern for issues of public theology is in part rooted in the work of Talcott Parsons and Robert Bellah. The influence of Bellah, although largely unacknowledged, is present throughout *The Naked Public Square*, specifically in Neuhaus' fundamental thesis that some agreed-upon authority which transcends the community must be present for the proper function of any viable society." Grenz, "Reconsecrating the Public Square," 66. Andrew Murphy points out that to engage in the public square requires "humility and charity from all sides." Murphy, "Naked Public Square Now: A Symposium," 17. He continues, "To take the notion of engagement as seriously as Neuhaus' book demands, we might be required to see the public square as not only reflecting the nation's diverse faith commitments but also as itself requiring a leap of faith in which we bring our deepest (and divergent) values to a vibrant political debate without any guarantee that our side will win on any particular issue." Murphy, "Naked Public Square Now," 17. Neuhaus's public square is a diverse one characterized by various religious and secular beliefs. The challenge is to work together with other religious leaders in order to construct liberal democratic principles for America.

124. Neuhaus, *Naked Public Square*, 188.

125. Neuhaus, *Naked Public Square*, 60.

> Such a moral legitimation does not mean declaring that the way things are is legitimate. . . . Moral legitimation means providing a meaning and a purpose, and therefore a framework within which the violation of that meaning and purpose can be criticized. The vision that is required cannot be produced by the political process itself. Politics derives its directions from the ethics, from the cultural sensibilities that are the context of political action. The cultural context is shaped by our moral judgments and intuitions about how the world is and how it ought to be. Again, for the great majority of Americans such moral judgments and intuitions are inseparable from religious belief.[126]

The role of the church is significant in this context. The church can serve as the source of moral legitimation that provides a meaning and purpose. Neuhaus declares, "the state must be supported and judged by the transcendent truth that the church proclaims, and the church must be checked in her propensity to exercise in 'the city of man' a political power that is not rightly hers."[127] Hence, the church should not succumb to the supposed dualism of private and public belief. Religious belief is not privatized conscience that has no significant bearing on the public square. On the contrary, the church is the public source of transcendent truth. The sphere of the gospel is not irrelevant to the sphere of the law.[128] The two kingdoms of "the City of God" and "the City of Man" are distinct, yet not divorced: They are a twofold manifestation of God's kingdom.

Neuhaus challenges Christians to engage with society in order to create a theonomous culture because the public square cannot remain naked. Moreover, the church cannot be silent because the church is the source of moral legitimation. Although there is no guarantee that Christians can always influence public issues, we cannot avoid the public square. With a spirit of compromise and humility, we must seek to participate in the public square as moral actors.

---

126. Neuhaus, *Naked Public Square*, 60.
127. Neuhaus, *Naked Public Square*, 165.
128. Neuhaus, *Naked Public Square*, 115.

The Promise of Gunton's Pneumatology for a Trinitarian Public Theology: Gunton's Contribution to Public Theology

Despite the richness of the public theologies offered by the theologians examined above, none of them pays much, if any, attention to pneumatology. As a result, their understanding of the work of the Spirit in public theology is superficial. Instead, the Spirit seems to be viewed merely as an extension of Christ. When Christ is mentioned, the Spirit appears to be implicitly included.[129] Consequently, the Spirit's relation to the Father and the Son is not thought out in any concrete way as to how they may be working together for the transformation of the creation. Indeed, it is not only pneumatology that is noticeably missing from their theories, but also God's trinitarian nature.

This presents a lacuna in contemporary approaches to public theology and reveals the need for a robust pneumatology in this theological endeavor. When pneumatology is overlooked, there is a tendency to perceive God in a unitarian or binitarian manner. Suffice it to say that this creates a serious deficiency in one's theology. Gunton rightly argues, "Because God is triune, we must respond to him in a particular way, or rather set of ways, corresponding to the richness of his being."[130] To fail to perceive God trinitarianly means that we begin on the wrong foot. Gunton continues, "In turn, that means that everything looks—and, indeed, is—different in the light of the Trinity."[131] Thus, we must approach God trinitarianly. Gunton's pneumatology provides a firmer foundation for public theological inquiry and helps settle several important questions whose answers must guide our

---

129. This point is especially clear in the case of Niebuhr. To be fair, Niebuhr has, in my opinion, the clearest understanding of the triune Creator in relation to the transformation of the world among the six theologians surveyed. Niebuhr clearly acknowledges the creating and redeeming work of the triune God in his median types. In regard to the Thomistic system, the Christ above culture typology, he argues, "The whole effort at synthesis here is informed by, if not grounded on, the conviction of which Trinitarian doctrine is a verbal expression; namely, that the Creator of nature and Jesus Christ and the immanent Spirit are of one essence. Man does not possess three ways to truth, but has been given ways to three truths; and these three truths form one system of truth." Niebuhr, *Christ and Culture*, 131. Nonetheless, the eschatological Spirit is perceived as the immanent Spirit rather than the transcendent Spirit. Accordingly, he fails sufficiently to distinguish the Spirit from Christ in their work of transforming the world.

130. Gunton, *Promise of Trinitarian Theology*, 4.

131. Gunton, *Promise of Trinitarian Theology*, 4–5.

hermeneutics: Who is God, what is he doing with the world, and how is he guiding the world to its ultimate end?

Trinitarian thinking is indispensable to "undo the old bifurcation between the cultural mandate and the great commission."[132] These issues have been approached apart from considering the Trinity so that the two commandments are not perceived within the divine intention of creation and redemption. As a result, the complementary nature of the two commandments is overlooked. We are not forced to choose one or the other, but the two go hand-in-hand in order to achieve the ultimate plan of God for the world.

One perceives the tendency to bifurcate these commandments, for example, in the case of D. A. Carson. His understanding of the creation story seems thin because he does not view it through the lens of God's triune nature and work.[133] Yet, he emphasizes the importance of a trinitarian theology of the Godhead in public theology, even including it as one of the non-negotiables of biblical theology. This is where Gunton's robust pneumatology can be helpful. Gunton argues that a weak pneumatology has plagued Western theology since the time of Augustine. There is a tendency in Western theology to perceive the Spirit as the bond of love that unites the Father and the Son. Hence, the bond of love is hardly perceived as a person, contrary to the nature of the triune God.

Yet, as Gunton argues, the Scripture attests that the Spirit is the eschatological Spirit. If one overlooks the work and person of the Spirit, one's theology is deprived of the third aspect of the creation story: the Spirit's perfecting work. Indeed, when one surveys Carson's non-negotiables of biblical theology, it seems clear that the Spirit's relation to the Father and

---

132. Smith, "Thinking Biblically about Culture," 23.

133. Smith rightly points to this weakness of Carson's theology. He argues, "Given the riches of biblical wisdom across its canonical sweep, Carson's plot summary of the story is puzzling. While he emphasizes the doctrine of creation—that 'God made everything' (45)—he nowhere attends to what has commonly been described as the 'cultural mandate,' the call embedded in creation for humans to *cultivate* the earth (Gen. 1:27–29)." Smith, "Thinking Biblically about Culture," 22; italics in original. Indeed, Carson rather quickly dismisses the cultural mandate as "peculiar responsibilities toward the rest of the created order" that we have as God's image bearers, without any elaboration. Carson, *Christ and Culture Revisited*, 46. Smith continues, "A weak theology of creation will lack a clear theology of culture as a task given to humanity as image bearers of God. This perhaps explains why, for Carson, 'culture' always seems to be a noun (something 'out there') rather than a verb (something we *do*)." Smith, "Thinking Biblically about Culture," 22; italics in original.

the Son is not taken into account.¹³⁴ Hence, a holistic trinitarian thinking is missing. But seen through a trinitarian lens, the distinct work of each person of the Trinity becomes clear. The Father, who is the fountainhead of the three persons, reaches out to the world through his two hands, the Son and the Spirit, as Gunton frequently reiterates. While the Son who is the mediator of creation and redemption works incarnationally by identifying himself with the world through becoming human and instituting a new beginning for fallen humanity, the Spirit works both transcendently and immanently in perfecting and transforming the creation (humanity and the created world) to bring all things into relation to the Father through the Son. Yet, their work should be understood as unified although they are distinct. They are united in one goal, namely, to transform the whole creation.

Hence, I argue that the old bifurcation of the cultural mandate and the great commission can be eliminated by viewing both in light of the unified work of the three persons of the Trinity. In my view, it is not enough to read the Bible canonically, we must also read it trinitarianly. When we read the Bible trinitarianly, it helps us to see who the triune God is and how he is working in order to bring ultimate redemption to the world. Gunton's trinitarian theology, which is illuminated by his robust pneumatology, enables us to shift our eyes to the triune Creator.

Similarly, Gunton's robust pneumatology leads us to conclude that the nature of culture is redemptive.¹³⁵ He presents a cogent argument for the eschatological Spirit who perfects and transforms the created world. Hence, it is not only humanity that will be redeemed, but also the created world because the creation will be "brought into the glorious freedom of the children of God" (Rom 8:21). Since culture is a significant aspect of the

---

134. This point appears more prominently in Carson's criticism of Vincent Bacote's cosmic pneumatology. He questions how "these complementary roles of the Spirit are properly related to each other (the Spirit's role in creation and the Spirit's role in redemption)." Carson, *Christ and Culture Revisited*, 215. I sympathize with Carson's concern that Bacote's cosmic pneumatology appears to stand alone, apart from Christ. Nonetheless, this is no indication that the Spirit's work in creation has no bearing on redemption. On the contrary, trinitarian thinking enables us to see the intricate relation between Christ and the Spirit in redeeming the creation.

135. Gunton argues, "Culture, we might say, is that set of activities in which those made in the image of God share in the divine perfecting of that which was made in the beginning." Gunton, "Reformation Accounts of the Church's Response to Human Culture," 80. Similarly, Niebuhr contends that culture is redemptive since it is "corrupted order rather than order for corruption." Niebuhr, *Christ and Culture*, 194. That is, culture is a creational good in itself. See footnote 44 in this chapter for further details on Niebuhr's view of culture.

created world, the Spirit uses it in his work of perfection and transformation; thus, culture is redemptive.

As examined above, Hunter contends that culture-making is not salvific or redemptive in character. He claims that it should by no means be taken as "building the kingdom of God." Furthermore, Hunter warns that Christians should not approach cultural engagement as a means of wielding power or achieving domination. In fact, culture cannot be changed by mere human effort. Instead, we should honor God by being faithful witnesses rather than attempting to change the world.

Perhaps the main difference between Gunton and Hunter is not primarily whether culture is redemptive, although they diverge on this point, but about how to understand the transformation. As noted above, Hunter and Hauerwas promote the more peaceful and non-violent approach toward cultural engagement that is aligned with the Anabaptist tradition. But, if one can prove that transformation arises from faithful witness and pacifism rather than triumphalism, it is possible that Hunter and Hauerwas would find common ground with Gunton.[136]

As I argued above, Gunton's pneumatology is robust because it is firmly grounded in the triune God. In divine love, the triune God reaches out to the creation through his two hands, the Son and the Spirit. This, I believe, frames the background for the nature of transformation by the Spirit. If the Spirit is the agent of transformation, the nature of the transformation should reflect the purpose of the divine mission. Gunton contends that the Son and the Spirit are agents of the Father's love. If so, whatever the Spirit perfects and transforms derives from the Father's love.

Indeed, Gunton argues that the purpose of the Spirit's work is reconciliation, not domination. If so, there is no place in cultural engagement for violence or oppression. The triune God does not transform the created world so that he can dominate or overpower those who oppose him. The world is already under his reign. But, he transforms the created world to bring about reconciliation, harmony and unity between God and humanity, between man and his fellow man, and between humanity and creation.

---

136. Hunter argues, "Within the dialectic between affirmation and antithesis, faithful presence means a constructive resistance that *seeks new patterns of social organization* that challenge, undermine, and otherwise diminish oppression, injustice, enmity and corruption." Hunter, *To Change the World*, 247; italics mine. This statement hints that, after all, Hunter expects some type of transformation to occur as a result of faithful presence.

Furthermore, although humanity is asked to participate in the divine transformation, we do not work apart from the Spirit who is the agent of transformation. On the contrary, we are to be directed by the Spirit. Thus, humanity has no ultimate power or ability to change the world, or even to perceive how to change the world aright. Unfortunately, many Christians fail to grasp this point and misconceive their role in the transformation of the world.[137]

It is the Spirit who transforms the world. And as Gunton argues, he transforms it by reconciling humanity with God, each other and the world. If so, humanity cannot change the world apart from the eschatological Spirit. The Spirit must first bring us to God. Only in the context of reconciliation does transformation of the world become possible. Therefore, we must forsake triumphalism and seek peace and love instead. Further, we must rely on the Spirit to lead us to the right path. It is not human power or ingenuity that changes the world, but our faithfulness to the Lord that brings godly change.[138]

The Spirit is elusive. The Spirit is like a wind that "blows wherever it pleases. You hear its sound, but you cannot tell where it comes from or where it is going" (John 3:8). We may not perceive the work of the Spirit as it happens. But, the Spirit is working among us to transform and perfect the created world. What is expected from us is our faithfulness to the Lord in the context of our reconciliation with him, each other and the world.

Gunton's full-bodied pneumatology also makes a significant contribution to public theology regarding the role of the church. As examined above, Neuhaus and Hauerwas differ on the nature of the church's role toward the world. Neuhaus seeks to establish a Christian presence in the public square. He argues that Christian belief should not be reduced to private belief. Rather, Christian belief is relevant to the public sphere. On the

---

137. Constantinianism is one example of such misconception.

138. As noted above, Hauerwas contends that "his [Niebuhr's] call to Christians to accept 'culture' . . . and politics in the name of the unity of God's creating and redeeming activity had the effect of endorsing a Constantinian social strategy." Hauerwas and Willimon, *Resident Aliens*, 40. This is one notable place where Gunton's full-bodied pneumatology can be helpful. The unity of God's creating and redeeming activity does not have to have the effect of endorsing a Constantinian social strategy if we understand the mission of the eschatological Spirit. The Spirit is sent by the Father through the Son to reconcile all creation with the Father, not to overpower it through force. But in light of the work of the eschatological Spirit, God's creating and redeeming activity need not be separated, nor be coercive, as the Spirit can work through culture and the church to bring peaceful restoration.

other hand, Hauerwas argues that Christians should not engage in politics. It is not the church's responsibility to transform this violent world into the peaceable kingdom of God. Rather, the church is called to be a faithful witness to the world and testify in such a way that the world sees its fallenness.

These theologians present persuasive arguments regarding whether to engage or not to engage with the world. Nonetheless, the eschatological Spirit is missing from their conceptions. Gunton holds, "The key to ecclesiology as to eschatology is pneumatology."[139] The church is constituted by the eschatological Spirit. If so, when one thinks about what the church's role should be in the world, the eschatological Spirit must be considered. Hence, Gunton's robust pneumatology can bring a fresh perspective to the role of the church in the public square.

Gunton maintains that the church is constituted by the eschatological Spirit by reconciling humanity with God, each other, and the created world. In so doing, he transforms and perfects the created world. If the church is constituted by the Spirit, the church must be eschatologically oriented. Hence, the nature of the church is eschatological, while the ultimate purpose of the church is reconciliation. Reconciliation begins with the church as the eschatological Spirit freely invites people to the church by reconciling them with God. Yet, the Spirit does not remain within the church. Instead, he goes out to bring people to Christ by reconciling them with God one at a time.

Further, Gunton argues that the church is a "community where that representative humanity becomes the form of the teleology of others."[140] Hence, the church is oriented outwardly. The church is not only the place for the reconciliation that is indispensable to the transformation of the world, it is also a community where humanity is nurtured and finds "a human way of being in and with the world."[141]

However, argues Gunton, "The heart of the constitution of the church by the Spirit is to be found in worship. Every act of worship that is in the Spirit is a constituting of the Church."[142] Despite the outwardness of the church in her orientation, the church is constituted inwardly. That is, the church cannot be the church unless there are acts of worship in the Spirit.

---

139. Gunton, *Father, Son and Holy Spirit*, 230.
140. Gunton, *Christ and Creation*, 111.
141. Gunton, *Triune Creator*, 205.
142. Gunton, *Transcendent Lord*, 15.

Though the church has an outward orientation, it is nonetheless rejuvenated by prayer and worship in the Spirit. This echoes Hunter's idea of the relation between the church and society.[143] Hunter argues for a "theology of faithful presence," but asserts that this approach requires social institutions that support Christians "to believe coherently and live with integrity."[144] For Hunter, and for Gunton, the church constitutes this "plausibility structure" for believers.

Similarly, Hauerwas argues that there is no Christian ethics apart from the Christian community. One can only practice Christian ethics within the Christian community. Therefore, although the church is oriented outwardly, Christians must remain within the church in order to be faithful witnesses to the world. And this is how the role of the church toward the world should be maintained.

Towards a Theoretical Framework for a Trinitarian Public Theology Informed by Pneumatology

Having examined Colin Gunton's contribution to public theology, we conclude that a robust pneumatology is necessary in order to further develop public theology. Public theology must be done with a view toward the transformation of the world. If so, hermeneutical questions such as the identity of the transforming agent and the purpose and object of the transformation need to be addressed. Doing so will enable us to suggest a basic theoretical framework for a trinitarian public theology. As discussed above, the eschatological Spirit is the agent of transformation. Yet, this aspect of the Spirit's work is underexplored.[145] Hence, building on Gunton's work, we can attempt a further contribution to public theology by further illuminating the work of the eschatological Spirit in the creation.

Moreover, this robust pneumatology must be firmly grounded in a trinitarian theology: the work of the Spirit must be perceived in relation to

---

143. Similarly, it also echoes Hauerwas.

144. Hunter, *To Change the World*, 202.

145. See Bacote, *Spirit in Public Theology*. Bacote's work is a unique exploration of cosmic pneumatology in relation to public theology that appropriates Abraham Kuyper's public theology. He lists several theologians who have done work in the area of cosmic pneumatology (e.g., Geiko Müller-Fahrenholz, Sinclair Ferguson, Jürgen Moltmann, Clark Pinnock, Mark Wallace and Colin Gunton). Yet, to my knowledge, no theologian has built on this work for the purpose of developing public theology in light of a trinitarian pneumatology.

the Father and the Son. It is only within this framework that we can have a holistic understanding of the mission of the triune God to reclaim the created world. In so doing, we will be able to discern how we should engage with culture as a participant in the divine redemption.

Given that the Spirit works within human culture to bring redemption, it is desirable to develop criteria for discerning the Spirit's work. In light of the Spirit's often subtle activity, it is difficult to discern how and where the Spirit may be working in transforming the world. Yet, if the eschatological Spirit is moving among us to transform the creation, we will sometimes be able to trace his footsteps. In *Father, Son and Holy Spirit*, published posthumously, Gunton wrote, "So also is it with all human culture where it is good, it is because it is enabled to be so by the power of the God who upholds all things in Christ."[146] He continued, "We are on the way to developing a criterion by which we may seek to judge whether or not any given cultural activity or artefact is the gift of the Spirit."[147] Unfortunately, due to his sudden passing, Gunton was not able to finish this task. With Gunton, I believe that such criteria can be constructed if pneumatology is trinitarianly conceived. As we move toward a trinitarian public theology, the work of the eschatological Spirit in relation to the Father and the Son must be explored. And as we learn more about the Spirit, we may be able to discern how he is working among us today.

What, then, is the promise of Gunton's pneumatology for trinitarian public theology? Gunton's pneumatology holds promise for eliminating the dualism between the spiritual and the material that has long existed in the history of Christianity. Further, Gunton's pneumatology posits that the Spirit is working to transform the world even in its fallen condition. This transforming work of the Spirit is reconciliation rather than conflict. Gunton's pneumatology argues for a promise of communion among human beings that mirrors the communion of the divine persons. We will be united through reconciliation as we forgive each other and are forgiven by God. In so doing, we will be perfected, albeit in a finite sense, in our communion with God, each other and the created world.

In addition to this, Gunton's pneumatology suggests a way to discern at least some of the Spirit's eschatological work in culture. Such discernment

---

146. Gunton, *Father, Son and Holy Spirit*, 121.

147. Gunton, *Father, Son and Holy Spirit*, 123. Gunton further adds, "Equally important, is the fact that the Spirit is free to enable those who by no means confess God's being and action to achieve the greatest of things" (123).

is challenging due to the Spirit's elusive nature. But this area has also been underexplored because a trinitarian pneumatology has been overlooked in the realm of public theology; yet one cannot discern the Spirit's work apart from the triune God. But Gunton's pneumatology, which is firmly grounded in the doctrine of the Trinity, enables us to suggest criteria for discerning the Spirit's work.

CRITERIA FOR DISCERNING THE SPIRIT'S WORK IN RELATION TO PUBLIC THEOLOGY

As mentioned in the previous section, it is difficult to discern the work of the Spirit due to his elusive nature. Yet, this does not mean that the Spirit's eschatological work is completely hidden from us. Amos Yong rightly argues,

> Christian discernment . . . is intricately tied to moral discernment as well as to the development of the human faculties of perception, understanding, and judgment in their broad senses. Growth in love and knowledge is inseparable from the acquisition of deep moral and perceptual insight, and all contribute to the continuing increase in the capacity of the Christian to accomplish moral and spiritual discernment.[148]

Thus, Christian discernment is a "skill that is developed over time."[149] One of the challenges of discerning the Spirit's work is acquiring the requisite sensitivity and wisdom. Yong contends that although discernment is one of the spiritual gifts (1 Cor 12:10), it takes time to develop. An essential aspect of nurturing our skills of discernment is to immerse ourselves in scripture and Christian living. Hence, discernment is not a supernatural ability that is instantly acquired, but rather a skill that is developed over time. If so, it is plausible to formulate criteria for discerning the Spirit's work. The criteria that I list in this section are by no means exhaustive. But, it is my hope that they move us forward in our attempt to discern the Spirit's work in culture in relation to public theology.

The first criterion is Scripturalness. Discerning the Spirit's eschatological work requires testing by the scripture. For example, when we encounter a social phenomenon that may look like the Spirit's work, it must

---

148. Yong, *Beyond the Impasse*, 145.
149. Yong, *Beyond the Impasse*, 146.

be examined in the light of God's revelation. Nonetheless, Yong cautiously adds that "such norms have to be sensitively applied to the concrete world of things."[150] It is one thing to apply biblical norms to current affairs, it is another to discern whether such norms are applied appropriately. Yong continues, "'Life in the Spirit' . . . requires reading both Scripture *and* the world accurately in order to ensure the appropriate applicability of scriptural norms to the world."[151] Christendom might have turned out differently had more caution been taken in applying biblical norms to the world appropriately.

The second criterion is the Trinitarianess. As Gunton has shown, it is imperative to perceive the eschatological work of the Spirit in light of the Trinity. The Spirit does not work alone. On the contrary, he works in accordance with the Son and Father. Yet, the Spirit is given his own distinct mission in relation to the Son and the Father. Therefore, in discernment, this balance (distinction in unity) must be maintained. It is not enough to discern the actions of the Spirit alone. Rather, we must discern whether a putative action of the Spirit is compatible with the work of the Father and the Son within the scheme of divine redemption.

The third criterion is communion-enabling. This criterion is derived from the nature and character of the third person of the Trinity. If the Spirit brings redemption to the world by creating an eschatological community, the actions of the Spirit must be characterized by communion. In other words, when we see reconciliation, love, and peace, it is plausible to argue that we are witnessing the Spirit at work. Michael Welker argues, "One can readily see with one's own eyes that love is the most complete of the forms of expression and communication in accordance with the Spirit. For in a differentiated way, love corresponds to the promised Spirit of righteousness and of peace."[152]

A fourth criterion is other person-centeredness expressed in love. When the eschatological Spirit is at work, people act for the benefit of others. The Spirit makes it possible for us to freely put others ahead of our own interests for the sake of the community.[153] Indeed, even a mundane thing like a father reconciling with his son or a son with his father (or a mother

---

150. Yong, *Beyond the Impasse*, 159.

151. Yong, *Beyond the Impasse*, 159; italics in original.

152. Welker, *God the Spirit*, 250.

153. Welker describes this as "free self-withdrawal for the benefits of others." Welker, *God the Spirit*, 252.

with her daughter) may be a sign of the work of the eschatological Spirit. Human love is fostered in our most basic relationships, such as family. If so, a reconciliation that takes place at home may go a long way in the eschatological work of the Spirit.

Welker argues that love is "in a way unmatched by any other power granted to human beings" because it is a "master in inventing exceptions that provide deliverance and promote life. Because love not only immerses itself in the beloved person, but also exercises a beneficial influence, both directly and indirectly, on that person's environment, love is continually building up new forms of life, both individual and communal."[154] Indeed, says Welker, "With its free self-withdrawal, love is contagious."[155] One can appreciate Welker's comments in relation to public theology. As argued above, the Spirit is the divine love. Hence, any actions of the Spirit should not contradict his nature. Yet, we often quickly dismiss the efficacy of love. We are more attracted to something powerful and heroic. But, the love that Christ exemplified on the cross is meek and humble. And if this is the love that the Spirit is testifying to in order to bring people to God, we should take a careful look at how we can promote God's love for the transformation of the created world. Indeed, all of the fruit of the Spirit (Gal 5:22) may be good criteria for discerning the work of the eschatological Spirit.

One potential pitfall of discerning the Spirit's work is confusing it with demonic activity. Yong argues that discernment includes "distinguishing between the divine, the human, and demonic."[156] Hence, there is always the possibility that what we are witnessing may be the result of demonic forces. Yong suggests that "evidence of demonic influence or infiltration consists in a thing's radical departure from its purposes and functions, thus affecting its relationships in a destructive manner."[157] Satan is cunning, and a master of deception. He disguises himself and can cause great destruction in the name of good.

In this light, we may also formulate negative criteria which suggest activities that are not of the Spirit but contrary to the Spirit's nature. For example, anything that does not produce the fruit of the Spirit is not the work of the Spirit (Gal 5:22). Attitudes or actions that display hatred, jealously, rage, selfish ambition, and the like are the work of the flesh rather than the

---

154. Welker, *God the Spirit*, 250.
155. Welker, *God the Spirit*, 250.
156. Yong, *Beyond the Impasse*, 157.
157. Yong, *Beyond the Impasse*, 158.

work of the Spirit (Gal 5:19–21). Our flesh thirsts for power, domination, and tyranny and seeks self-importance rather than humility and edification.[158] Indeed, when we neglect to "balance truth-telling with listening, justice with peace," the Spirit will not be among us "because the Spirit is the Spirit of truth (Jn. 16:12–13) and also the Spirit of love (Rom 5:5)."[159]

Further, the "spirit" that denies the Father and the Son is not the Spirit of God (1 John 4:1–3). Yong argues, "We discern the Spirit by discerning the Christ, but then also discern the Christ by the Spirit."[160] Although elements of humility, justice, peace, and other moral goods may characterize certain social movements or activities, if these also explicitly deny core Scriptural truths, they are not the work of the Spirit, but may be the work of the Enemy in disguise. As Jesus said, we must be alert for false prophets who come to us in sheep's clothing (Matt 7:15).

To process of discerning the Holy Spirit's work will necessarily involve balancing all of the preceding criteria, rather than taking one or two in isolation. For example, although the Nazi party created a community—the "people's community" (*Volksgemeinschaft*) based on national unity—this community was motivated by racial denigration and thus not a result of the work of the Spirit. In any particular case under examination, both positive and negative criteria (e.g., community creating vs. debasing) must be taken into account in determining whether the Spirit is working.

In sum, we must rely on the triune God and Scripture for spiritual discernment. Prayers that seek wisdom for spiritual discernment are necessary, while love and obedience prepare our hearts to be sensitive to his direction.

CONCLUSION

In this chapter, we have examined Colin Gunton's contribution to public theology and how it enables us to move forward in developing a trinitarian public theology. First, we discussed the history of public theology in the

---

158. Anselm Min argues that the biblical account of the Spirit's relation to the Father and the Son echoes his work in social movements. She argues, "The Holy Spirit is self-effacing, selfless God whose selfhood or personhood seems to lie precisely in transcending herself to empower others likewise to transcend themselves in communion with others." Min, *Solidarity of Others in a Divided World*, 118.

159. Kim, "Case Study," 96.

160. Yong, "Holy Spirit and the World Religions," 203.

United States to show that public theology has been received both positively and negatively. Further, I provided a definition of public theology flowing Stephen Holmes and drawing upon Gunton's robust pneumatology in order to supplement what is currently lacking in public theology. In my definition, I emphasize the importance of the triune God in public theology and sensitivity to the work of the Spirit who is the agent of transformation.

Second, we discussed the basic principles of our engagement in the public square. I argued that to seek the welfare of the city is the basic principle of our engagement, which ultimately leads to human flourishing. Whereas Christians are citizens of the City of God, this does not negate our responsibilities to the City of Man. Hence, Christians are called to promote human flourishing which is the objective of public theology.

Third, we examined Gunton's contribution to public theology. In order to set the stage for this, we first examined six prominent public theologians and thinkers in the United States to discover whether pneumatology plays any significant role in their public theology. As a result, we concluded that none of them gives significant attention to the eschatological Spirit and consequently their public theology is not robustly trinitarian due to the absence of the Spirit's work. In contrast, we discussed how Gunton's robust pneumatology that is firmly grounded in the triune God can make a significant contribution toward developing a trinitarian public theology (e.g., in unifying the cultural mandate and the great commission, in the nature of culture and transformation, and in the role of the church). As a way forward, I argued that a robust pneumatology is necessary for a trinitarian public theology. I also argued that pneumatology must be understood in the light of the triune God.

Finally, I proposed four criteria for discerning the work of the eschatological Spirit. The first is Scripturalness. To discern the work of the eschatological Spirit, it must be tested by the scripture. The second is the Trinitarianess. The Spirit's work must be perceived in the light of the Trinity to discern whether the activity in its nature and purpose is compatible with the Spirit's relation to the other persons of the Trinity. The third is communion-enabling. The actions of the Spirit must be characterized by fostering communion, reflecting the communion of the triune God. The fourth is other person-centeredness expressed in love. In addition, I proposed negative criteria which indicate activities that are not of the Spirit. The first is the work of the flesh which is contrary to the nature of the Spirit. The second is social activities or movements that contradict Scriptural testimony and deny key truths of God's revelation. We must rely on God and his word, not only human knowledge or perception, to guide us in discerning the Spirit's work.

Gunton's robust pneumatology provides the resources necessary to move toward a more robust, holistic and trinitarian public theology. By recapturing the work of the eschatological Spirit over the creation, Gunton enables us to explore the relation between the trinitarian God and the created world. Gunton's pneumatology clearly delineates the Spirit as the agent of transformation in relation to the Father and the Son. In so doing, he succeeds in giving the eschatological Spirit a personal identity while maintaining unity among the three persons. As a result, Gunton's pneumatology helps us to identify the modes of the Spirit's work in the world.

This represents a fresh approach to public theology. To my knowledge, no public theologian has approached public theology from the standpoint of the nature and particularity of the Spirit's work in the creation. We have not been viewing the world through the eyes of the Spirit, nor wisely discerning how the Spirit may be working among us to transform the world. As a result, our attempts to discern the Spirit's work have been largely arbitrary. In Gunton's words, we have tended to view it "in terms of what we happen to find attractive or appealing at the present time."[161]

Similarly, this fresh approach enables us to look beyond traditional modes of Christian cultural engagement that have been counterproductive. Drawing on trinitarian resources, Gunton identifies the Spirit as the divine love who transforms the world by reconciliation. If so, anything that is contrary to reconciliation or does not promote harmony and love may be a sign that the Spirit's work is not present. It may be political activity that promotes peace and unity in society, or simply an act of kindness toward others. Gunton's pneumatology shows that the transformation of the world happens when we reconcile with God, others and the creation. This means that the sphere of transformation by the Spirit is human relationships. This, in my opinion, significantly widens the approaches that Christians can take for cultural engagement. By the same token, it may enable us to discern the Spirit's work in places we never expected it.

While Gunton did not have the opportunity to find "adequate means of identification,"[162] it is fair to say that he paved the way for us to further identify the Spirit's work. In this sense, we can say that the promise of

---

161. Gunton, *Father, Son and Holy Spirit*, 121.
162. Gunton, *Father, Son and Holy Spirit*, 121.

Gunton's pneumatology lies in the encouragement to find adequate means of identifying the Spirit's work in relation to the Father and the Son. Gunton's contribution to public theology should not be overlooked because his pneumatology provides the resources needed to pursue further a trinitarian public theology.

Chapter 7

CONCLUSION

This study began with a simple yet puzzling question: Why has the Holy Spirit's work in creation been underexplored in the history of public theology? If the Holy Spirit is the agent of transformation in creation, why have theologians neglected the Spirit's activity in the context of public theology? I have suggested that there are several theological reasons why this has been the case.

The Holy Spirit has historically been conceived primarily as the bond of love between the Father and the Son rather than the third person of the Trinity (e.g., in Augustine). As a result, the Spirit has often lacked a personal identity apart from the other persons of the Trinity, especially the Son. Consequently, the Spirit has been viewed in terms of immanence rather than transcendence. In addition, the Spirit's work has been perceived as preserving and maintaining rather than transforming and perfecting creation. Indeed, the Spirit's work is often tied to common grace (e.g., Calvin). All of this, in my view, has caused the eschatological aspect of the Spirit's work in creation to be overlooked.

Stepping back a bit further, one begins to see that the underlying issue of these problems is rooted in the general lack of trinitarian theology in public theology. As I argued above in chapter 1, public theologians have generally failed to approach their work from a trinitarian perspective. As a result, the relation between the trinitarian God and the created world has not been examined in general. The relation between the Spirit and Christ has also been largely neglected in particular. But taking God's trinitarian nature into account is a crucial first step in constructing a biblically faithful, holistic public theology.

Colin E. Gunton rightly states, "Everything looks—and, indeed, is—different in the light of the Trinity."[1] Gunton's theology therefore begins with the question: Who is this God? I have thus argued that Gunton's robust pneumatology that is trinitarianly formulated overcomes the primary shortcoming that exists in public theology and ultimately provides what is lacking in public theology. This is in essence what I consider to be the promise of Gunton's pneumatology for public theology. In order to accomplish this end, I first examined Gunton's pneumatology in light of the doctrine of the Trinity (chaps. 2–5). I then applied Gunton's pneumatology to public theology in order to determine whether his pneumatology could offer a significant contribution to the area of public theology (chap. 6).

In chapter 2, I examined Gunton's understanding of the Spirit which is trinitarianly formulated and eschatologically conceived. To accomplish this, I identified how Gunton's doctrine of the Trinity contributes to unveiling the eschatological Spirit: that is to say, the One who works towards realizing the Eschaton and who is the agent of transformation. Against the Augustinian conception of the Trinity, Gunton's doctrine of the Trinity places emphasis on the relational aspect of the Trinity. Gunton therefore concludes that the eschatological Spirit is a personal Spirit rather than a static substance. Gunton further argues that the eschatological Spirit is a transcendent Spirit who brings perfection to the world for God's glory. In the end, I concluded that Gunton's pneumatology can shed new light on our world and our life in it.

Having established the theological and biblical basis for Gunton's eschatological Spirit, in chapters 3 through 5 I discussed how the Spirit actually works with the Father and the Son in order to bring transformation to the world. In chapter 3, I examined Gunton's doctrine of God, who is the triune Creator. The purpose of this section was to show how the relation of God's being and action provides a sufficient basis for the eschatological Spirit. Specifically, we saw how the action of God which derives from his being (the divine love) is mediated to creation through otherness. As a result, I concluded that Gunton's doctrine of God does provide strong support for the eschatological Spirit since the Spirit's action reveals a triune God who works together to achieve one goal: the restoration of the world.

---

1. Gunton, *Promise of Trinitarian Theology*, 4–5.

CONCLUSION

In chapter 4, in order to further unfold the action of the triune Creator toward the world, I examined how the divine love is actualized in the two hands of the Father, the Son and the Spirit, in Gunton's trinitarian theology. I explored the mediatory work of the Son and the Spirit to identify the various aspects of their work in the transformation of the world. In this context I explored the nature of the immanent work of the Son (e.g., incarnation) and the transcendent work of the Spirit (e.g., particularity). As a result, the intricate relation between the Son and the Spirit was identified. From this I concluded that God is God for us who comes among us to bring transformation to the world. Whereas the Son is the mediator of creation and redemption, the Spirit is the mediator of transformation. The Spirit particularizes those who come to God in order to renew the creation in accord with the Son's work in creation and redemption.

In chapter 5, I considered Gunton's anthropology in relation to the eschatological Spirit. In this section I shifted focus from the relations among the triune God to the relation between the eschatological Spirit and the church, as well as the relation between the eschatological Spirit and humanity. I explored how the Spirit works with the church and humanity in order to bring transformation to the world. Further, I investigated the nature of the relation between the church and humanity. In the end, I concluded that the eschatological Spirit enables the church to be a place for the re-formation of the image of God as the Spirit reconnects humanity with God, each other and the creation. Consequently, the church is enabled by the Spirit to engage culture in order to orient human life to God. In so doing, the church offers the sacrifice of praise to God for the restoration of the creation.

In chapter 6, I proposed how Gunton's pneumatology that is trinitarianly formulated and eschatologically conceived can contribute to the development of a full-bodied, holistic and trinitarian public theology. To accomplish this end, I first discussed briefly the history of public theology and the principles of our engagement in the public square in order to provide a basic overview of public theology. Then, I discussed six prominent U.S. public theologians and thinkers to discern whether pneumatology plays any significant role in their public theology. As a result, I concluded that none of them gives significant attention to the eschatological Spirit and consequently their public theology is not robustly trinitarian enough due to the absence of the sufficient focus on the Spirit's work. In turn, I examined how Gunton's robust pneumatology provides the necessary resources to address the deficiency in public theology owing to the absence of an adequate theology of the eschatological Spirit. Last, I explored the necessity and the content of criteria for discerning the work of the eschatological Spirit.

In the light of the above, I concluded that Gunton's pneumatology provides the necessary resources for moving toward a trinitarian public theology. Gunton's pneumatology that is firmly rooted in trinitarian theology enables us to approach public theology from a perspective that takes into account the triune God. Consequently, such an approach helps resolve long-standing theological problems (e.g., unbiblical dualism, the role of the church in culture, and others). Further, it enables us to see the world through the eyes of the eschatological Spirit to discern where and how the Sprit may be working among us. While Gunton himself did little work in proposing means for discerning the Spirit's activity, he paved the way to further identify the Spirit's work in the transformation of the world.

As noted earlier, Gunton held that in the light of trinitarian theology, everything looks different. Similarly, we can say that in the light of pneumatology that is firmly grounded in the Trinity, many things look different, especially the nature and work of the eschatological Spirit. This in turn brings a fresh approach to public theology, placing it in the sphere of the Trinity. Hence, this study, which set out to identify how Gunton's pneumatology can contribute to a full-bodied, holistic and trinitarian public theology, has accomplished its goal.

Gunton once wrote that if God is trinitarian, we must approach him trinitarianly. Much of Gunton's contribution to public theology derives from his trinitarian approach to understanding God's identity and character. Moreover, Gunton takes a relational approach to the doctrine of the Trinity rather than a classical Western one. As examined in chapter 2, he emphasizes the relational aspect of the Trinity. He argues that the being of God is constituted by the persons' relatedness in communion. Hence, the divine being is not a mysterious substance underlying the three persons, but persons who have relations with each other.

Nonetheless, relational models of the Trinity have been criticized. Many theologians who defend classical models of the Trinity express their concern that the relational models are not a faithful reflection of the traditional doctrine. Although the jury is still out on this intramural trinitarian debate, it is fair to say that Gunton's relational model of the Trinity makes a significant contribution to the field of public theology.[2]

---

2. For more details on the debate between classical and relational models of the Trinity, see Holmes, *Two Views on the Doctrine of the Trinity*.

CONCLUSION

In addition, Gunton's relational approach to the triune God has produced insights that bear on many critical areas in Christian theology, such as the eschatological Spirit, the relation between the triune God and the world, and the relation between the Son and the Spirit in transformation. If so, relational approaches may have the potential to further develop Christian theology and resolve some of the theological impasses that the church has encountered over the years.[3]

Similarly, Gunton's theological methodology based on the concept of "being and becoming," which we examined in chapter 3, serves as a key factor in understanding the nature and purpose of the eschatological Spirit. Gunton's attempt to mend the divorce between the immanent and economic Trinity in conceptualizing the triune God helps us to perceive the eschatological Spirit in a fresh way.[4] As argued in chapter 6, drawing from the triune God, Gunton identifies the Spirit as the divine love who transforms the world by reconciliation. If so, anything that is contrary to reconciliation or does not promote peace and unity may be a sign that the Spirit is not behind it. The Spirit's work must be perceived in relation to the Father and the Son. It is only within this framework that we can understand the divine intention of redemption toward the creation.

As stated above, criteria for discerning the Spirit's work have been underexplored by Gunton, due in part to the Spirit's elusive nature. Yet Gunton's pneumatology, firmly grounded in the doctrine of the Trinity, provides resources for formulating such criteria. On that basis, I proposed four criteria for discerning the work of the eschatological Spirit including Scripturalness, Trinitarianess, communion enabling, and others-centeredness expressed in love. In addition, I proposed negative criteria which indicate

---

3. At the same time, a word of caution is in order. As we examined in chapter 5, a relational ontology can cause theological dilemmas if caution isn't exercised. As I noted there, Gunton seems to conflate the distinction between God and humanity by falling into a kind of projectionism. Nonetheless, this does not discredit Gunton's contribution. Rather, this shows that although relational approaches can be fruitful in conceptualizing the triune God, we must not go beyond what Scripture and the orthodox doctrine of the Trinity allow us to say. See Thomas McCall's treatment of the relational Trinity in "Relational Trinity," 113–58.

4. With this blessing come concerns that were raised in chapter 4. Despite Gunton's relentless effort to keep distance between the economic and immanent Trinities, he seems, after all, to conflate the two. This point is especially apparent regarding the work of the Spirit. Unfortunately, it appears that Gunton fails to approach the axiom of God's act and being—that is to say that God's being and action should not be divorced—with sufficient caution and balance.

activities that are not of the Spirit. These include the works of the flesh (Gal 5:19–21) and social activities or movements that contradict Scriptural testimony and deny key truths of God's revelation.

These criteria for discerning the Spirit's work, in my view, are an exciting opportunity for those interested in the work of the Spirit in the secular world. As pointed out earlier, the Spirit's work has mainly been understood immanently in terms of sanctification, inspiration, and empowering. Yet, as Gunton's robust pneumatology shows, there is also a transcendental aspect of the Spirit's work. If so, we should identify its nature and character in order to obtain a more holistic view of the Spirit's activity.

Furthermore, such criteria can bring us a greater understanding of how the eschatological Spirit is working in order to bring transformation to the world, giving us a glimpse of what is to come.[5] This can enable us to be more sensitive to the Spirit's leading in cultural engagement. As argued in chapter 6, we must rely on the Spirit to lead us to the right path. It is not human power or ingenuity that changes the world, but our faithfulness to the Lord, who empowers us to bring about godly change. The Spirit is the agent of transformation. And we must be directed by him.

One area in which the Spirit may be working in the United States is racial issues. Starting from the Abolitionism movement during the Civil War to the recent protests over the deaths of unarmed African-Americans at the hands of white police, it is plausible to argue that the Spirit has been working to bring reconciliation to this deep wound in American society. Racial reconciliation is needed to restore peace and unity in our cities and communities. As Christians help bring this about, we seek the welfare of the city under the guidance of the Spirit.

Reconciliation is not easy in any case because it requires courage to admit our shortcomings and willingness to forgive those who have offended us. Hence, when such reconciliation takes place, it is the work of the eschatological Spirit: Mere human will or ingenuity cannot overcome our pride, ambition, or self-centeredness which arises from our sinful nature.

---

5. Suffice it to say that such transformation is only an anticipation of what is to come at the end. As Richard Mouw rightly argues, "Are we as Christians called to transform culture in the present age? . . . We are called to *await* the coming transformation." Mouw, *When the Kings Come Marching In*, 129; italics in original. Yet, while we wait, we should not wait idly. Rather, we should seek the welfare of the city as the Spirit guides. We live in a broken world. But, this world is a world "in which the kingdom of God has been inaugurated but has not yet reached its fulfillment." Middleton, *New Heaven and a New Earth*, 19.

It is only the Spirit who has the power to reconcile us with God, others and the creation. As Gunton argues, transformation begins to take place as the Spirit brings these things about. If so, more than ever, we must depend on the Spirit to guide us to the right path in cultural engagement. A prerequisite of transformation is a meek and humble heart, just as Christ demonstrated on the cross. Only when such reconciliation takes place will a society be transformed in ways that anticipate the world to come.[6]

What, then, is the promise of Gunton's pneumatology for a trinitarian public theology? First, it is the eschatological Spirit who transforms the whole creation in concert with the Father and the Son. This means that it is the divine intention to save not only human beings, but also the created world. Second, it is the transforming work of the Spirit which brings reconciliation rather than conflict. Third, it is the ability to discern at least some of the Spirit's anticipatory eschatological work in culture. And ultimately, it is a promise of a future transformation of the whole creation as we, a community of believers, seek the welfare of the city empowered and directed by the transforming work of the Spirit.

---

6. One such example in recent times, I believe, is the church shooting which took place at the Emmanuel African Methodist Episcopal Church in Charleston, South Carolina, on the evening of June 17, 2015. The young gunman, Dylan Roof, killed nine people during a prayer service. Later, he was indicted on thirty-three federal hate crimes charges. As much as such a heinous crime shocked the nation, what followed the killing astonished the country the most: The victims' families, appearing in front of Roof at the court, forgave him for killing nine black attendees of the meeting. David Brooks of the *New York Times* called this extraordinary act an example of living faith and the one uplifting part of this horrific crime. In the following days and weeks calls were made to remove the Confederate flag from the state capitol—the same flag Roof had posed with in a widely circulated photo. On June 22, the governor of South Carolina, Nikki Haley, also called for the removal of the Confederate flag, which eventually came down on July 10, 2015. On June 24, the governor of Alabama, Robert Bentley, single-handedly ordered the removal of the Confederate flag from the state capitol grounds. Many other actions to remove the Confederate flag have taken place in various states, including Mississippi and Tennessee. I believe that this was a moment when the Spirit worked among people to move toward reconciliation. The victims' families' extraordinary courage to forgive Roof and the humbleness they demonstrated at the court—even apologizing for their slowness to forgive him—are signs of their obedience to the Spirit's lead in reconciliation. At the same time, the nation's hearts and minds were opened by their testimony, pointing to the grace and love of God. Surely the Spirit was at work in these events, bringing about transformation and reconciliation.

BIBLIOGRAPHY

Allen, Diogenes, and Eric O. Springsted. *Philosophy for Understanding Theology*. 2nd ed. Louisville, KY: Westminster John Knox, 2007.
Allen, Leslie C. *Ezekiel 20-48*. WBC. Dallas: Word, 1990.
Anizor, Uche. "A Spirited Humanity: The Trinitarian Ecclesiology of Colin Gunton." *Themelios* 36 (2011) 24-41.
Augustine. *The City of God*. Garden City, NY: Image, 1958.
Awad, Najeeb G. "Personhood as Particularity: John Zizioulas, Colin Gunton, and the Trinitarian Theology of Personhood." *Journal of Reformed Theology* 4 (2010) 1-22.
Ayers, Lewis. "(Mis)Adventures in Trinitarian Ontology." In *The Trinity and an Entangled World: Relationality in Physical Science and Theology*, edited by John Polkinghorne, 130-145. Grand Rapids: Eerdmans, 2010.
———. "'Remember that You are Catholic' (serm. 52.2): Augustine on the Unity of the Triune God." *Journal of Early Christian Studies* 8 (2000) 39-82.
Bacote, Vincent. *The Spirit in Public Theology: Appropriating the Legacy of Abraham Kuyper*. Grand Rapids: Baker Academic, 2005.
Barth, Karl. *Church Dogmatics*. Vol. 1.1 of *The Doctrine of the Word of God*. Edited by G. W. Bromiley and T. F. Torrance. London, 1995. Repr. London: T. & T. Clark, 2006.
Basil of Caesarea. *On the Holy Spirit*. Crestwood, NY: St. Vladimir's Seminary Press, 1980.
Benne, Robert. *The Paradoxical Vision: A Public Theology for the Twenty-First Century*. Minneapolis: Fortress, 1995.
Berger, Peter L. *The Heretical Imperative: Contemporary Possibilities of Religious Affirmation*. Garden City, NY: Anchor, 1979.
Berger, Peter, and Thomas Lackman. *The Social Construction of Reality: A Treatise in the Sociology of Knowledge*. New York: Anchor, 1967.
Breitenberg, E. Harold. "To Tell the Truth: Will the Real Public Theology Please Stand Up?" *Journal of the Society of Christian Ethics* 23 (2003) 55-96.
Budziszewski, J. "Evangelicals in the Public Square." In *Evangelicals in the Public Square: Four Formative Voices on Political Thought and Action*, edited by J. Budziszewski, 15-38. Grand Rapids: Baker Academic, 2006.
Cady, Linell E. "H Richard Niebuhr and the Task of a Public Theology." *Anglican Theological Review* 72 (1990) 379-398.
Calvin, John. *Institutes of the Christian Religion*. Grand Rapids: Eerdmans, 1989.
Carson, D. A. *Christ and Culture Revisited*. Grand Rapids: Eerdmans, 2008.
Chia, Roland. "Trinity and Ontology: Colin Gunton's Ecclesiology." *International Journal of Systematic Theology* 9 (2007) 452-68.

Coakley, Sarah. "Why Three? Some Further Reflections on the Origins of the Doctrine of the Trinity." In *The Making and Remaking of Christian Doctrine: Essays in Honour of Maurice Wiles*, edited by Sarah Coakley and D. A. Pailin, 29–56. Oxford: Clarendon, 1993.

Cole, Graham A. *God the Peacemaker: How Atonement Brings Shalom*. Edited by D.A. Carson. New Studies in Biblical Theology 25. Downers Grove, IL: InterVarsity, 2009.

———. *The God who Became Human: A Biblical Theology of Incarnation*. Edited by D.A. Carson. New Studies in Biblical Theology 30. Downers Grove, IL: InterVarsity, 2013.

———. *He Who Gives Life: The Doctrine of the Holy Spirit*. Wheaton: Crossway, 2007.

———. "A Responsible Lifestyle in Old Testament Perspective: A Consideration of Some Popular Proposals." *Reformed Theological Review* 41 (1982) 1–10.

Collins, Paul M. *The Trinity: A Guide for the Perplexed*. London: T. & T. Clark, 2008.

Crisp, Oliver. "Did Christ have a *Fallen* Human Nature?" *International Journal of Systematic Theology* 6 (2004) 270–88.

Crouch, Andy. *Culture Making: Recovering Our Creative Calling*. Downers Grove, IL: InterVarsity, 2008.

Cumin, Paul. "The Taste of Cake: Relation and Otherness with Colin Gunton and the Strong Second Hand of God." In *The Theology of Colin Gunton*, edited by Lincoln Harvey, 65–85. London: T. & T. Clark, 2010.

Diogenes, Allen, and Eric O. Springsted. *Philosophy for Understanding Theology*. 2nd ed. Louisville, KY: Westminster John Knox, 2007.

Dozeman, Thomas B. *Commentary on Exodus*. Grand Rapids: Eerdmans, 2009.

Dunn, James D. G. *Romans 1–8*. WBC 38A. Dallas: Word, 1988.

Durham, John I. *Exodus*. WBC. Waco, TX: Word, 1987.

Enns, Peter. *Exodus*. NIV AC. Grand Rapids: Zondervan, 2000.

Fermer, Richard M. "The Limits of Trinitarian Theology as a Methodological Paradigm." *Neue Zeitschrift für Systematische Theologie und Religionsphilosophie* 41 (1999) 158–186.

Fitzmyer, Joseph A. *Romans: A New Translation with Introduction and Commentary*. TAC 33. New York: Doubleday, 1993.

Flett, John G. *The Witness of God: The Trinity, Missio Dei, Karl Barth, and the Nature of Christian Community*. Grand Rapids: Eerdmans, 2010.

Forrester, Duncan B. *Truthful Action: Explorations in Practical Theology*. Bloomsbury: T. & T. Clark, 2000.

Forster, Greg. *The Contested Public Square: The Crisis of Christianity and Politics*. Downers Grove, IL: IVP Academic, 2008.

Gaffin, Richard. "Atonement in the Pauline Corpus." In *The Glory of the Atonement: Biblical, Historical and Practical Perspectives*, edited by Charles E. Hill and Frank A. James III, 140–62. Downers Grove, IL: InterVarsity, 2004.

Gastafson, James M. "Preface: An Appreciative Interpretation." In *Christ and Culture*, xxi–xxxv. New York: HarperCollins, 2001.

Gingerich, Mark. "The Church as Kingdom: The Kingdom of God in the Writings of Stanley Hauerwas and John Howard Yoder." Διδασκαλία 19 (2008) 129–43.

Green, Bradley G. *Colin Gunton and the Failure of Augustine: The Theology of Colin Gunton in Light of Augustine*. Eugene, OR: Pickwick, 2011.

———. "Colin Gunton and the Theological Origin of Modernity." In *The Theology of Colin Gunton*, edited by Lincoln Harvey, 165–81. London: T. & T. Clark, 2010.

―――. "The Protomodern Augustine? Colin Gunton and the Failure of Augustine." *International Journal of Systematic Theology* 9 (2007) 328–41.
Grensted, Laurence W. *A Short History of the Doctrine of Atonement*. Theological Series 4. Manchester: The University of Manchester at the University Press, 1920.
Grenz, Stanley J. "Reconsecrating the Public Square." *Fides et Historia* 18 (1986) 65–75.
Gunton, Colin E. *Act and Being: Towards a Theology of the Divine Attributes*. Grand Rapids: Eerdmans, 2003.
―――. *The Actuality of Atonement: A Study of Metaphor, Rationality and the Christian Tradition*. Grand Rapids: Eerdmans, 1989.
―――. "And In One Lord Jesus Christ . . . Begotten not Made." *Pro Ecclesia* 5 (2001) 261–74.
―――. "Atonement and the Project of Creation: An Interpretation of Colossians 1:15–23." *Dialog* 35 (1996) 35–41.
―――. *The Barth Lectures*. London: T. & T. Clark, 2007.
―――. "Barth, the Trinity, and Human Freedom." *Theology Today* 43 (1986) 316–30.
―――. *Becoming and Being: The Doctrine of God in Charles Hartshorne and Karl Barth*. London: SCM, 2001.
―――. "The Being and Attributes of God. Eberhard Jüngel's Dispute with the Classical Philosophical Tradition." In *The Possibilities of Theology: Eberhard Jüngel in his Sixtieth Year*, edited by John Webster, 7–22. Edinburgh: T. & T. Clark, 1994.
―――. "Between Allegory and Myth: The Legacy of the Spiritualising of Genesis." In *The Doctrine of Creation: Essays in Dogmatics, History and Philosophy*, edited by Colin E. Gunton, 47–62. Edinburgh: T. & T. Clark, 1997.
―――. *A Brief Theology of Revelation*. Edinburgh: T. & T. Clark, 1995.
―――. *Christ and Creation*. Carlisle, England: Paternoster, 1992.
―――. *The Christian Faith: An Introduction to Christian Doctrine*. Oxford: Blackwell, 2002.
―――. "Christology: Two Dogmas Revisited—Edward Irving's Christology." In *Theology through the Theologians*, 151–68.
―――. "Christ the Sacrifice: Aspects of the Language and Imagery of the Bible." In *The Glory of Christ in the New Testament: Studies in Christology in Memory of George Bradford Caird*, edited by L. D. Hurst and N. T. Wright, 229–38. Oxford: Clarendon, 1987.
―――. "*Christus Victor* Revisited. A Study in Metaphor and the Transformation of Meaning." *Journal of Theological Studies* 36 (1985) 129–45.
―――. "The Church on Earth: The Roots of Community." In *On Being the Church: Essays on the Christian Community*, edited by Colin E. Gunton and Daniel W. Hardy, 48–80. Edinburgh: T. & T. Clark, 1989.
―――. "The Community of the Church in Communion with God." In *The Church in Reformed Tradition: Discussion Papers Prepared by a Working Party of the European Committee*, edited by Colin E. Gunton et al., 38–41. Geneva: World Council of Reformed Churches, 1995.
―――. "Creation and Mediation in the Theology of Robert W. Jenson: An Encounter and a Convergence." In *Trinity, Time and Church: A Response to the Theology of Robert Jensen*, edited by Colin E. Gunton, 80–93. Grand Rapids: Eerdmans, 2000.
―――. "The Doctrine of Creation." In *The Cambridge Companion to Christian Doctrine*, edited by Colin E. Gunton, 141–57. Cambridge: Cambridge University Press, 1997.

———. *The Doctrine of Creation: Essays in Dogmatic, History and Philosophy*. Edinburgh, T. & T. Clark, 1997.

———. "The End of Causality? The Reformers and Their Predecessors." In *The Doctrine of Creation: Essays in Dogmatics, History and Philosophy*, edited by Colin E. Gunton, 63-82. Edinburgh: T. & T. Clark, 1997.

———. *Father, Son and Holy Spirit: Essays toward a Fully Trinitarian Theology*. London: T. & T. Clark, 2003.

———. "God, Grace and Freedom." In *God and Freedom: Essays in Historical and Systematic Theology*, edited by Colin E. Gunton, 119-33. Edinburgh: T. & T. Clark, 1995.

———. "The God of Jesus Christ." *Theology Today* 54 (1997) 325-34.

———. "Immanence and Otherness: Divine Sovereignty and Human Freedom in the Theology of Robert W. Jenson." *Dialog* 30 (1991) 17-26.

———. *Incarnation and Imagery: Words, the World and The Triune God*. Edited by Martin Rogers. Farmington Papers 4. Oxford: The Farmington Institute for Christian Studies, 1999.

———. *Intellect and Action: Elucidations on Christian Theology and the Life of Faith*. Edinburgh: T. & T. Clark, 2000.

———. "Introduction." In *Theology of Reconciliation*, edited by Colin E. Gunton, 1-11. New York: T. & T. Clark, 2003.

———. *The One, the Three, and the Many: God, Creation, and the Culture of Modernity*. Cambridge: Cambridge University Press, 1993.

———. "Person and Particularity." In *The Theology of John Zizioulas: Personhood and the Church*, edited by Douglas Knight, 97-107. London: T. & T. Clark, 2010.

———. "Pneumatology." In *Dictionary of Ethics, Theology, and Society*, edited by Paul A. B. Clarke and Andrew Linzey, 644-47. London: Routledge, 1996.

———. *The Promise of Trinitarian Theology*. 2nd ed. London: T. & T. Clark, 2003.

———. "The Reformation Accounts of the Church's Response to Human Culture." In *Public Theology in Cultural Engagement: God's Key to the Redemption of the World*, edited by Stephen R. Holmes, 79-93. London: Paternoster, 2008.

———. "Relation and Relativity: The Trinity and the Created World." In *Trinitarian Theology Today: Essays on Divine Being and Act*, edited by Christoph Shwöbel, 92-112. London: T. & T. Clark, 1995.

———. "Salvation." In *Cambridge Companion to Karl Barth*, edited by John Webster, 143-58. Cambridge: Cambridge University Press, 2000.

———. "The Spirit as the Lord: Christianity, Modernity and Freedom." In *Different Gospels*, edited by Andrew Walker, 74-85. London: Hodder and Stoughton for the C.S. Lewis Centre, 1988.

———. "The Spirit in the Trinity." In *The Forgotten Trinity: 3. A Selection of Papers Presented to the BCC Study Commission on Trinitarian Doctrine Today*, edited by Alastair I. C. Heron, 123-35. London: BCC/CCBI, 1991.

———. "The Spirit Moved over the Face of the Waters: The Holy Spirit and Created Order." *International Journal of Systematic Theology* 4 (2002) 190-204.

———. "Theology in Communion." In *Shaping a Theological Mind: Theological Context and Methodology*, edited by Darren C. Marks, 31-36. Farnham: Ashgate, 2002.

———. *Theology through the Theologians: Selected Essays 1972-1995*. Edinburgh: T. & T. Clark, 1996.

———. "Time, Eternity, and Doctrine of the Incarnation." *Dialog* 21 (1982) 263-68.

———. "Towards a Theology of Reconciliation." In *Theology of Reconciliation*, edited by Colin E. Gunton, 167–74. New York: T. & T. Clark, 2003.

———. "Transcendence, Metaphor and the Knowability of God." *Journal of Theological Studies* 21 (1980) 501–16.

———. *The Transcendent Lord. The Spirit and the Church in Calvanist and Cappadocian.* The Congregational Lecture. London: Congregational Memorial Hall Trust, 1988.

———. "The Trinity in Modern Theology." In *Companion Encyclopedia of Theology*, edited by Peter Byrne and Leslie Houlden, 937–57. London: Routledge, 1995.

———. "Trinity, Ontology and Anthropology: Towards a Renewal of the Doctrine of the Imago Dei." In *Persons, Divine and Human: King's College Essays in Theological Anthropology*, edited by Christoph Schwöbel and Colin E. Gunton, 47–61. Edinburgh, T. & T. Clark, 1991.

———. *The Triune Creator: A Historical and Systematic Study.* Grand Rapids: Eerdmans, 1998.

———. *The Triune God: A Doctrine of the Trinity as though Jesus Makes a Difference.* Volume 1, *A Christian Dogmatic Theology*. Unpublished manuscript, 2003.

———. "The Triune God and the Freedom of the Creature." In *Karl Barth: Centenary Essays*, edited by S. W. Sykes, 46–68. Cambridge: Cambridge University Press, 1989.

———. "Universal and Particular Atonement in Atonement Theology." *Religious Studies* 28 (1992) 453–66.

———. "When the Gates of Hell Fall Down: Towards a Modern Theology of the Justice of God." *New Blackfriars* 69 (1989) 488–96.

———. *Yesterday and Today: A Study of Continuities in Christology.* 2nd ed. London: SPCK, 1997.

Hamilton, Victor P. *Exodus: An Exegetical Commentary.* Grand Rapids: Baker Academic, 2011.

Hanby, Michael. *Augustine and Modernity.* London: Routledge, 2003.

Harris, Harriet A. "Should We Say that Personhood is Relational?" *Scottish Journal of Theology* 51 (1998) 214–34.

Harrower, Scott. *Trinitarian Self and Salvation: An Evangelical Engagement with Rahner's Rule.* Eugene, OR: Pickwick, 2012.

Hauerwas, Stanley. *Dispatched from the Front: Theological Engagements with the Secular.* Durham: Duke University Press, 1994.

———. "The Naked Public Square Now: A Symposium." *First Things* 147 (2004) 11–12.

———. *The Peaceable Kingdom: A Primer in Christian Ethics.* Notre Dame: University of Notre Dame Press, 1983.

———. *Performing the Faith: Bonhoeffer and the Practice of Nonviolence.* Grand Rapids: Brazos, 2004.

Hauerwas, Stanley, and William H. Willimon. *Resident Aliens: A Provocative Christian Assessment of Culture and Ministry for People who Know that Something is Wrong.* Nashville: Abingdon, 1989.

Helm, Paul. "Colin Gunton's Point." *Helm's Deep Philosophical Theology.* http://paulhelmsdeep.blogspot.com/2011/09/colin-guntons-point.html.

Höhne, David A. *Spirit and Sonship: Colin Gunton's Theology of Particularity and the Holy Spirit.* Farnham: Ashgate, 2010.

Holmes, Stephen R. *The Quest for the Trinity: The Doctrine of God in Scripture, History and Modernity.* Downers Grove, IL: IVP Academic, 2012.

———. "Towards the *Analogia Personae et Relationis*: Developments in Gunton's Trinitarian Thinking." In *The Theology of Colin Gunton*, edited by Lincon Harvey, 49–64. London: T. & T. Clark, 2010.

Holmes, Stephen R., et al., eds. *Two Views on the Doctrine of the Trinity*. Grand Rapids: Zondervan, 2014.

Hunter, James Davison. *To Change the World: The Irony, Tragedy, and Possibility of Christianity in the Late Modern World*. New York: Oxford University Press, 2010.

Jeffery, Steve, Mike Ovey and Andrew Sach, *Pierced for Our Transgressions*. Nottingham: InterVarsity Press, 2007.

Jenson, Robert W. "Christ as Culture 1: Christ as Polity." *International Journal of Systematic Theology* 5 (2003) 323–29.

———. "A Decision Tree of Colin Gunton's Thinking." In *The Theology of Colin Gunton*, edited by Lincoln Harvey, 8–16. London: T. & T. Clark, 2010.

———. *Ezekiel: Brazos Theological Commentary on the Bible*. Grand Rapids: Brazos, 2009.

———. *Systematic Theology*. Volume 2 of *The Works of God*. Oxford: Oxford University Press, 1995.

Johnson, Keith E. "Imitatio Trinitatis: How Should We Imitate the Trinity?" *Westminster Theological Journal* 75 (2013) 317–34.

———. *Rethinking the Trinity and Religious Pluralism: An Augustinian Assessment*. Downers Grove, IL: IVP Academic, 2011.

Jüngel, Eberhand. *God's Being is in Becoming: The Trinitarian Being of God in the Theology of Karl Barth*. Grand Rapids: Eerdmans, 2001.

Kärkkäinen, V. M. "Pneumatology." In *Global Dictionary of Theology*, edited by William A. Dryness and Veli-Matti Kärkkäinen, 659–69. Downers Grove, IL: IVP Academic, 2008.

Keener, Craig S. "Holy Spirit." In *The Oxford Handbook of Evangelical Theology*, edited by Gerald R. McDermott, 159–76. New York: Oxford University Press, 2010.

———. *Romans*. NCCS. Eugene, OR: Cascade, 2009.

Kilby, Karen. "Perichoresis and Projection: Problems with Social Doctrines of the Trinity." *New Blackfriars* 81 (2000) 432–45.

Kim, Kristeen. "Case Study: How Will We Know When the Holy Spirit Comes? The Question of Discernment." *Evangelical Review of Theology* 33 (2009) 93–96.

Knight, Douglas. "Metaphor to Mediation: Colin Gunton and the Concept of Mediation." *Neue Zeitschrift für Systematische theologie und Religionsphilosophie* 43 (2001) 118–36.

Kuyper, Abraham. "Common Grace." In *Abraham Kuyper: A Centennial Reader*, edited by James D. Bratt, 165–201. Grand Rapids: Eerdmans, 1998.

———. "Sphere Sovereignty." In *Abraham Kuyper: A Centennial Reader*, edited by James D. Bratt, 461–90. Grand Rapids: Eerdmans, 1998.

Lehenbauer, Joel D. "The Theology of Stanley Hauerwas." *CTQ* 76 (2012) 157–74.

Leithart, Peter J. *Between Babel and Beast: America and Empires in Biblical Perspective*. Eugene, OR: Cascade, 2012.

———. *Defending Constantine: The Twilight of an Empire and the Dawn of Christendom*. Downers Grove, IL: IVP Academic, 2010.

Letham, Robert. "Triune God." In *The Oxford Handbook of Evangelical Theology*, edited by Gerald R. McDermott, 99–115. New York: Oxford University Press, 2010.

———. *The Work of Christ*. Leicester: InterVarsity, 1993.

MacLeod, Donald. "The Doctrine of the Incarnation in Scottish Theology: Edward Irving." *Scottish Bulletin of Evangelical Theology* 9 (1991) 40–50.
Marty, Martin E. "Foreword." In *Christ and Culture*, xiii–xix. San Francisco: Harper and Row, 2001.
McCall, Thomas. "Relational Trinity: Creedal Perspective." In *Two Views on the Doctrine of Trinity*, edited by James S Sexton, 113–58. Grand Rapids: Zondervan, 2014.
McElroy, Robert W. *The Search for an American Public Theology: The Contribution of John Courtney Murray*. New York: Paulist, 1989.
McGrath, Alister. *Christian Theology: An Introduction*. 5th ed. Oxford: Wiley-Blackwell, 2011.
McNall, Joshua. *A Free Corrector: Colin Gunton and the Legacy of Augustine*. Baltimore, Maryland: Fortress, 2015.
———. "Gunton and Augustine." In *T. & T. Clark Handbook of Colin Gunton*, edited by Andrew Picard, Myk Habets and Murray Rae, 269–84. London: T. & T. Clark, 2023.
Middleton, Richard J. *A New Heaven and a New Earth: Reclaiming Biblical Eschatology*. Grand Rapids: Baker Academic, 2014.
Min, Anselm Kyongsuk. *The Solidarity of Others in a Divided World*. New York: T. & T. Clark, 2004.
Molnar, Paul D. *Divine Freedom and the Doctrine of the Immanent Trinity: In Dialogue with Karl Barth and Contemporary Theology*. Edinburgh: T. & T. Clark, 2002.
Moo, Douglas J. *Romans*. NIV AC. Grand Rapids: Zondervan, 2000.
Moore, T. M. *Culture Matters: A Call for Consensus on Christian Cultural Engagement*. Grand Rapids: Brazos, 2007.
Mounce, Robert H. *Romans*. TNAC 27. Nashville: B&H, 1995.
Mouw, Richard J. "Cultural Discipleship in a Time of God's Patience." *Scottish Bulletin of Evangelical Theology* 28 (2010) 80–91.
———. *When the Kings Come Marching in: Isaiah and the New Jerusalem*. Grand Rapids: Eerdmans, 2002.
Murphy, Andrew. "The Naked Public Square Now: A Symposium." *First Things* 147 (2004) 16–17.
Nausner, Bernhard. "The Failure of a Laudable Project: Gunton, the Trinity and Human Self-Understanding." *Scottish Journal of Theology* 62 (2009) 403–20.
Neuhaus, Richard John. "The Naked Public Square: A Metaphor Reconsidered." *First Things* 23 (1992) 78–81.
———. "The Naked Public Square Now: A Symposium." *First Things* 147 (2004) 24–26.
———. *The Naked Public Square: Religion and Democracy in America*. 2nd ed. Grand Rapids: Eerdmans, 1986.
Niebuhr, Richard H. *Christ and Culture*. New York: HarperCollins, 2001.
———. "The Doctrine of the Trinity and the Unity of the Church." *Theology Today* 3 (1946) 371–84.
Noll, Mark A. "The Public Church in the Years of Conflict." *Christian Century* (1991) 552–59.
Ottati, Douglas F. "Christ and Culture." *American Presbyterians* 66 (1988) 320–25.
Paget, Michael. "Christology and Original Sin: Charles Hodge and Edward Irving Compared." *Churchman* 21 (2007) 229–48.
Pérez, Ángel C. "The Trinitarian Concept of Person." In *Rethinking Trinitarian Theology: Disputed Questions and Contemporary Issues in Trinitarian Theology*, edited by Giulio Maspero and Robert J. Wozniak, 105–45. London: T. & T. Clark, 2012.

Phan, Peter C. "Systematic Issues in Trinitarian Theology." In *The Cambridge Companion to the Trinity*, edited by Peter C. Phan, 13–29. New York: Cambridge University Press, 2011.

Pinnock, Clark H. "The Role of the Spirit in Creation." *The Asbury Theological Journal* 52 (1997) 47–54.

Rauser, Randal. "Rahner's Rule: An Emperor without Clothes?" *International Journal of Systematic Theology* 7 (2005) 81–94.

Reese, Naomi N. "Émile Durkheim." In *Dictionary of Christianity and Science*, edited by Paul Copan et al., 195–96. Grand Rapids: Zondervan Academic, 2017.

———. "Social Sciences." In *Dictionary of Christianity and Science*, edited by Paul Copan et al., 632–33. Grand Rapids: Zondervan Academic, 2017.

———. "Sociology." In *Dictionary of Christianity and Science*, edited by Paul Copan et al., 633–34. Grand Rapids: Zondervan Academic, 2017.

Sanders, Fred. "Entangled in the Trinity: Economic and Immanent Trinity in Recent Theology." *Dialog: A Journal of Theology* 40 (2001) 175–82.

———. *The Image of the Immanent Trinity: Rahner's Rule and the Theological Interpretation of Scripture*. New York: Peter Lang, 2005.

Schaeffer, J. H. F. *Createdness and Ethics: The Doctrine of Creation and Theological Ethics in the Theology of Colin E. Gunton and Oswald Bayer*. Berlin: De Gruyter, 2006.

Schwöbel, Christoph. *Persons, Divine and Human: King's College Essays in Theological Anthropology*. Edited by Christoph Schwöbel and Colin E. Gunton. Edinburgh: T. & T. Clark, 2002.

———. "The Shape of Colin Gunton's Theology: On the Way Towards a Fully Trinitarian Theology." In *The Theology of Colin Gunton*, edited by Lincoln Harvey, 182–208. London: T. & T. Clark, 2010.

———. "A Tribute to Colin Gunton." In *The Person of Christ*, edited by Rae Murray and Stephen R. Holmes, 13–18. London: T. & T. Clark, 2005.

Sider, Ronald J. *Just Politics: A Guide for Christian Engagement*. Grand Rapids: Brazos, 2012.

Smith, James K. A. "Thinking Biblically about Culture." *Perspectives* 24 (2009) 21–23.

Spence, Alan. "The Persons as Willing Agent: Classifying Gunton's Christology." In *The Theology of Colin Gunton*, edited by Lincoln Harvey, 49–64. London: T. & T. Clark, 2010.

Stackhouse, Max L. "Christian Social Ethics in a Global Era: Reforming Protestant Views." In *Christian Social Ethics in a Global Era*, edited by Max L. Stackhouse et al., 11–73. Nashville: Abingdon, 1995.

———. *Globalization and Grace*. Volume 4 of *God and Globalization*. London: Continuum, 2000.

———. "Liberalism Revisited: From Social Gospel to Public Theology." In *Being Christian Today: An American Conversation*, edited by Richard John Neuhaus and George Weigel, 33–53. Washington, DC: Ethics and Public Policy Center, 1992.

———. "Public Theology." In *Dictionary of the Ecumenical Movement*, edited by Lossky Nicholas et al., 1131–33. Geneva: WCC Publications, 1991.

———. "Public Theology and the Future of Democratic Society." In *The Church's Public Role: Retrospect and Prospect*, edited by Dieter T. Hessel, 63–88. Grand Rapids: Eerdmans, 1993.

———. *Public Theology and Political Economy: Christian Stewardship in Modern Society*. Grand Rapids: Eerdmans for Commission on Stewardship, National Council of the Churches of Christ in the U.S.A., 1987.

———. *Shaping Public Theology: Selections from the Writings of Max L. Stackhouse*. Edited by Scott R. Paeth et al. Grand Rapids: Eerdmans, 2014.

Terry, Justyn. "Colin Gunton's Doctrine of Atonement: Transcending Rationalism by Metaphor." In *The Theology of Colin Gunton*, edited by Lincoln Harvey, 130–45. London: T. & T. Clark, 2010.

Thiemann, Ronald F. *Constructing a Public Rheology: The Church in a Pluralistic Culture*. Louisville, KY: Westminster John Knox, 1991.

Torrance, T. F. *The Christian Doctrine of God*. Edinburgh: T. & T. Clark, 1996.

Van Til, Henry R. *The Calvinistic Concept of Culture*. Grand Rapids: Baker Academic, 2001.

Vanhoozer, Kevin. "The Atonement on Post Modernity." In *The Glory of Atonement*, edited by Charles Hill and Frank James, 367–404. Downers Grove, IL: InterVarsity, 2004.

Volf, Miroslav. *A Public Faith: How Followers of Christ Should Serve the Common Good*. Grand Rapids: Brazos, 2011.

———. "Soft Difference: Theological Reflections on the Relation between Church and Culture in 1 Peter." *Ex Auditu* 10 (1994) 15–30.

Webster, John. "Gunton and Barth." In *The Theology of Colin Gunton*, edited by Lincoln Harvey, 17–31. London: T. & T. Clark, 2010.

———. "Systematic Theology after Barth: Jüngel, Jenson, and Gunton." In *The Modern Theologians: An Introduction to Christian Theology since 1918*, edited by David Ford and Rachel Muers, 249–64. Malden: Blackwell, 2005.

Welker, Michael. *God the Spirit*. Minneapolis: Fortress, 1994.

Whitney, William B. *Problem and Promise in Colin E. Gunton's Doctrine of Creation*. Studies in Reformed Theology. Boston: Brill, 2013.

Winter, Bruce W. *Seek the Welfare of the City: Christians as Benefactors and Citizens*. Grand Rapids: Eerdmans, 1994.

Wood, Charles M. "How Does God Act?" *International Journal of Systematic Theology* (1999) 138–52.

Wright, Terry J. "Colin Gunton on Providence: Critical Commentaries." In *The Theology of Colin Gunton*, edited by Lincoln Harvey, 146–64. London: T. & T. Clark, 2010.

———. *Providence Made Flesh: Divine Presence as a Framework for a Theology of Providence*. Eugene, OR: Wipf & Stock, 2009.

———. "Reconsidering *Concursus*." *International Journal of Systematic Theology* 4 (2002) 205–15.

Yoder, John Howard. "How H. Richard Niebuhr Reasoned: A Critique of Christ and Culture." In *Authentic Transformation: A New Vision of Christ and Culture*, edited by Glen H. Stassen et al., 31–89. Nashville: Abingdon, 1995.

Yong, Amos. *Beyond the Impasse: Toward a Pneumatological Theology of Religion*. Grand Rapids: Baker Academic, 2003.

———. "The Holy Spirit and the World Religions: On the Christian Discernment of Spirit(s) 'after' Buddhism." *Buddhist-Christian Studies* 24 (2004) 191–207.

www.ingramcontent.com/pod-product-compliance
Lightning Source LLC
Chambersburg PA
CBHW070328230426
43663CB00011B/2256